WITH INTENT TO DESTROY

WITH INTENT TO DESTROY

Reflecting on Genocide

◆

COLIN TATZ

VERSO

London • New York

First published by Verso 2003
© Colin Tatz 2003
All rights reserved

1 3 5 7 9 10 8 6 4 2

Verso
UK: 6 Meard Street, London W1F 0EG
USA: 180 Varick Street, New York, NY 10014–4606
www.versobooks.com

Verso is the imprint of New Left Books

ISBN 1–85984–550–9

British Library Cataloguing in Publication Data
Tatz, Colin Martin
    With intent to destroy: reflecting on genocide
    1. Genocide
    I. Title
    364.1′51

    ISBN 1859845509

Library of Congress Cataloging-in-Publication Data
Tatz, Colin Martin.
    With intent to destroy: reflecting on genocide / Colin Tatz.
    p. cm.
    ISBN 1-85984-550-9
    1. Genocide. I. Title.

HV6322.7.T38 2003
304.6′63–dc21

2003053516

Typeset in 10.5/12.5 Bembo by SetSystems Ltd, Saffron Walden, Essex
Printed in the UK by Bath Press

In memory of a South African mentor,
Edgar Brookes,
and, in appreciation, this book is for
Yehuda Bauer

CONTENTS

DEFINITIONS OF GENOCIDE

In international law

Article II

In the present Convention, genocide means any of the following acts committed with intent to destroy, in whole or in part, a national, ethnical, racial or religious group, as such:

(a) Killing members of the group;
(b) Causing serious bodily or mental harm to members of the group;
(c) Deliberately inflicting on the group conditions of life calculated to bring about its physical destruction in whole or in part;
(d) Imposing measures intended to prevent births within the group;
(e) Forcibly transferring children of the group to another group.

Article III

The following acts shall be punishable:

Genocide;
Conspiracy to commit genocide;
Direct and public incitement to commit genocide;
Complicity in genocide.

The United Nations, *Convention on the Prevention and Punishment of the Crime of Genocide, 1948*

Article 6 of the *Rome Statute of the International Criminal Court*, effective from 1 July 2002, states that: 'For the purpose of this Statute, "genocide" means any of the following acts committed with intent to destroy, in whole or in part, a national, ethnical, racial or religious group, as such' and then adds, verbatim, the terms of Article II above.

In the social sciences

Genocide . . . is the destruction of the essential foundations of the life of national groups, with the aim of annihilating the groups themselves. The objectives of such a plan would be the disintegration of the political and social institutions, of culture, language, national feelings, religion, and the economic existence of national groups, and the destruction of personal security, liberty, health, dignity, and even the lives of the individuals belonging to such groups.

Raphael Lemkin, 1944

Genocide is the deliberate destruction of physical life of individual human beings by reason of their membership of any human collectivity as such.

Pieter Drost, 1959

Genocide is defined as a structural and systematic destruction of innocent people by a state bureaucratic apparatus.

Irving Louis Horowitz, 1976

Genocide is any act that puts the very existence of a group in jeopardy.

Henry Huttenbach, 1988

The concept of genocide applies *only* when there is an actualised intent, however successfully carried out, to physically destroy an entire group (as such a group is defined by the perpetrators).

Steven Katz, 1989

Genocide is the sustained purposeful action by a perpetrator to physically destroy a collectivity directly or indirectly, through interdiction of the biological and social reproduction of group members, sustained regardless of the surrender or lack of threat offered by the victim.

Helen Fein, 1993

Genocide is a form of one-sided mass killing in which a state or other authority intends to destroy a group, as that group and membership in it are defined by the perpetrator.

Frank Chalk and Kurt Jonassohn, 1990

Genocide is the sustained purposive action perpetrated by the state, or actors condoned by the state, on a captured victim group as defined by the perpetrator(s), leading to the physical destruction of the group.

Jennifer Balint, 1991

Genocide in the generic sense means the mass killing of substantial numbers of human beings, when not in the course of military action against the military forces of an avowed enemy, under conditions of the essential defencelessness of the victims.

Israel Charny, 1994

In the dictionaries

Genocide: annihilation of a race.

The Shorter Oxford, 1973

Genocide: extermination of a national or racial group as a planned move.

The Macquarie, 1985

Genocide: 1. the use of deliberate systematic measures (as killing, bodily or mental injury, unlivable conditions, prevention of births) calculated to bring about the extermination of a racial, political, or cultural group or to destroy the language, religion, or culture of a group. 2. one who advocates or practices genocide.

Webster's Third New International, 1971

PROLOGUE

Nations in transition, from colonialism or from a war or from the domination of one tribe over another, need social consensus and ways of feeling good about themselves. Many feel uncomfortable about some, or even much, of their earlier history. They don't want reminders of murder and massacre, let alone of genocide, whether done to them or by them. When they first established their nation states, the two quintessential victim groups of the twentieth century – the Jews and the Armenians – didn't want to know about genocide. They didn't teach that history, as if to demonstrate that they hadn't 'gone as if sheep to the slaughter' and that they were, indeed, nations of virility and valour. Once they had learned that without history there is no present and no future, then both states undertook educational and spiritual journeys into their genocides.

On the culprit side, postwar, democratic, reunified Germany is still weighed down by the *Schuldfrage* (guilt question). Turkey, still struggling to achieve its ninety-five-year-old dream of becoming the beacon of democracy in the Near East, does everything possible to deny its genocide of the Armenians, Assyrians and Pontian Greeks.

But Australia, the United States and Britain are not nations in transition, at least not in the manner of Germany or Turkey. Why then do these nations – especially Australia and the United States – experience paroxysms, ranging from upset to extreme angst to even more extreme anger, when the (literal) spectres of genocide appear as facets of their proudly democratic histories?

Bad history, ugly history, doesn't remain buried for long. In the 1990s, the relatively well-known fates of Native Central and North Americans were systematically researched, collated and presented in books such as David Stannard's *American Holocaust* (1992) and Ward Churchill's *A Little Matter of Genocide* (1998). These works came to prominence in conjunction with an aptly titled Massachusetts text on Holocaust education for high schools, *Facing History and Ourselves*, by William Parsons and Margot Strom (1994).

However, more recently, Samantha Power, in explaining how far outside the American universe of obligation or concern were 'foreign' genocide victim groups and places, managed to avoid entirely the issue of domestic American genocide. In her *New York Review of Books* essay, which preceded her 2002 book, *A Problem from Hell*, she explains American inertia, lack of political will, absence of morality and crass expediency when that major power could have acted in several ways to mitigate, or even halt, the mass killings of Armenians, Jews, Kurds, Bosnians and Rwandans. She demands to know how 'Rwandan Hutus in 1994 could freely, joyfully, and systematically slaughter some eight thousand Tutsi a day for one hundred days without any foreign interference'. She points to the facts that this genocide 'occurred *after* the cold war; *after* the growth of human rights groups; *after* the advent of technology that allowed for instant communication; *after* the erection of the Holocaust Museum on the Mall in Washington DC' (Power 2002, her emphases). She insists that Americans face these facts, but she doesn't even mention their own history of genocide of Native Americans.

Imperial and colonial Britain has a rich reservoir of history. Some of that history is a record of achievement and beneficence; some of it, or even much of it, was appalling in its legacy of societal destruction and its maleficence. Mike Davis's *Late Victorian Holocausts* (2001), for example, is not a conventional colonial history, but he links, in dramatic fashion, the 'New Imperialism' with the catastrophic crop failures of the 1870s and 1890s; these combined to produce a death toll of some 50 million as colonial states, especially Britain, forcibly incorporated millions into their economic and political structures.

In Australia, the new millennium began with an asylum-seeker problem of some magnitude. The asylum-seekers were skilfully confused with would-be terrorists, in an Australia which had never had to confront that problem. As a means of coercion, terrorism isn't new. But systematic terrorism has arrived in or near countries not inured to it, at least not in the manner of Ireland and Israel. The 'war against terrorism' is now upon us, and the response to it is in part realistic, in part hysterical. The year 2003 began with draconian anti-terrorist legislation in several democracies, and with daily doses of national media campaigns to 'be alert' but not 'alarmed'. The Australian version of this campaign began with the insistence that 'Australians are friendly, decent, democratic people ... [who] will remain that way'. In times of stress and hysteria, there is impatience, nay, dismissal of anything and everything that stands in the way of patriotic, bellicose fervour.

Yet the 'friendly, decent, democratic people' found a way to place some 1,100 asylum-seekers in remote mainland detention centres, and a similar number 'off-shore' – 'the Pacific solution' – on islands like Nauru. Riots, burnings, suicides, homicides, attacks on warders and a change in the private management firm responsible for these 'systems' have not altered the government's claim that 'detention centres are not jails', notwithstanding their utter remoteness and the razor-wire boundaries, even for the hundred or more detainees classified as children.

The millennium also began with the celebration of the centenary of federation and a dedication to reconciliation with the Aboriginal and Islander peoples. Yet Australians shy away from admitting exactly what it is that has to be reconciled, and why. A middle power, a stable democracy, this 'land of the fair go' and 'the level playing field' insists that its peoples 'move on' – yet steadfastly, obstinately, refuses to acknowledge what it is that they must move on from.

The past is, indeed, a foreign country. So, too, for most white Australians, white Americans and Britons, is genocide. Catastrophes of mass death occur outside their universe of concern in far-off, unpronounceable places like Oswiecim (Auschwitz), Treblinka, Sobibor, Belzec, Majdanek, Phnom Penh, Dhaka, Srebrenica, Sarajevo, Pristina, Goradze, Kigali and Goma. Such people and places are the essence of a remote 'other'. They are simply not relevant to people like us. And, as we will see, if they are or were relevant, it was 'all a long time ago'. Uncomfortably, Indonesia's genocidal practices in East Timor are much closer to Australia in terms of time, geography, national interest, sphere of influence and political relationship.

Over the past forty-two years, I have (as an immigrant) observed the search for an Australian identity of independence, accompanied by the growth of a confident nationalism free of Mother England. I have also seen both movements begin to flag, even crumble, when confronted by increasingly strident Aboriginal assertions and other ethnic challenges to the assimilationist mould. The old shibboleths about 'one people' sharing the same hopes, loyalties, customs and beliefs began to fragment some time ago. Even the Jewish community, once notable for its integration and its pursuit of 'ideological non-distinctiveness' from mainstream Australia, has been re-shaped by an influx of 'foreign' Jews, many of whom are unwilling to surrender their own history for a 'look-only-to-the-future-and-forget-the-past' philosophy.

Genocide is now in the vocabulary of Australian politics, albeit grudgingly, or even hostilely. Whether owing to the frustration attending three Holocaust war crimes trials which ended in acquittal or abortion in Adelaide in the 1990s, or by the coming to light of an Australian awareness, perhaps complicity, in the events of East Timor in the 1970s (and later), or the public's first knowledge of the wholesale removal of Aboriginal children, the dreaded 'g' word is firmly with us. It isn't likely to go away because we wish it so, or because of a crusade to deny it, or at least to exorcise it. The purpose of my university and public courses, and of this book (among others), is to keep it here – not to produce anger, shame, guilt, or some international opprobrium but to prod Australians into facing their history and thus to facilitate a 'moving on', free of the chronic suppuration that arises from suppression.

With Intent to Destroy is an integrated collection of essays about the grave (and gravest) aspects of race politics – in Europe, South Africa and Australia – that have assailed me during four decades as student, researcher, teacher and writer. They are inevitably personal and admittedly selective – I make no claims to radical historical discoveries or to any attempt to cover all potential genocides here – and they reflect my situation as an immigrant, South African, Australian Jew. What they do cover is an evolution (rather than a revolution) in my thinking about racism and the termini to which, regrettably yet inevitably, racist behaviour so often leads.

The book is also an attempt to integrate what have become increasingly separate fields: Holocaust studies and genocide studies. Schism is perhaps too strong a term, but diverging and divergent paths are assuredly what we have at present. The Holocaust and its literature overwhelm, and there are good and proper reasons why this is so. Scholars of that event should have no reason or need to denigrate comparative genocide studies as somehow trivialising or minimising that *tremendum*. Nor is it valid to assert that the Holocaust agenda is history while the genocide approach is sociology. And there is no need or cause for genocide scholars to ignore, or evade, the lessons and legacies of the Holocaust in their pursuit of other case histories.

The first chapter relates the breaking of a protective membrane around me, allowing in that darkness which I see, and which others see, as the nature of the Holocaust. It is a highly personal journey, evoking many long-suppressed memories and influences of a murderous and spiteful South Africa, especially during World War II. Those years, and the post-1948 'invigoration' of an apartheid that had long been there in harsh practice, explain my mainsprings and my lifelong interest in race politics.

The second chapter offers an approach to the study of genocide through the event which for most Westerners, at least, remains the paradigm case study – the Holocaust, or *Shoah*, or *Churban*, or Judeocide. It is, in many ways, the result of instruction over several years at Yad Vashem (The Martyrs' and Heroes' Remembrance Authority) in Jerusalem, where I was truly confronted by the Holocaust, by its explicability and its inexplicability, and by Yehuda Bauer's presentation of its dialectical contradictions. The conclusions I have reached as a result of that confrontation are presented as a set of 'thoughts', springboards for further consideration, on the historical, philosophical, religious and psychological aspects of the Holocaust.

An attempt to understand something of the 'anatomy' of genocides – their origins, ideological bases, socio-political contexts, the techniques and technologies used, precedented and unprecedented aspects – gives rise to the case-study chapters which follow and which focus primarily on Germany, Australia and South Africa. They each illustrate important aspects of the study of genocide: the structural process in the case of Germany, whereby antisemitism was transformed into an industrialised engine of genocide; the matters of definition and interpretation in the case of Australia; and the question in South Africa of whether or not the apartheid regime can be described as genocidal.

These chapters are followed by some reflections on responses to geno-cide, both official and not so official – a seeming inability or refusal on the part of the Turkish authorities, for instance, to concede the Armenian genocidal massacres, the denialism[1] which has featured so strongly in Australia and which continues to be raised in respect of the Holocaust, and the vogue for apology as a way of 'laying things to rest'.

A concluding chapter discusses why and how both the narratives and the analyses of various genocides might be disseminated. Teaching about such calamities is hardly fun but it isn't all that difficult. Rather, what is disturbing is the reluctance of curriculum-setting people, in schools and universities, to take the subject on board. I reflect on genocide, and on both the exhilaration and the pain involved in thinking about it, writing about it, and teaching it.

I

BREAKING THE MEMBRANE: JOURNEY TOWARDS GENOCIDE

Two British writers bear the name Alexander Baron. The Jewish novelist, who was born in 1917 and died in 1999, was the author of, among other works, an acclaimed trilogy of World War II novels.[1] The other, a self-proclaimed poet, was very much alive in 2003, spouting his antisemitic venom.[2]

The title of this chapter derives from a memorable response by novelist Alexander Baron to an interviewer. 'What impact did the destruction of European Jewry have on your work?' he was asked. 'A personal incident', he replied, 'broke through whatever membrane of resistance had formed in my mind' and thereafter he was 'completely invaded by the knowledge of what had happened'. 'Not a single day passes without some thought or picture of the *Churban*[3] assailing me' (Baron, 1980: 66–72).

The membrane metaphor resonates with me: a tough, fibrous, protective tissue that both divides from, and serves to connect to, other structures. As a child during World War II, I was both divided from, yet sharply connected to, the world of Nazis. We were good at division in racist South Africa. There was a galaxy of 'thems' and 'usses', too often expressed in mean-spirited language: three kinds of whites – the Afrikaners, known to Jews as *chatesim* (an untranslatable, ugly term); the English-speaking *goyim*, more contemptuously termed *yoks*; and *unsere menschen*, 'our people', the Jews, 90 per cent of whom were *Litvaks*, of Lithuanian origin; and then the great majority, three kinds of blacks – Cape Coloureds,[4] Indians and Africans (variously, *slamaaiers*, coolies, *sammies*, *kaffirs*,

natives, Bantu, *schvartzes*). The Afrikaners, of course, had their own lexicon of contempt: *kaffirs*, *rooineks*, *jewboys*. Languages abounded among
abundant servants: Sotho, Tswana, Venda, Xhosa, Zulu. Yet almost no
white household comprehended any of them, or could distinguish one
from another.

Sixty, rather than six, degrees of separation in all things: buses, bus stops,
train carriages, trams, schools, lines at post offices, the football and cricket
grounds, elevators, cinemas, cafes, blood banks, ambulances, hospitals,
entrances, exits. Schoolyard enemies, although white, lived in their areas,
we in ours. Playground games took on racist tones, with more playing of
'cowboys and Indians' than 'good guys *versus* bad guys', the only good
Indian a dead Indian, as we echoed the John Wayne or Gary Cooper
frontier philosophy. There was also 'Allies and Axis', though Axis meant
Nazis, always jackbooted, black-clad SS ghouls with fanged Alsatians,
courtesy of Hollywood B-grade propaganda movies. Japan, a world too
far, we simply didn't know or care about.

Living with, and raised by, an immigrant grandmother meant being her
interpreter, especially of the English-language press. How well, for instance,
can a nine-year-old elaborate in Yiddish the June 1944 Normandy beach
landings? Not very. But a bubble of doubt began to form within the
boundaries of my secure and protective membrane. We had a *Pears'
Cyclopaedia*, complete with gazetteer. Each day, from 1941 onward, following the evening BBC radio World News, she'd ask me to show her, on
the map of Lithuania, Poland or Russia, where the Nazis had got to. I'd
show her Vilna, or Kovno, or Ponevezh, Shadove, Telz. She'd weep.
'What's wrong?' I'd ask. 'Our family is gone,' she'd cry. Gone? One didn't
comprehend 'gone' at that age. On reflection, how perspicacious, almost
prescient, she was: how could she have known what most of the world
didn't know at those points in time?

Then, in April–May 1945, the usual Saturday movie matinee at what
South Africans curiously call 'the bioscope': advertisements, animal cartoon,
serial (Zorro, Superman), newsreel (Movietone News, Pathé News), sing-
along with the Wurlitzer, ice cream, toffee apples and candy floss at the
interval, and then the movie. But this time a voice-over asked all children
under fourteen to leave or 'cover your eyes' when the newsreel came on.
This ten-year-old stayed, fingers splayed to peek at whatever it was. It
proved to be bulldozing corpses at Belsen. The end of near-innocence,

near because between *Pears*, the BBC and my grandmother's tears, I sensed that something was particularly amiss for Jews. But even then the newsreels didn't quite convey those 'Jews' to me: *musselmänner*, a term I learned much later, corpses but yet not corpses, because these dehumanised, skeletal 'things' were not human enough to identify with. That bubble was now stretching a little, beginning to tense my membrane.

The years 1939 to 1945 were crushed between *Crown and Swastika*, in the words of the title of Patrick Furlong's excellent 1991 book on the opposition to South Africa's entry into World War II and the virulent antisemitism of Afrikaner nationalism and the right-wing movements. White South Africa was fervently divided between those who supported Deputy Prime Minister General Jan Smuts's pro-war and pro-British position and those who stood by the Prime Minister, General J.B.M. Hertzog, vigorously opposed to this 'foreign war'. Smuts won a slim parliamentary majority and assumed power, leaving some 40 per cent of the Afrikaner population violently anti-war, or supportive, many actively, of a Nazi victory. Hertzog retired but flirted with ultra-right politics. His Minister of Justice, and then of Defence, Oswald Pirow, founded the New Order, based, he claimed, not on Franco's Spanish but on Salazar's Portuguese national socialism, somehow a 'lesser' variety. It was the same Pirow to whom Hitler had said in November of 1938 – a date significantly earlier than the one generally accepted as the start of the 'Final Solution' – that he knew how to deal with the race 'problem': 'One day the Jews will disappear from Europe.' Hitler's only other confidant on this issue, at that time, was the Czech Foreign Minister.

Others formed Blackshirts, Greyshirts, the South African Fascists, the Gentile National-Socialist Movement. The most dangerous organisation was the *Ossewabrandwag*, the Ox-Wagon Sentinels (or Guard), led by J.F.J. (Hans) van Rensburg. Its 'active' pro-Axis wing was called, not surprisingly, the *Stormjaers* (Storm Troopers). Known by their abbreviation as the *OB*, these men, and the other 'shirts', attacked synagogues, Jewish shops, soldiers in uniform, blew up post offices and railways, and printed and distributed Nazi leaflets and propaganda. I remember going to the Rand Easter Show, akin to the Royal Easter Show in Sydney, always fearful of bomb attacks or conscious of soldiers being waylaid and bashed by Afrikaner students, usually from the town of Potchefstroom. I watched in awe as Jewish teenagers formed vigilante groups to protect prayer and property, as we walked to Friday night Sabbath services in the 'safety' of large groups.

Here, indeed, was a special kind of alienation, of belonging but not quite belonging, of Jews hoping, believing, even preaching, that they were mainstream South Africans but somehow sensing that they had no place in this white South Africanism. The chapter titles on Jewish stereotyping in Milton Shain's *The Roots of Antisemitism in South Africa* (1994) are noteworthy: among others, 'From Pariah to Parvenu', 'Shirkers and Subversives' and, significantly, 'Outsiders and Intruders'. Their whiteness was just barely salvation or redemption in this society so suffused by hate.

In 1945 came the beginning of the end of a primary schooling taught solely by old men and women. All able-bodied men had been 'up north', as active service was called, somewhere between Abyssinia and Egypt and Libya and in the push into Italy, and women were in the armed support services or in munitions factories. Many of their sons had been housed for the duration in St George's Orphanage. They were tough, hungry, lonely, brutalised kids – to whom one paid playground protection money in the form of sandwiches made to order – caraway rye, with *shmaltz* (chicken fat), salami and pickles. Jewish kids they hated and belted, our lunches they revered.

A new deputy principal arrived, a giant of a man, not yet demobilised, in full major's gear, Sam Browne belt, insignia, medals, glory – Phil Green. We begged him to tell us about the war, the 'Allies and the Axis', the heroes, the RAF pilots, the Spitfires, Hurricanes and Mosquito bombers. Instead, for six weeks he chastened us and lectured us on the infamies that men commit upon other men in the name of race. Our little ceremony of innocence was drowned. Membranes were rupturing further as I thirsted for more from Green, my first mentor in humanism. Something was very much awry in my own and my family's views about the hier- and lower-archy of the races. There was a world of horror out there that no one would talk about – not at home, not in *cheder* (the after-hours Hebrew school), not in *shul* (the synagogue).

High school in 1946 gave few explanations about our immediate yesterday's world. Perhaps two of our teachers, like Green, had courage enough to question South Africa's direction in the light of the past decade. One was Ted Gordon, a South African Jew who had served in the Royal Navy; the other was more aggressive and outspoken, the hater of fascism,

Cecil Williams. He later became a theatre director, and a member of *Umkhonto we Sizwe* (Spear of the Nation), the military arm of the African National Congress, the man who drove Nelson Mandela secretly into South Africa on the very day and at the exact time of his recapture (Mandela, 1995: 365, 369, 371–2). But, again, the school was drawn, quartered, sequestered. The Jewish boys from Yeoville Boys' primary were kept in separate forms at King Edward VII until the third senior year of high school, maintaining the cloister of the war years. King Edward's was a public school with private school pretensions, the 'gentlemen in green'.

We had compulsory physical education until fifth (and final) form, each session replete with indoor ball games, and boxing or wrestling matches, often between Christian A and Jewish A, Christian B and Jewish B. In third form in 1948, we believed that the creation of Israel would earn us a little more respect, perhaps lessen such crudities as some teachers calling all Jewish boys 'Lazarus'. But it didn't. 'We'll send you back to Palestine' crowed a pair of Afrikaner Nationalist Party-supporting teachers, as their Dr Daniel Francois Malan, antisemitic theologian, took office on a crude, or rather, even cruder, racist ticket.

Yet one could, in all youthful naïveté, still maintain a strange, not quite rational loyalty, as in rooting for national cricket and rugby teams, for expatriate soccer players in the English League, particularly in the Charlton Athletic team, for golfers like the great Bobby Locke. All white, of course. Perhaps the strong focus on sport allowed an ideal (of sorts) to survive: that the national motto 'United we stand' might just have some meaning; that somehow, somewhere, some day, all that overt antisemitism, that vicious, often murderous racism, that cosmic divide of class and colour, would go away; that Phil Green could find place and space for his humanity.

During the 1950s I learned much more about South Africa, as student and as school teacher. I studied at the Pietermaritzburg campus of Natal University, a two-campus institution then segregated in every possible sense. Generally, faculty members were, as far as race was concerned, 'orthodox' white South Africans, but I had the fortune to be taught, and mentored, by two eminent opponents of apartheid, Edgar Brookes and Arthur Keppel-Jones. Brookes was a humanist, devout Christian, poet, historian, and a senator who represented the Zulu people of Natal during the years of special 'native representation' in the all-white Parliament (between 1937 and 1959, Africans could elect four white senators and three white members of the House of Assembly). Keppel-Jones's *When Smuts Goes* (1950) was a more prophetic than satiric account of South African political life between 1947 and 2015. In 1955 he assured me he was not a seer but 'merely an observer of the train tracks of South African history, following them to their termini' – a phrase that would remain with me when I came to look at Germany and other genocidal societies in later years.

The University Counsellor, who was also College Warden, disliked me. As a devoted Nationalist and supporter (or member) of the *Broederbond* (the secret Afrikaner society, the Band of Brothers), he disliked my Jewishness, my Johannesburg urbanness, the 'liberal' curriculum and teachers I chose. Despite this, he did me one favour. When I applied for a scholarship to do the Honours programme, he called me aside to whisper that if I wanted the bursary I would need a grade at least 15 per cent better than the next candidate: that, he explained, was the Jewish entrance fee to life – another good lesson. I got the marks, and from him, a knowing smile and a pat.

While working the night shift at the offices of the *Natal Witness*, I discovered a stash of antisemitic pamphlets in a hidden cupboard. This *Witness*-printed material was vile stuff, ranging from blood libels[5] to world domination. This was not in Bloemfontein or Potchefstroom, the heart-lands of Afrikanerdom, but in the epicentre of English-speaking King, Crown and Country – the province of Natal. That newspaper was to resurface in my life some forty-three years later.

On graduation, I returned to Johannesburg, to teach at a private secondary school. There I shared a staffroom with Julian Visser, a former *Ossewabrandwag* officer who had been sentenced to death for blowing up a post office in the town of Benoni. (This had been commuted to a life sentence, then a pardon when the Nationalists came to power.) The syllabus of one of the matriculation examinations allowed for a discussion of the 'Native Question and Native Policy'. For all the enlightenment of the school's directors, grades were grades, they said, and they were not about to be jeopardised by antagonising examiners who admired or revered 'the South African way of life'. The choice was clear: use Afrikaner ideology textbooks on the topics, or don't teach that topic.

All this, plus that long-standing feeling that, somehow, I, as a Jew, didn't fit, didn't belong, couldn't belong in that milieu, was about to lead to a major decision.

In early 1960, amid the paranoia and horrors of life after Sharpeville – the killing by police of sixty-nine unarmed Africans and the wounding of many more, all because they refused to carry their 'pass books', the ID booklet that only black Africans were required to carry – it seemed to me that I had six choices.

First, to identify with mainstream (racist) Afrikaner nationalism and ideology. Impossible.

Second, to identify fully with someone else's (liberation) nationalism, in those days black nationalism rather than specifically Inkatha or African National Congress or Coloured or Indian nationalism. Not possible. I wasn't a joiner and I didn't have the guts, if that's what it was, to be a Baruch Hirson or a Ben Turok, eminent (and imprisoned) white opponents of the apartheid regime, sacrificing marriage and children for a cause not fully my own.

Third, to join the Communist Party, the South African branch of which had always been more concerned with human rights and an economic place in the sun for blacks rather than with the overthrow of colonial capitalism. It was a real challenge and a choice, but one I rejected for many reasons, not the least of which was my not needing that false camaraderie which accompanied Jews when they joined the Russian Revolution in 1917. That joining, it seemed to me, was as much about their need for legitimacy as human beings and their social acceptance (for the first time) as it was about fighting oppression.

Fourth, to put on blinkers and pretend that there was nothing amiss around me. Out of the question.

Fifth, to write critiques of the system while still being, if not complicit in it, then at least a companion to it. That, of course, was what I was doing: attempting to teach the 'Native Question' as part of the matriculation syllabus; writing my book, *Shadow and Substance*, on the history of South Africa's racial policies, while living in a rent-controlled apartment in an exclusively white suburb; boasting of being servantless while conveniently ignoring the inclusion with the rent of the services of a man called Moses, a 'boy' aged sixty, who lived in the servants' quarters, minus wife and children, and who cleaned, swept and polished five days a week for a minimal wage (in a building co-owned by a member of the Communist Party and superintended by Sonia Bunting, widow of the founder of the South African CP). I couldn't continue living that kind of lie.

It was that sort of rationalised complicity or collaboration, something I later describe as companionship, that led me to the sixth and final alternative: to remove myself from the environment altogether. This I did, at the end of 1960. I didn't flee, I left. I remember quite vividly the trigger to my racing off to the passport and booking offices. A regular blood donor, I went to give my pint. As the attendant detached the bottle, she affixed a label showing a white circle. 'Is that what I think it is?' 'Yes,' she replied. 'We've been told to practice for the new legislation which will forbid the transfusion of the blood of any one racial group member into a person of another racial group.' The legislation was passed soon enough. I don't recall whether the Nazis, steeped in the 'mythus of blood' as they were, ever went that far. I do recall Dr Maurice Shapiro, head of the Johannesburg blood bank, telling me in Canberra early in 1961 how he had the hopeless task of explaining the legislation to a forthcoming international haematology conference in Japan.

I went to Australia, specifically to the doctoral programme at the Australian National University in Canberra. There, and in the field, I studied Aboriginal administration in northern Australia. An anthropology of white bureaucracy, perhaps, looking at why (Minister for Territories) Paul Hasluck's fine-sounding policy precepts, although often ambiguous and contradictory, either never came to fruition or wound up in practice being the antithesis of what was intended in theory (Tatz, 1964).

Australians, I found, were capable of some pretty deep-seated racist notions and practices, most of which were 'explained' to me, or explained away, as being wrong-headed, perhaps misguided, but generally excusable because they were always well intentioned. I was constantly assailed by contentions that white South Africans were men and women of malevolence and bad faith, as opposed to Australians, who were full of benevolence and good faith. A nonsense and a mischief, of course, but there was none of that messianic South African ideological imperative which said that their God had given their Dutch Reformed Church adherents a 'divine mission' in life to bring blacks to civilisation through apartheid.

At the University of New England in the early 1970s, the culmination of a decade's work in Australia – in Canberra and at Monash University in Melbourne – began to bear fruit. During that decade, I had been very much involved in doing what I couldn't or wasn't allowed to do in South Africa, namely, to attempt to influence change in racial oppression. This was a 'living out' of an earlier frustration: where it had been impossible for me to influence the course of events in South Africa, Australia provided me with an opportunity to make serious efforts in that direction, with some realistic hope of success.

I distinctly remember my membrane's vulnerability in Armidale. Here I was pontificating about racism, its origins, its evolution over centuries, its 'scientific' phase in the nineteenth century, and yet at no time was I talking about Jews and antisemitism as being integral to race politics. Slowly I reached the point of learning and teaching about antisemitism, but always stopping at or about 1941. I remember the resistance which stopped me from passing through to 1942 and beyond – those pictures of the naked women at the edge of the soon-to-be burial pits, in pathetic clasp of dignity in their ultimate indignity, the distorted features of those medically experimented on, Primo Levi's *sommersi*, the drowned ones, the pyjama-striped ones hanging on the wire. By now I knew very well where my relatives in Ponevezh and Shadove had gone, but I couldn't articulate any of it. Suppression of these images was almost total. I'd say to students: 'You read the 1942 to 1945 materials, and I'll meet you again at the Nuremberg Trials, and beyond.'

At Sydney's Macquarie University in the 1980s I taught Aboriginal politics, race politics, South African politics, politics and sport, but still the death factory domain of the Holocaust remained, for me, in a 'too-hard' basket. In 1985, I went to Israel to play golf for Australia in the Maccabiah Games. After the sport, I stayed there on sabbatical and, perhaps a half-a-dozen times, visited Yad Vashem, Israel's official Holocaust memorial and research centre. This was either exorcism or 'flooding': whichever it was, I was having to stare down the barrels of those Nazi years that began with mobile gas vans in Chelmno in December 1941. I met Shalmi Barmore, then director of education at Yad Vashem. We talked, he listened and urged me to come to Israel the following year to attend their intense, three-week-long 'Seminar on Holocaust and Antisemitism'. If I had to name a 'best thing I ever did', it was to attend that course so admirably led by Yehuda Bauer, one that tore through my tissues of resistance and allowed everything from *Pears'* gazetteer, Belsen footage, Phil Green, the Sentinels of the Ox-Wagon, Christian A versus Jewish A, black Australia, New Zealand and Canada to merge into a stream of Holocaust consciousness.

Yad Vashem was, and is, exhilaration: a strange word, indeed, to use about the *Shoah*, but apt because of the reconstruction of events, actors, times, dates, motives, memos and because of the almost forensic dissection of what Bauer referred to as a historical event occasioned by real people and, hence, explicable. Myths fell away, every preconception a wrong conception. My guides helped me reach the heart of darkness and, like Baron, I was assailed daily by the images, the ideas, the ordinary and the extraordinary men and women, no longer as a nightmare but as a stimulus for a search for that minuscule, but essential, pinpoint of malignancy that sets a genocide in motion, and for the supportive surrounding environment that makes for fertile growth.

My search for the malignancy had begun, as an undergraduate, with reading Churchill's World War II memoirs. An episode he described there set off alarm bells about the system in South Africa. At Teheran at the end of 1943, he, Stalin and Roosevelt were dining in the context, *inter alia*, of a decision on unconditional surrender. 'What', asked Roosevelt of Stalin, 'should we do when we get to Berlin?' Unhesitatingly, 'Uncle Joe' replied: 'Fifty thousand must be shot', referring to Hitler's SS and military 'technicians'. Churchill was enraged, muttering darkly that he would rather be taken out into the garden there and then and be shot 'than sully my own and my country's honour by such infamy' (Churchill, 1952: 293–4, 543). What appealed to me was not any magical quality about British justice but Stalin's (and Roosevelt's) sharp specificity of where to locate responsibility for the cosmos of death unleashed by the Nazi regime. Stalin, of course, was as prepared as the Nazis to engage in mass killing without trial.

Later, I read Dwight MacDonald's collection of essays on the 'responsibility of peoples'. The first essay, written pretty much white-hot in March 1945, apportioned blame to the specially trained SS: 'particular kinds of Germans, specialists in torture and murder, whom it would be as erroneous to confuse with the general run of Germans as it would be to confuse the brutality-specialists who form so conspicuous a part of our own local police force with the average run of Americans' (MacDonald, 1957: 21, 33–8). He was very much against a collective German guilt, disparaging 'Teutonophobes' like diplomat Lord Vansittart and the crime writer Rex Stout, and contending that if everyone is guilty, then no one is really guilty. But, curiously, there followed chapters that involved trivialising the Holocaust by comparing it to other crimes, like the bombing of Dresden and brutal and bastardly treatment of the pygmy peoples of the Congo by the Belgians.

I asked nearly all the lecturers at Yad Vashem where they located 'responsibility' for the Holocaust. Each had a different view, ranging from a 'one-man' theory, to forty or fifty ideological 'true believers' in the Nazi hierarchy, to MacDonald's and Stalin's specially trained 50,000. No one said 'Germany', or 'the German people'. I asked many questions about other genocides, particularly the Armenian. No one answered, claiming headache and preoccupation enough with trying to understand the Holocaust. Yehuda Bauer reflected, more strongly as each year went by, on the Armenian genocide being 'a cousin', and then a 'half-brother', to the Judeocide.

My Macquarie colleagues didn't demur when, in 1987, I sought approval to introduce a new third-year undergraduate course, the Politics of Genocide. But one senior professor, in the politest way possible, wanted assurance that the course would have 'balance'. I replied that if that meant I would invite an ex-camp commandant to present an alternative point of view, the answer was 'no'; accordingly, the course had no such 'balance'. Within forty-eight hours of a national newspaper story that genocide, as such, was to be taught for the first time in Australia, the Turkish ambassador sought audience with me. After federal police had 'cased' my office for Armenian assassins, His Excellency arrived – to ask, very politely, why he shouldn't tell the world that Macquarie was running a propaganda outfit, unworthy of a major university. We agreed that he should send an English-speaking academic, who I insisted must have seen the archives of the Ottoman Empire (said to have been opened to the public), to give a two-hour presentation, for 'balance'. The Turks sent a specialist in postwar Turkish foreign policy who hadn't seen any archives, even those that turned out to be only pre-1894. The man had two restaurants in San Diego and we exchanged some delightful recipes. The students dismissed him, very politely, and his last-ditch defence was that all that couldn't have been genocide because the word wasn't invented until 1944, a facile argument I was to hear later about Australia's Aborigines.

The course, I am happy to say, is still alive and well some seventeen years on. Much of the debate and discussion among students and staff focuses, unsurprisingly, on the definition of genocide. In the end, the students are urged to use the only legally valid instrument, namely, Article

II of the Convention on the Prevention and Punishment of the Crime of Genocide. New or re-definitions by lawyers and social scientists are of interest and, in some contexts, of some value, but our emphasis on accountability leads us to a strictly forensic approach. However, for my own work in Aboriginal affairs, and especially in the matter of the 'stolen generations', I have come to value, and to use, the ideas asserted by Christian Pross in *Cleansing the Fatherland* (Aly *et al.*, 1994). While lamenting his inability to 'develop new definitions of the Nazi program and the Nazi perpetrator', he summarises nineteenth-century race theory in a way in which I would wish to see genocide studied, namely, as an ideological tool or as ideological justification for recourse to biological 'solutions' to social or political problems. On the one hand, we have the terse legal Article II(e) 'forcibly transferring children of the group to another group' – which is what Australia did, until the 1980s, with the intention (irrespective of how well or badly motivated) of causing these children to cease being Aboriginal. On the other, the Pross approach encourages investigation of the whole ragbag of 'racial hygiene', and into the entire panoply of 'scientific' thought about race hierarchy being regarded as justification for resorting to, variously, biological elimination or assimilation, to resolve the perceived problem.

My students tend to express impatience with my friend Israel Charny's view of genocide. He sees it, in the generic sense, as the 'mass killing of substantial numbers of human beings, when not in the course of military action . . . under conditions of the essential defencelessness and helplessness of the victims' (Charny, 1994). They understand his concerns about the essentially defenceless and helpless people, but he insists on mass killing of substantial numbers – which applies well to Australia's nineteenth-century private settlers' killing of Aborigines, but not to the 'sophisticated' removal of children by the state. Many also refuse to share his vision that the accident at the Chernobyl nuclear reactor was 'genocide resulting from ecological destruction and abuse'.

Comparing, in teaching and research, the Holocaust with the Armenian and Australian genocides, is not simply to accommodate the sensitivities of other victim groups through an anthology of tolerance for all victim groups (or through a litany of intolerance of all perpetrators). At Yad Vashem, it is quite acceptable to assert the uniqueness of the Holocaust: audiences there don't demur. Sydney is somewhere else. It is an essentially non-Jewish milieu, where one has to prove the singularity of that event – and, in the end, having traversed an array of other ghastly case studies, the students know the degrees of genocide pretty well and how those differences can be articulated.

With these ideas in mind, I founded, at Macquarie University, the Centre for Comparative Genocide Studies in 1993. In 2000, we decided to transfer our work to another institution, and so we affiliated with the Shalom Institute, located at the University of New South Wales. We incorporated our new body as the Australian Institute for Holocaust and Genocide Studies (AIHGS). Our continuing work encompasses the millennia of antisemitism, including the long saga of blood libels; the Nazi war crimes trials, including analysis of the materials used in the three Australian cases in the 1990s; the killing units in Lithuania; the treatment of the Romany peoples by the Nazis; the attempted appropriation of the Holocaust, particularly by Polish politicians and officials who seek to equate the Nazi attempt to dismantle the Polish state with the Nazi attempt to eliminate world Jewry; the issue of impunity in the perpetration of genocide; the emergence of fraudulent claims about Australian involvement as victims (O'Brien, 1997: 4–9);[6] the Vatican and the Holocaust; the great similarities between the Armenian and Jewish genocides; the fate of the Assyrians and the Pontian Greeks, especially in Smyrna in 1923; the issue of whether or not to define events in East Timor as genocide; the 'autogenocide' in Cambodia; and, not least, genocide, as legally defined in the Convention, in Australia over the past two centuries.

A notable achievement is something that seemed unlikely at our Centre's inception, namely, that a southern-hemisphere university could make a major contribution to genocide studies, given the locus of European, African and Asian killing fields and given the focus elsewhere of American university and museum money and activity. That the Centre (now Institute) is sought after as a clearing house, a place of advice, information, research, teaching models and a vehicle of publication astounds us: either there is a dearth of centres of excellence or this Institute has done it well, or both. There are few academic, intellectual and emotional obstacles to our work. Yet one major obstacle does remain – money. Australia has no culture of major endowment to academia, at least not in the humanities and social sciences, no ethos of the *alma mater*. There are also no visionaries who see the need for continuing research and education about genocide. People understand commemorations, shrines, memorials of a physical nature, but in the more enduring sense of what really matters – study, analysis, diagnosis, prognosis, even prevention – people in this 'lucky country' don't invest in death.

Has there been a consistent focus in my writing and teaching these past fifteen years? Yes, a profound appreciation of genocide as the ultimate form of racism. Looking back, I have to say that my personal journey to genocide studies was initially slow, some forty years from the Belsen newsreels to enlightenment in Jerusalem. It was also, initially, an essentially Jewish journey, traumatised by and unwilling to confront the Holocaust while teaching about other dimensions of race relations almost as if they were in a separate universe, unrelated causally to, and uninfluenced by, that singular event.

Experience of ugly race relations was part of my life, almost from infancy. Serious study of race relations began in Pietermaritzburg in the 1950s. It is ironic that that 'Sleepy Hollow' – the city of my student days, once described by a visiting American as 'half the size of New York cemetery and twice as dead' – should have become the flashpoint of so much racial violence in the 1980s and 1990s; ironic, too, that it should re-emerge in my life, in quite bizarre fashion, more than forty years later.

In 1997, while at Natal University to accept an honorary degree, I made a semi-nostalgic visit to the *Natal Witness*. I agreed to the editor's request to reproduce a 'return-of-the-native-son' feature I was to write for the *Sydney Morning Herald* on return. The 2,000-word piece discussed changes since previous visits, the abolition of apartheid in social amenities, the slide into tolerance at the inter-personal level between racial groups, the inherent but as yet potential greatness of the new constitution. There was analysis of the gulf between the new 'rainbow country' idealism and the old realities of gross inequalities in education, health, wealth, leisure, sport. Inevitably, I commented on the serious crime statistics and criticised the ability of the Truth and Reconciliation Commission to arrive at the truth or to reconcile victims or their relatives with what had been perpetrated. The University, for which I had both affection and gratitude, was precariously balanced, wanting to maintain Oxbridge standards while radical students trashed buildings and demanded that if one student passes then all must pass.

Soon after the *Witness* publication, a letter from the University's Principal expressed his Executive's outrage at my ingratitude, my erroneous reference to the trashing of the campus, and my disparagement of the new South Africa. Perhaps, he concluded, they had erred in conferring the title of Doctor of Laws on me. I replied that his own officers had shown me the 'trashing spots'; however, I needed to know whether the newly awarded degree should be deleted from my CV; and I was entitled to know in what way the new South Africa differed from the old in matters of censorship, hypersensitivity and evasion of truth. The award was 'safe', he replied, because the honour was for services rendered to Australian Aborigines, not to the overthrow of apartheid as a 'way of life'. In some respects, how little had changed.

The conceptual wholeness, the bringing together of tributaries which are very much part of the one river, has been an enriching experience. It appears that each new set of discoveries, treatments and approaches produces yet another set. One begins with an (attempted) comprehension of the motives, intent, scale, implementation and operation of the Holocaust. To understand, it is necessary to look at similar phenomena, and so I attempt to unravel the Armenian, Pontian Greek, Rwandan, Burundian and Aboriginal experiences. All cases provoke their own particular brand of denial, and stimulate a need to find appropriate methods for combating that perpetuation of the evil. All cases produce a struggle for reliable and trustworthy memory. Czech novelist Milan Kundera laments that 'the bloody years . . . have turned into mere words, have become lighter than feathers, frightening no one' (Kundera, 1985: 4). In most instances, the victims' memory, however grim, is a social cement that enables them to cohere as a people. It is part of what I call both their 'inside' and their 'outside' history. Memory is also their internal narrative, their chronology, of what befell them. In that important sense, memory is what they need, or want, to commemorate, revere, pass on. Denial, or negation, or disparagement of that memory produces an unbearable hurt.

By contrast, that hurt is sometimes partly assuaged by an apology from the state in which the events were perpetrated. 'Apologetics', the most recently emerging sub-field of genocide, is significant. For perpetrators, or their descendants, it can be 'a relatively low-level piece of Western manners and morals' (Minogue, 1998: 11–20). The Vatican has apologised for its 'tepid' response during the Holocaust; East Germany said 'sorry' to the Jews minutes before reunification and Poland followed suit. 'One cannot dwell constantly on memories and resentments', intoned François Mitterrand in

1994, even as he found the flowers to half-atone for the deportation of so much of French Jewry. The sincerity, depth of feeling, or the tenor of what Kenneth Minogue (1998) calls 'a curious kind of moral sentiment among white Europeans, one that demands purging by apology', is not what is important to the victims or their descendants. Apology, contrary to the beliefs of the John Howard-like politicians of this world, is not always about a slide from moral considerations into political and economic demands for reparation. For the victim groups, it is important that there be an open acknowledgement that something terrible indeed happened. In the absence of such acknowledgement, the victims' trauma continues, aggravated by a denialism that says that nothing ever happened to them. Public apology is one small counter to denialism. On a personal level, it can be, albeit belatedly, some kind of balm for the survivors. For the perpetrator societies, it is usually about a regret, however fleeting, passing or superficial, that they were once the sort of people, or the sort of nation, that they now wish they had not been at those points in time.

2

APPROACHES TO GENOCIDE

While arguments continue over the usefulness (or otherwise) of describing the Holocaust as a unique or singular event, it remains, for those in the West, at least, the yardstick by which all mass killings are judged. For me, it represents the paradigm case and remains the best 'way in' to an understanding of genocide.

Holocaust history – the chronology and the major actors (the perpetrators, the victims and the bystanders) – is well-enough known. Paradoxically, while the distance from the events themselves expands, so too does the search for explanations. The thoughts, notes and commentaries I present here are intended as a set of inquisitive approaches to the study of this genocide, springboards to understanding how it might be freshly addressed. I pose several questions that trouble me, present a number of conundrums and offer few clear-cut answers. As a way of breaking down the potentially vast range of material to consider, I have used four rough categories through which these approaches can be channelled: history, philosophy, religion and, with some reluctance, psychology.

HISTORY

Holocaust and antisemitism

Both these words are, regrettably, euphemistic and inappropriate. Possibly the first Western scholar to use 'holocaust' in a genocidal context – to refer to the Turkish genocides of Hellenic, Armenian and Assyrian populations in Asia Minor between 1914 and 1924 – was Melville Chater in his 1925 article 'History's greatest trek'.[1] He was referring specifically to the burning of Smyrna (Izmir) by Kemal Ataturk's army in September 1922, the culmination of years of massacres and deportations of Christians. The word had, of course, been used by Greeks in antiquity in a non-genocidal context, but here the usage clearly referred to the Turkish theatre of actions. Winston Churchill used the word in connection with the Armenians: 'whole districts blotted out in one administrative holocaust'. That was in 1929. The word comes from the Hellenic *olokautoma*, meaning the destruction of everything by burning.

Holocaust, with a capital H, was Elie Wiesel's chosen term because he wanted the Jewish destruction to be tied to God in that the word derives from ritual sacrifice, from an offering wholly burned by fire in exaltation of God. *Shoah* and *Churban*, the Hebrew words for 'catastrophe' and 'destruction', suggest a more human, secular realm of death. Rightly so: there was no Jewish ritual or offering, as in Abraham's binding of Isaac. There was only a Nazi ritual and a routine of manufactured death. Nor did any angel of mercy intervene on God's behalf to offer an alternative sacrificial body. There was only the total, systematic annihilation of the Jewish collective existence. That, says Arno Mayer (1990: vii), was Judeo-cide – a more pointed and pertinent term, in my view.

In 1879, the German agitator Wilhelm Marr coined the term 'Anti-Semitism' in order to contrast not Jew and Christian, but Jew and German. There was, and is, no 'Semitism' to be anti. Neither hyphen nor capital S is needed for antisemitism, the institutionalised attitudes and actions against Jews. What is meant is the old-style *Judenhass*, Jew-hatred, a stark term we should learn to use. Conor Cruise O'Brien suggests we use 'anti-Jewism', an ugly term for an ugly reality.

In the end, we are stuck with Marr's terminology, now entrenched in many languages, as in the more modern German *antisemitismus*. But the term has to cover a multitude of antisemitisms, a wide range of anti-Jewish sentiments, attitudes and behaviours.

Language, or in this case English, is deficient. There is a need for adjectives so that we can distinguish political antisemitism, national, social, cultural, legal, literary and certainly racial antisemitism. And within each of those sub-species, there are different kinds, and differing orders, of behaviour. There are perhaps the above-mentioned seven genres of antisemitism, and at least ten or more levels or degrees of gravity, with verbal insults as one level of the social genre, and ideological justification of the extermination of Jews as quite another in the racial genre. The notion of disestablishing or destroying the Jewish state – in the name of anti-Zionism – is yet another (neo-genocidal) variety in the universe of Jew-hatred.

The unique versus universal issue

I believe that Holocaust scholars and Holocaust courses, including those at Yad Vashem, should not simply assert the singularity, the uniqueness, of the event. A doubting, even a hostile, world should be shown that it is unique or, to use the latest term, unprecedented. There are, certainly, levels and degrees of genocide. A scale of measurement would help conceptualise the differences, both qualitative and quantitative, between for example what the Athenians did to all the people of Melos in 416 BCE, what mediaeval Europe did to people who were classed as witches, and what the Turks did to 1.5 million Armenians in 1915–16.

This would be akin to the American criminal justice system's recognition of the differences in intent between murder 1 and 2, and manslaughter 1 and 2. Genocide is not a flat word that covers, equally, all systematic attempts to attack the essential foundations and institutions of a targeted people. While the Genocide Convention mistakenly equates the unequal acts constituting the crime, this should not prevent scholars from categorising genocides. Look at the three million dead Polish non-Jews and the three million dead Polish Jews and ask whether this is the same phenomenon. Hitler sought to dismantle the Polish nation state by a genocide of the intelligentsia, a policy that left 90 per cent of the population alive. But the Nazis used the full apparatus of the state to fulfil their first priority – in the end, their only priority – to kill all Jews because they were Jews. Both were genocides: the arithmetic of the Polish dead was the same, but the scale, scope, motive and intent were different.

Of Germany, Talmon talks of the 'remorselessly applied decision to eliminate everyone, but everyone' (1980: 2–3). According to the liberal German historian Eberhard Jäckel, 'never before had a state . . . decided that a specific human group, including its aged, its women, its children and infants, would be killed as quickly as possible, and then carried through this regulation using every possible means of state power' (1969: 47–66). This practice excluded the possibility that Jews might surrender, join the perpetrators, collaborate, convert to the Nazi faith or sell themselves into slavery to save their lives. For the Nazis, wrote historian (and survivor) Saul Friedländer, the Jew was 'irredeemably evil in his very being' (1977: 5). Emil Fackenheim (1985) contends that Jewish history is filled with expulsion, exile, inquisition, pogrom, massacre and mass murder because of what Jews did, or believed, or practised religiously or culturally. For him, the 1935 Nuremberg laws signalled a fatal change: henceforth, Jews would be 'dealt with' simply because they were Jews.

The issue is not whether the Judeocide was unique or universal; it is unique *and* universal. Genocide has always been part of human history. Some instances have been similar in scope and scale to the Armenian and Jewish genocides, some different. These genocides have all been tragic, yet in each we detect some vaguely rational purpose, whether economic, nationalistic, punitive, linguistic or political. The Holocaust is a genocide, and hence part of the universal phenomenon, but it is the only one of its kind – if for no other reason than that the murdering of people became an end in itself, that the murder served no purpose other than murder, and that the enormous resources consumed in the killing contravened both rational and national self-interest. There can be no better illustration than that of the Nazi dedication of armed men, machinery and railways to death marches and camps for unarmed, dispirited and almost lifeless civilians while they were simultaneously fighting, for their very survival, another enemy, a determined foe which had the very real potential to destroy them, and did.

There is a serious problem in the universal approach. It is common for non-Jews to teach or exhibit materials encompassing the fates of the Armenians, the Romany people, the Ukrainians and the Cambodians. By omitting the critical factors of the murderers' intent, motive, scale and methodology, they tend to flatten, even trivialise, the Holocaust. If all mankind commits genocide, and if all genocide is simply genocide, why is this Jewish catastrophe so special? This increasingly common impatience with Jewish memory seems to rest on a double fulcrum: a conscious or unconscious dislike of Jews, and a conscious effort to bypass having to look too closely at *that* history.

It is common for Jews, especially in the United States, to engage in 'Museums of Tolerance'. The attitude underlying that approach is defensive, negative, perhaps even destructive. 'Weep for the human fate', it says to the viewer, 'and if you have a few tears left over when you get to the end of the hall, spare them for the Jews'. The real challenge is to show the Judeocide's uniqueness, without special pleading and without diminishing the deaths of others.

Jewish self-interest

A reality of Jewish life has been an exaggeration, or plain misunderstanding, of that which gives non-Jews cause for antisemitism. Historical, traditional, *völkisch*, Christian and Muslim antisemitism are such that no new or other *raison d'être* is necessary. Fatally, almost, Jews persist in avoiding any public activity which they believe may give rise to antisemitism. Thus, the American Jewish leadership delayed publication of details of the 'Final Solution' lest Americans might come to feel that they were engaging in a 'Jewish war'. The leaderships' notion was that this 'belief' might create additional antisemitism, or a new kind of antisemitism! The South African leadership asked a refugee ship, the *Stuttgart*, to turn back in 1936 because its arrival would cause antisemitism – in a society already overtly, actively and deleteriously antisemitic in thought, word and deed. So, too, rabbis and community leaders in Australia practised their policy of ideological and community 'non-distinctiveness' by insisting to the federal government that the preservation of local 'freedom and civilisation' would be in jeopardy if 'hordes' of European refugee Jews were allowed in. Foreign Jews, according to Australian Jews, would create antisemitism. 'Assimilable' physical types should be admitted, and then only in small numbers.

Jewish communities, too, need a more realistic perception of the nature of antisemitism.

Intentionalism, functionalism or inevitabilism?

For perhaps twenty years now there has been a serious debate, both theoretical and personal, both abstract and highly emotional, about what is called 'intentionalism', the 'straight path' to Jewish destruction, *versus* 'functionalism', the 'twisted path' to the 'Final Solution'. The late Lucy Dawidowicz (1975) represents the former school, arguing that the destruction of Jews was intended from the outset, an outset that might even date from Hitler's attendance at military academy in 1919. It was consistent dictatorial will that made it happen. Karl Schleunes (1970) best represents the latter school which sees the Nazi era as a political system in which normal, sound administration was replaced by propaganda. It sees the disintegration of traditional bureaucracy into a crooked maze of ill-conceived and uncoordinated task forces. It depicts the fragmentation of decision-making and the blurring of political responsibility. Into that chaos, in that 'twisted path' of the war setting, some forty or fifty 'true believers' in the SS put into action a war of extermination against the Jews which was not only inconsistent with, but also detrimental to, their other war of territorial conquest.

Functionalism is thus seen to be the better path to the exculpation of a nation. Chaos, ambiguity, blurred lines of accountability and responsibility all point to the fanatical will of the few rather than of the many, of more tangible and identifiable perpetrators rather than the ghastly prospect that a whole nation was somehow involved. My view of functionalism is that it embraced most of the nation, as discussed later in this chapter.

The impact of Hitler and Nazism on German village life has been ignored by all but a few scholars. Walter Rinderle and Bernard Norling (1993) have assessed the Nazi impact on Oberschopfheim, a Catholic village in south-western Germany. Their academic study, like William Sheridan Allen's (1984 [1965]) study of 'Thalburg' (in reality, Northeim) tells us not about coercion but about acceptance, even willing adoption, of the Nazi credo by the peasants. Perhaps the best source for an appreciation of German peasant willingness comes from the German writer, Hans Helmut Kirst. His novel, *The Fox of Maulen* (1968), sometimes published as *The Werewolves*, is a caustic account of the rapid leap by ordinary Germans from (alleged) 'resignation' to 'recruitment' to 'perpetration'. In that sense, functionalism, as fortuitous advantage-taking in an unforeseeable gap in the smokescreen of war, does not hold water. Was there merely a set of aberrant circumstances – postwar depression, reparations, hunger, the need for restored dignity – that mixed so fatally for all concerned? These dichotomies of interpretation are all too simple.

Can we not view all this in another way? Can we not follow German history, as Keppel-Jones claimed he could do with South African history in 1950, as on a set of railway tracks, leading to that inevitable terminus?

I see a series of building blocks being assembled, aggregated and accreted: from the days of *völkisch* antisemitism, church contempt and Christian antisemitism, to the rise of 'scientific' racism, the anthropology of race, the attractions of fascism and the revolt against modernity, the emphatic insistence on an ethnic nationalism, the eugenics movements, the beginnings of *rassenhygien* (racial hygiene), the attempts in 1895 to prevent further Jewish migration to Germany, the antisemitism rampant in the German universities in the 1910s and 1920s, and so on. I see an engine that had been assembled by the ideas and actions of various designers, engineers, fuel makers and lubricant manufacturers, one that needed only a driver to switch it on. In short, the Holocaust was not inevitable; but all the ingredients needed to make it happen, to allow it to happen, to enable it to happen, were already in place.

Genocidal machines of this capacity are not part of the tele-fantasy world of the *X-Files*. They do not land overnight from outer space, wreak their evil, and then depart. Nor do they get shot down, once and for all, by the good guys.

Resistance: five questions and no answers

1. In February 1943, several hundred German women demonstrated outside Gestapo headquarters in Berlin for the release of their *Mischlinge* husbands. (*Mischlinge* meant progeny of Jewish and non-Jewish unions, in varying degrees of *Mischung*, 'blend' or 'mixture'.) They were not set upon, assaulted or imprisoned. Their husbands were released and survived the war and the Nazi mission of extermination. Why did this protest work? And since it did work, why was there not more action like it? And how come the Nazis allowed well over 100,000 *Mischlinge* to serve in the Wehrmacht, even to rise to the higher echelons, as in the case of the Luftwaffe's General Erhard Milch?[2]

2. If the *Judenrat* (Jewish Council) in Minsk and the Jewish leadership in Slovakia could not only *not* collaborate but resort to armed defiance, why did the Amsterdam *Judenrat* co-operate with the Nazis in the way it did? Why did the Vilna Ghetto and its leadership support Rumkowski-like responses, as described below? Do these contradictions tell us something about specific Jewish communities, at a particular time and place, or about Russian, Slovakian, Dutch or Lithuanian Jews in general, or about Russian, Slovakian, Dutch or Lithuanian societies?

3. Why is Jewish resistance always perceived and presented as guns and grenades, as if there were no other forms of resistance? Resistance, says Bauer in lectures, was 'any group action consciously taken in opposition' to Nazi decrees. Agreed. But surely resistance was also involved in the individual engaging in forbidden prayer, or in having a child in impossible circumstances, or in the individual determined on *überleben*, an attitude that said 'I will outlive them'? (Bauer has subsequently revised several of his views about the nature of resistance (2002: chapter 6).)

4. Why do people at museums like *Lochomei Hagetaot* (the Ghetto Fighters' House) in Israel virtually set aside Zionism and its historic achievements by trying to prove a direct causal connection between the Warsaw Ghetto uprising and the creation of Israel? There were hundreds of group actions of rebellion, defiance, opposition and uprising. Why are so few celebrated in the manner they deserve?

5. Why is it – given that we know how difficult or impossible and/or ineffective any resistance was – that some commentators persist in further victimising the Jews by castigating them for their alleged meekness rather than commending what occurred?

I have no answers to these questions, and many others like them, which confront me. But perhaps there is some value in simply asking them.

The role of academics

Biologists, eugenicists, anthropologists, psychiatrists and lawyers provided the building blocks, or the engine parts, of the genocidal apparatus. There are clear-cut steps in race politics, including this case study of the Holocaust. These steps are accompanied or attended by sentience, rationality, logic, premeditation, and high levels of consciousness and articulation.

Even allowing, for a moment only, Saul Friedländer's (1977) notions of 'utter irrationality' and 'insane impulses', there had to be, and there were, six, possibly seven, sequential steps in Nazi race policy and practice: (1) formulation of an idea, followed by (2) exposition, (3) justification, (4) adoption, (5) legitimisation, (6) implementation and, subsequent to the events, (7) rationalisation (as explanation, justification or exculpation). There is, in some quarters, an eighth step: denialism. The professors, or their predecessors, were responsible for the first three essentials, and it is they who, yet again, take care of the seventh and eighth.

I am not wedded to the 'free speech' or 'First Amendment' philosophy, much more prevalent in the United States than in Australia. With the benefit of a legal education, I learned very early on that there are no absolute rights: I cannot live wherever I choose to live, I cannot practise any ritual I wish to in the name of religion, I cannot assemble wherever I wish to assemble, and I cannot say, in word or on web, whatever I feel like saying. Australia's admired social critic Phillip Adams never tires of berating anti-vilification laws: 'How can we honestly put people in jail for saying things?' he asks. Apart from implementation, all other steps, or factors, in the equation are 'mere words'. If one follows the steps above, it is plain that words can be, and have been, fatal.

Meta-history

In his essay 'A Plea for the Dead', Elie Wiesel says: 'the events of those days flowed from no law and no law flows from them'; it is 'a mystery that passes our comprehension and represents our defeat' (1965: 152). The Holocaust 'outruns our perceptions'. In the face of this destruction, there can only be silence. My response is yes, initially. But Bauer rightly argues that this was a human event in history: it happened, it was done by people and it must therefore be explicable. We now have, in English alone, perhaps 5,000 books attempting to explain it. Yad Vashem and its network of scholars have done much to unravel the mystery – and Wiesel has hardly been silent. His collected works are called *Against Silence* (1985).

There has been criticism of historians who press for answers. Wiesel contends that there is no longer anything to understand, no longer anything to know: 'It is not by playing with words or with corpses that you will understand or know.' In answer, Michael Marrus argues that, while

Auschwitz was indeed another planet, silence is a counsel of despair. If the Holocaust were beyond history, beyond examination and explanation, then it would become irrelevant to our daily lives.

PHILOSOPHY

'Philosophy' may not be the ideal word to describe the material in this section. But I can't find a better one for my search for some truth and wisdom in a domain that seems to defy clear, rational explanation. I have been an avid reader of Morris Ginsberg, formerly at the London School of Economics and Politics, whose writings on justice in society (1965) informed and assisted much of my earlier research and writing. A sociologist and a social philosopher, Ginsberg was interested in the law, and it is in his sense of speculation about the need for moral and reasoned explanations that I use the word 'philosophical'.

Darwin and Darwinism

Darwin was not a racist. As man advances in civilisation, he wrote, so the simplest reason would tell him that he ought to extend his social instincts and sympathies to all the members of his nation, and then on to the men of all nations and races. But his science destroyed one of the greatest props upholding the ethic of 'thou shalt not kill'. Darwinism, wrote Talmon (1980: 14–16), deprived man of his uniqueness in the order of creation; man was no longer created by God; there is no order in the universe – there is only the struggle of all against all, one in which the strong, the fit and the talented rule.

An effect of Darwinism was the removal of whatever brakes and reins the churches had had on murderous violence towards non-Christians and, in particular, towards the Jews. From the fourth century onward, the Christian canon had followed St Augustine's doctrine that Jews should be brought low, harassed, demeaned and expelled, but not killed. They were needed to witness the second coming of Christ, an event they had to see to realise the wrongness of their original rejection of him as the Messiah. The admonition not to kill saved hundreds of thousands of Jews from what was otherwise a pretty murderous Christianity. In a real sense, the

Darwinian 'enlightenment' eliminated God from 'the order of the universe' and thus facilitated the pathway to slaughter – in the name of 'science'.

Otherness in life and in death

Since the 1980s, 'other', 'others', 'significant others' and 'otherness' have become vogue words. Edward Said did not discover the concept: he simply brought a well-worn idea to public attention. In 1934, Mordecai Kaplan explained the 'otherness' of Jews as primary, especially when they are in danger. Otherness, not 'Chosenness', is a more comprehensive and embracing essence of Jewishness than formal religion. It encompasses history, literature, language, social organisation, folkways, sanctions, standards of conduct, aesthetic values and social ideals (Kaplan, 1934: 177–8). He might well have added a code of ethics, the role of Jews in human affairs and a land-based nationalism (Zionism). This totality is 'Jewishness'. As a construct, it incorporates devout 'non-Jewish' Jews like Isaac Deutscher and humanistic Jews like Yehuda Bauer. (In 1958, Deutscher explained his 'non-Jewishness' or, rather, his 'non-Judaicness': 'I am, however, a Jew by force of my unconditional solidarity with the persecuted and exterminated. I am a Jew because I feel the pulse of Jewish history; because I should like to do all I can to assure the real, not spurious, security and self-respect of the Jews' (Deutscher, 1968: 51).)

Jew-hatred often rests on the notion of God's election of Jews as His 'Chosen People'. This is myth, albeit real enough for the early Christians who sought to proclaim the Jews as *Israel carnalis*, the people of the flesh, as opposed to Christians who were now the chosen people, and hence *Israel verus*, the true people of Israel. If there was, or is, any validity to Jews as 'chosen', then it rests on the concept that Jews were chosen by God to observe not ten, but 613 commandments.[3]

But it is this very quality of positive otherness, rather than the more religious notion of 'chosenness', that the world has turned into its value opposite. Jews have always been depicted as both other and unlike, by badges, special dress, special areas of residence, and citizenship status. From the thirteenth or fourteenth century onwards in Europe, Jews were demonised and depicted in church art as tailed, horned, beastly and Satanic. But by the time of the living corpses in the Warsaw Ghetto and a myriad other such places, by the time of the striped ones strung out on the Belsen barbed wire, Jews had indeed become 'other' – but this time, quite visibly, three-dimensionally, other than human.

The value of Jews

Discussing the bystanders, the individuals and the nations, Friedländer says that they may have been motivated by self-interest, pseudo-ideological choices or traditional antisemitism. But whatever the motivation, the result, except in the instances of righteous gentile behaviour, was always 'a choice in which the Jew was less than any other consideration he was weighed against' (Friedländer, 1977). Everybody should stop and ponder that – always less! In the documentary film *Auschwitz and the Allies*, Ben Ami says, 'Jews were of no value to the Germans, except as hair and gold teeth.' They were of no value to the Allies. 'Even if I had been able to sell one million Jews, who would have bought them?' Eichmann asked – not (says Wiesel) without truth. It seems that, in the eyes of the world, the Jew will always be less than any other consideration, except, dialectically, when he is more than any other consideration in his alleged evil, his cunning, his 'control' of the world's media and his aim to control the world's economies. Faced with this eternal value placed on my own group, I have come to share with so many fellow Jews the belief that self-reliance is the only choice. This may look like, but is not intended as, a contradiction of Bauer's view that it is only non-Jews who can fight antisemitism with any degree of success.

The Jewish 'race'

The German rather than the Nazi biomedical vision saw Jews as a biologically determined race, whose characteristics were both immutable and dangerous. There have been two Jewish responses to what geneticist Benno Müller-Hill (1988) calls this 'murderous science'. First, the Hitlerian legacy is such that a great many Jews still define themselves as a race when, by any anatomical or anthropological classification of mankind, they are no such thing. Second, while many Jews, in one breath, reject that vision of themselves as a race, in the next they proclaim their Jewishness as a biological (hence 'racial'?) inheritance from their mother (only). (Traditional, Orthodox Jewry accepts a person as Jewish if the mother is Jewish, since maternal parenthood cannot be doubted.)

There is a contradiction and, yet, for most religious Jews, a simultaneous truth. Presumptuous as this may sound, I believe that *Halakhah*, the venerated written and oral Jewish law, needs to be given a fresh interpretation if it is to disavow the racial categorisation of Jews which was born out of the 'scientific' racism of the nineteenth century. To claim that a group of people share a common ancestry may be scientifically justifiable; to claim that they share inherent virtues or vices which make them inherently better or worse than other people is quite unwarranted.

The responsibility of people

Justice across the generations is one of the most difficult of all moral philosophical questions. How do we judge who was responsible and accountable for 215 years of Aboriginal oppression? In Germany, what period do we judge: only the twelve years from 1933 to 1945, or over a hundred years, or the whole German nation from 1848? Lord Vansittart, in *Lessons of My Life* (1943), believed the latter. Was it the maniacal Hitler, as most assert? Was it the forty or fifty SS elite, the 'true believers', as Bauer once told me? Was it the 50,000 specially trained SS, as Stalin told Roosevelt in 1943? Was it the English, French and German academicians of the nineteenth and early twentieth centuries, as I often argue (Tatz, 1989)?

What is the meaning of responsibility? Is it only legal, in Eichmann's criminal sense? Tim Mason (1981: 23–40) insists that we must counterbalance the intentionalist arguments because they have great flaws. He looks at the logical and moral possibility that systems and institutions, as well as the persons who exercise power within them, may be responsible for terrible crimes. But if this is the case – and based on my work in South Africa and Australia, I believe it is – then all economic, social, political, legal, religious, administrative and educational systems are involved. If whole systems are involved, infinitely more people are culpable. Therefore, almost all who comprised the German nation – or the South African or Australian nations – bore degrees of responsibility. This is precisely what Ernst Nolte (1985, 1986, 1988) is so busy denying. It was not the systems and institutions, he argues, but the aberrant 'them' Germans who manipulated the systems, as opposed to the 'us' Germans who had nothing to do with it.

Moral/metaphysical guilt

Did I participate in the ugly reality of South African apartheid while being a speaker-researcher opposing that ideology? Yes. I wrote critically, yet I employed servants, people disbarred from conjugal rights and the company of their children, at the 'ruling rates' of pay. Was I morally, metaphysically, guilty? Yes. Is this moral guilt real, or is it just my need to indulge in some moral miasma because I need to, or want to, in order to make myself 'look good'? It is, indeed, real. Is this moral guilt a nursery, a necessary, preparatory seedbed in which legal-criminal activity can later occur? Yes. Was there an avenue out of any further complicity or companionship? As I explained in chapter 1, one mechanism for escaping culpability, and subsequent guilt, was to leave the arena of complicity.

Wiedergutmachung

This is the German word for reparation and restitution, 'making good again'. There is no system for the restitution of limbs, organs, families, children, lives. One can give back the giveable, such as stolen art, something now much in vogue. One can restore the restorable, such as a destroyed synagogue. For the rest, as international lawyer Grotius said in 1625, there is only the common denominator of money, as with those Swiss banks and German industries now busy with tokenistic payments some fifty-eight years down the track.

Is that all? We academics and teachers have to do more than merely insist that reparation is made. We must each make our own special contribution towards achieving the reality of the cliché 'it must never happen again'. We need to do more than build shrines in the hope that such exhibits will ward off repetition. Much of the world is too busy either trivialising, relativising, flattening, deflecting, appropriating, forgetting, distorting or denying the event. Questions must always be asked. We can press Christians, in general, to come to terms with their culpability, if not before and during the Holocaust era, then certainly in the cases of Rwanda and Bosnia. We can press Germans to do even more to face their history.

In secondary and tertiary education classes, we can promote the centrality of genocide rather than leave it in darkness. We can introduce the study of antisemitism and its consequence (Judeocide), and other genocides, into professional curricula. Architects, engineers, biologists, pharmacists, medical practitioners, lawyers and teachers need to know how their disciplines have been perverted, in genocidal eras, in the management and operation of mass murder.

Objectivity and subjectivity

The 1951 Japanese film *Rashomon* is a sharp lesson in how differently the participants in, and witnesses to, the same event (a mediaeval murder and a rape) see, feel and interpret it. It teaches us about the unknowability of truth. The Holocaust is replete with the knowable, the unknowable and the seemingly unfathomable. Conundrums and contradictions abound. As with quicksilver, when we think we have hold of a blob of truth, we don't. A dialectic approach would allow us to see tensions and conflicts, to appreciate the most difficult of Holocaust phenomena, namely, that some apparently contradictory views are often simultaneous truths. Perhaps the most puzzling, and poignant, of Holocaust topics in this context is the behaviour of righteous gentiles, those who saved Jews for no reward and who, in so doing, put their own property or lives at risk. A fair number of them hated Jews.

Despite constant protestations to the contrary, all science and research is subjective. 'Value-freeness', or neutrality, is a false god and more so in the field of human history than in any other. Louis de Jong, the Dutch historian, exemplified in *The Netherlands and Nazi Germany* (1990) how careful, meticulous history can be unashamedly, unapologetically subjective. Is there objectivity in the works of German historians Ernst Nolte and Andreas Hillgruber, the men who argue that the Holocaust was only one of several genocides, that Hitler was merely imitating Stalin's 'Asiatic' policies, that the Holocaust was not an 'original' genocide, and that what the Nazis did was no different in genre from the American actions in Vietnam (Nolte, 1988; Hillgruber, 1986)? For men of intelligence, their argument is both specious and pathetic.

Judgment

Judgment of perpetrators occurs in many places and forms, in history books, in literature, film, art, in popular culture and, of course, in the forensic records of such trials as have taken place.

Judgment of the victims, however, is an excruciating exercise. Many Jews and non-Jews of a younger generation raise the question in class or in social discussion: why did the Jews not do more? why did they not resist? kill a few Nazi guards? Judgment of the victims has even been raised by some who survived. Elie Wiesel insists that we must not judge the Jewish victims.

Historians have a clear-cut duty to tell the story, to analyse the elements of the story, and then to evaluate and judge the characters. Assessing Chaim Rumkowski, the 'Elder' or 'King of the Jews' in the Lodz Ghetto, the man who delivered children to the Nazis on the rationale that adults could bear children later (if they survived), the man whose policies, if not for a Russian technical hitch, might have saved 69,000 Jews, Bauer judged that he would first have pinned a medal on him – and then hanged him (Bauer, 2002: 132, and in lectures at Yad Vashem).

Shalmi Barmore, my tutor at Yad Vashem when he was director of education there, said that he does not have the moral or philosophical tools to make that kind of judgment. At that ghastly level, not many of us do. But we must judge, and on 'lesser' levels we can do so, for example, on the behaviour of Jewish leaderships in America, Australia and South Africa during the war years.

The singular person and the collective abstraction

The survivors have a valid point: their individual maiming, torture and degradation are real enough, and so is the commonplace feeling of guilt at having survived, of luck that came their way but not to the six million others. Yet historians talk in collective terms, in sweeping concepts like 'the Jews', 'the Poles', 'the bystanders'. For many survivors, to make general and abstract that which for them is individual and physical is a kind of blasphemy.

Their narrative is critical. For many years, the Yad Vashem seminar on the Holocaust and antisemitism tried to avoid including survivors in the programme because they tended to personalise issues in classes, forever seeking explanations about their individual experiences. I vividly recall taking a survivor of five camps to the Jerusalem course: this woman was desperate for an explanation of her fate. After continuous interruption by her of 'abstract' lectures, someone suggested that she be allowed to address the seminar. This was highly effective. Thereafter, the historical abstractions continued, but in a group now more informed, and warmed, by that survivor's story. Only in this way can we bridge the gulf that so often exists between the survivors and those whose profession it is to explain how they were able to survive.

RELIGION

Theodicy, the vindication of the justice of God, especially during the Holocaust, is of major moment to Christians. Regular conferences are given on the topic, often under such rubrics as 'The Crisis in Christianity' and 'Where were the Churches during the Holocaust?'. Books and articles with titles like 'The concept of God after Auschwitz' (by Hans Jonas, 1968) are still much in vogue; others, like 'The concept of man after Auschwitz' (by Jack Bemporad, 1968), much less so.

For those who want to pursue these issues in greater depth, there is no better exposition than Yehuda Bauer's 2002 book. Clinically, logically, he dissects the views of the late Lubavitcher Rebbe (Rabbi) Menachem Mendel Schneersohn and many others, on God and the Holocaust. Bauer says that not one of them is able to answer the question of why the children were killed. He concludes by saying that 'the theology of the Holocaust is fascinating, but it is a dead end'. I am not a theodicist; rather, a secularist and humanist who is inquisitive enough to still want to look for, and perhaps even find, some explanations in an area of study with which I am not fully comfortable, or at home, and in which I certainly lack the wisdom and knowledge of a Bauer.[4]

'A true Christian cannot be an antisemite'

This is the opening tenet of Professor Jules Isaac's *The Teaching of Contempt: Christian Roots of Anti-Semitism*, published in English in 1964. Isaac, the venerable French historian, who influenced and befriended Pope John XXIII, published his *Genèse de l'antisémitisme* in 1956. In the *Contempt* book, he pointed out that all authorities agree that antisemitism is, by definition, unChristian, even anti-Christian: 'A true Christian cannot be an anti-Semite; he simply has no right to be one.' He quotes the philosopher Jacques Maritain as decrying this phenomenon as 'an anti-Christian madness' and Pope Pius XI as saying to a group of Belgian pilgrims in 1938 that 'Anti-Semitism is inadmissible . . .'. A Decree of the Holy Office, on 25 March 1928, stated, 'The Apostolic See . . . condemns in an especial manner the hatred against the people once chosen by God, that hatred, namely, which nowadays is commonly called anti-Semitism.' Protestant churches have the same viewpoint, expressed graphically by a resolution of the World Council of Churches in Amsterdam in 1948: 'We call upon all the churches we represent to denounce anti-Semitism, no matter what its origin, as absolutely irreconcilable with the profession and practice of Christian faith. Anti-Semitism is sin against God and man' (Isaac, 1964: 21–3).

In the light of centuries of teaching and preaching contempt, and in the behaviour of churches during the Holocaust, the historical verdict is that but a fraction of Christianity was, and is, Christian. That must remain a Christian problem.

Jews and the crisis in Christianity

Yad Vashem and Franklin Littell have convinced me that other people besides Jews have to face their histories. Emil Fackenheim, German-born rabbi and religious existentialist, writes that to allow the gulf between Jew and Christian to widen is to give Hitler a posthumous victory – because he succeeded so well in widening the gulf between them that Christians became oblivious of Jews as human beings (Fackenheim, 1970, 1985). At this stage, I am not sure that most of us can respond in the way these Christian theologians wish, and so help them face their histories. Most Jews cannot cope with their own religious and emotional responses to the Judeocide, let alone find the capacity, now, to help Christians resolve their crisis of credibility, their sins of antisemitism. And when Christians do respond, as did the Vatican in 1999, the *responsum* is fraught with omissions and evasive elisions, as I discuss later.

Excommunicated Jews

One aspect of religious practice has emerged in Holocaust history: excommunication. A perennial in the literature is the hypothetical question: what if Pope Pius XII had threatened or actually excommunicated the Nazi (Catholic) hierarchy? Or what if the Vatican had placed all German Catholics under interdict, that is, an ecclesiastical censure of all Catholics which bars them from the sacraments, religious services and Christian burial?

Few people know that there is a form of Jewish excommunication, and only Rabbi Fackenheim has raised it in the Holocaust context. Can a Jew cease being Jewish? Again, we have dialectical contradictions. For Jewish orthodoxy, birth or conversion alone creates Jewishness, notwithstanding that a Jewish person may eschew, deny and disavow all that is involved in being Jewish. So, when is a born, practising Jew no longer a Jew? When, answers Fackenheim, such a Jew betrays, maims or kills a fellow Jew during the Holocaust or, obviously, in a pogrom or genocide outside that event. (He doesn't say anything about an ordinary Jewish murderer, but pinpoints a Jew who kills another Jew because that person is Jewish.) As a rabbi, he would impose *herem*, that is, excommunication, at least in a metaphorical sense. (In the *halakhic* (traditional Jewish law) sense, *herem* is extremely rare.) Fackenheim has the tools for such judgment. Have Orthodox leaders? Have we, as citizens, students, readers?

Jewish unity only in death?

Many Jews still believe that their fate at the hands of the Nazis lay in their religious Jewishness, in their Judaicness. There are two propositions to consider. First, it did not matter to the Nazi regime whether Jews were integrated or separated, assimilated or agnostic, ultra-Orthodox or Reform, or were by then practising Christians with a Jewish parent or grandparent. Their kind of Jewishness made not one iota of difference to the German–Jewish relationship. Any kind of Jew deserved to be killed. Second, Jewish resistance in the ghettos and in the death camps transcended all differences about shades of religiosity, Zionism or socialism. Only in death was there Jewish unity, a particularly bitter irony since it is our (quite mythical) monolithic, homogeneous, conspiratorial unity in life that allows for the simplistic notion of Jewish 'otherness'. Perhaps the Nazis recognised that only in the total, indivisible mass graves was there 'final proof' of Jewish oneness and sameness?

Some rabbinical responses during the Holocaust

Rabbi Kalman Klonymos Shapira, an ultra-Orthodox Polish *Hasid* (pious man) from Piazsno, maintained a contemporary Sabbath commentary for his disciples. Found in a buried milk can in 1960, his *Esh Kodesh* ('Holy Fire') covers the period September 1939 to July 1942 (Schindler, 1990). He begins with theodicy, affirmation of the divine, with the classical notion of suffering as being educational. Normal theology recedes when he asks God why He does not respond. He moves on from *Kiddush Hashem*, sanctification of the Divine Name and the acceptance of martyrdom, to a broader concept – *Kiddush Hakhayim*. The latter term was coined by Rabbi Yitzchak Nissenbaum, who died in the Warsaw Ghetto in 1943. It means both the sanctification and the protection of our lives. In earlier Jewish martyrdom, the Jew had the option of choosing life, even if it meant negating Judaism. During the Holocaust, the choice became the manner in which the Jew would accept and prepare for death. But as the darkness goes on, he asks God where He is and what value there is in Him if there are no victims left alive to respond. He concludes, or his life concluded, in Majdanek, the Nazi concentration camp on the outskirts of Lublin, with a plea to his congregation not to give in, not to give Hitler a cheap victory and always to remember God.

Rabbi Yissakhar Shlomo Teichtal, an ultra-Orthodox rabbi in Budapest, was an eye-witness. A strong anti-Zionist in the 1930s, his entire theology changed. Instead of helping our Zionist children, he wrote, we mourned them, discouraged them, cut them off. His message, in his *Em Habanim Semekhah* ('The Joyful Mother of Children'), was clear: our exile victimised us and we did not even see the exile; we struggled among ourselves and we regarded everything other than 'us' as an anathema. Some of the blood now being spilled must be blamed on the Jewish leadership who refused to see that in Zionism lay redemption and salvation (Schindler, 1984, 1990). The Rabbi was killed by a Ukrainian prisoner in January 1945 on a train carrying people from Auschwitz to Bergen-Belsen. His last act was one of *hesed* (loving kindness) as he attempted to intervene on behalf of a fellow Jew whose morsel of bread was taken forcibly from him.

The influential Zionist leader Stephen Wise, an American Reform rabbi, was at the centre of events when the details of the 'Final Solution' came through. He sought backroom, quiet influence on American and Jewish responses to the news. Peter Bergson, of the *Irgun*, the underground armed organisation formed in Palestine in 1931, sought maximum publicity of the slaughter. Wise, at that time and place, went so far as to equate Bergson with Hitler. It is such fellow-hatred, amid such carnage, that fills me not so much with confusion as with despair at, and disappointment in, the Jewish condition.

Some rabbinical responses after the Holocaust

In 1970, Emil Fackenheim wrote 'never, within or without our Jewish history, have men anywhere had such a dreadful, such a horrifying, reason for turning their backs on the God of history'. Yet, he concludes, after nearly two millennia, the molested, slandered and slaughtered Jews held fast to a God of history with a faith which, while shakeable, remained, in fact, unshaken.

There are, of course, other views which Fackenheim castigates as spurious. Thus we have another *Hasidic* leader, the Satmar Rebbe, Yoel Teitelbaum, saying that the Jews were supposed to stay in exile until the Messiah came: they did not, and by responding to Zionism, they sinned and were duly punished. Rudolf Kastner, a Budapest Zionist, negotiated with the Nazis to have a trainload of 1,684 Jews taken safely out of Hungary in 1944.[5] One of those on board was Teitelbaum, who went first to Palestine as a refugee, and then on to New York in 1947. There he headed the *Satu-Mare* (Szatmar or Satmar) movement, a strong and influential Orthodox Jewish movement in Williamsburg. As Rebbe, he wrote books in which he not only fulminated against the existence of Israel, but also described the Holocaust as 'God cutting off the rotting arm of Judaism'. He pre-dated Schneersohn's 'God-as-surgeon' contention by some twenty years. Fritz Klein, one of the senior Nazi doctors, claims to have been a good doctor obeying the Hippocratic oath (Lifton, 1986). By killing Jews, he claimed, he was curing! As a doctor, he said, if he found a gangrenous excrescence in a body he would remove it; he found Jews to be a gangrenous excrescence on the German body politic – so he removed it. What difference is there, in mentality and metaphor, between the diagnostic rabbi and the curative surgeon?

Fackenheim calls this 'surgical concept' a slander on more than a million children in an abortive defence of God. The Italian Rabbi Hartum said Jews were punished for their crime of assimilation. They would have died slowly, within fifty years, of assimilation; instead, as some kind of boon, they died sharply by the sword of the Nazis. In 1990, Rabbi Eliezer Shach, an eminent presence in Jerusalem, could say, in that city, that the Holocaust was divine retribution for the accumulated weight of the years spent growing away from Judaism.

Bauer, in a personal note to me, laments that 'any perusal of even the *haredi* [God-fearing] daily papers in Israel will show you that it is a dogma that God willed the Holocaust – and then you have to explain why, and then get tangled up in unpleasantness'. The 'unpleasantness' is nothing less than the furor following the dictum that Hitler was God's agent or lieutenant who 'amputated the poisoned limb of an increasingly secularist Jewish society', a notion attributed to the late Lubavitcher Rebbe, Menachem Mendel Schneersohn, head of a powerful group of *Hasidic* Jews with headquarters in New York.

Bauer (2002: 210–11) concludes:

> Schneersohn's words are important not only because of the central position of the Habad movement in the fundamentalist world (and in Jewish and Israeli politics) but also because the Rebbe said, or strongly hinted, what other *haredi* leaders may have feared to say: that the Holocaust was the act of a just God, that it was caused by Jewish sins, and that Hitler was God's scourge, an extension of God's arm or, in other words, his messenger. The acceptance of such an ideology would make redundant all the Holocaust research and all attempts at explaining what occurred.

For Rabbi Richard Rubenstein, there could be no God after Auschwitz. For others, there is the fallback position: 'it is written' that before the Messiah returns, there will be, or must be, a catastrophe, and the Holocaust was 'it'. With extremes such as these, there is hardly room for a 'united' Jewry, let alone a Jewry that can confidently respond to Christian cries for help in understanding God's position in all of this.

The new secular religion

There is a plethora of new Holocaust organisations, museums, exhibitions, memorials, courses and seminars of staggering dimensions. The 'Remembering for the Future' conference at Oxford in 1988 drew 650 educators, and there is now a three-volume set of proceedings from these Elisabeth Maxwell-inspired events (Roth and Maxwell-Meynard, 2000). Elie Wiesel has lamented that in intellectual circles in New York, San Francisco and elsewhere, 'no evening is a success without Auschwitz'.

One result of this 'surfeit' has been the publication of books that come close to being disdainful of the Holocaust while claiming passionately not to be. Peter Novick and Norman Finkelstein have each published sustained attacks on 'the Holocaust industry' and its role in American life. Novick alleges that Jews maintained their victim status because it was in their political interests to do so: 'Jews were intent on permanent possession of the gold medal in the Victimization Olympics' (2000: 8–15, 189–203). Finkelstein, in a less weighty and more virulent work, alleges, among other things, that Novick's book is in 'the venerable American tradition of muckraking', and that there has been a crass exploitation of Jewish suffering to 'shake down' Swiss banks, and others. The Nazi *holocaust* was the actual event, he says, but the *Holocaust* is its 'ideological representation', one exploited by Zionists (Finkelstein, 2000: 3, 4, 90–120, 151–4). Both books deplore denialism but point their finger, and anger, at 'the self-proclaimed guardians of Holocaust memory'. Tim Cole is also concerned with the *Shoah* as 'big business', with the Holocaust as 'an icon in the West', one bought and sold as all manner of myth and kitsch (1999: 1–19). There are, of course, such 'guardians', and I have my own negative views about them; but I sometimes have some trouble distinguishing whether these critics are attacking this 'guardianship' or the subject being guarded.

This massive Jewish death is not a fad, an avenue for interested intellectuals to gain kudos, only to be discarded when 'discovery' of the event wears off, or wears thin. Nor should it be used as an instrument of abuse, in the manner of the late Rabbi Kahane, who argued that the extent of Jewish suffering justifies Jewish actions against others, such as the mass deportations of Arabs from Israel.

PSYCHOLOGY

I have little faith in psychological explanations of genocide but since they have been used by others, I include the category here. Some of the literature seeks to explain, but only succeeds in explaining away, the criminal character of genocide, war crimes and crimes against humanity. Individual diagnoses of perpetrators doesn't help pinpoint responsibility and accountability, or lead in any useful way to forecasting, let alone preventing, genocidal behaviour.

Psychopolitics

A critical, almost inquisitorial, as well as politico-historical, approach to genocide is needed. Psychopolitics, for example examining Hitler's or Himmler's psyches for motivation and explanation, tells us nothing. If anything, it exculpates, and it certainly confuses issues. Bruno Bettelheim, when reviewing Robert Jay Lifton's *The Nazi Doctors* (1986), deliberately did not read the parts of the book on psychological probing: that, he wrote, might explain away rather than explain (Ascherson, 1987). We need to understand what Himmler did, and ignore his curious and incomprehensible comment, in 1943, to senior SS officers in Poznan, that throughout 'this most difficult of tasks' – the extermination of Jews – 'we have stayed decent', and 'we have suffered no harm to our inner being, our soul, our character' (Arad *et al.*, 1981: 344–5).

Confusion arises when we give serious attention to, for example, Alice Miller's analysis of psychological factors in Hitler's childhood (1991). As a psychotherapist, she tries to explain what made Hitler do what he did, and she believes she can 'explain' him. The problem with psychopolitics is that it cannot diagnose incipient psycho- or sociopaths: you cannot put them through airport security frames in their teenage years and hope that a bleep will identify a latent *genocidaire*. Added to which, Himmler had a happy childhood.

The question of insanity

The Nazi state was dedicated to the exclusion of 'bad, alien' blood and of Jewish intellectualism that allegedly disrupted, debilitated, distorted and

destroyed 'intuitive, instinctive truth'. Into that state came what Saul
Friedländer (1977: 10) calls 'the pathology' of their 'exterminatory drive'.
It was not the killing that was pathological: it was the obsession. He
wonders whether we miss a vital point, namely, the 'dimension of the
utterly irrational impulse, of some kind of insanity'.

To talk of mental illness in this context is not only to suspend judgment
but to diminish or exclude responsibility and accountability. And to say
that this is 'unfathomable' is to put an end to questioning. 'Insanity' puts
paid to the painful questions about how 'ordinary men' come to commit
such acts, about the driving forces behind such actions, such as conformity,
obedience, and so on.

Do we have to ask questions? Yes, of course, especially as the quintessential catchphrase about all cases of genocide is that 'it must never
happen again'. If that is, indeed, the universal response, then every facet of
the genocide in question must be narrated, questioned, analysed, dissected,
magnified and explained.

Conclusion: doing and knowing

Elie Wiesel, survivor of Auschwitz and Nobel Laureate for Literature, says
he does not know what to do with the Holocaust:

> We do not know how to handle it. We did not know what to do before it
> occurred: we were totally disoriented while it occurred; and now after it
> we have acquired a unique knowledge from it that may crush us. We
> simply do not know what to do with such knowledge. It goes deep into
> the nature of man and has extraordinary implications about the relationship
> between man and man, man and language, man and himself, and, ulti-
> mately, man and God. We don't know: at the beginning that is the answer
> to it, and I am afraid at the end as well.
>
> Wiesel, 1985: 287

Wiesel has moved from his earlier stance that 'the time has come for all of
us to learn and to be silent'. 'What can be done?' he asks. To which he
replies, 'Teach, I say. Teach and teach again.'

To teach what we know is one answer. Another is to go on probing, to
uncover what Wiesel has mystified, to fathom the 'extraordinary implications' about relationships within mankind, between man and God. We are

obliged to go beyond the act of teaching: obliged to try to know that which we do not, to comprehend the incomprehensible. Bauer always reminds us that this epochal event was a historical one, occasioned by humans upon humans: it must, therefore, be explicable in terms of human nature and human behaviour in this corporeal world. 'Who said the Truth was meant to be revealed?' is a proverbial question. To which a wise old rabbi replied: 'It has to be sought, that's all.'

3

GERMANY: THE GENOCIDAL ENGINE

Much of the earlier literature on modern Europe, Germany and World War II – by notable historians A.J.P. Taylor and Alan Bullock, among others – generally ignored antisemitism and relegated the Judeocide to mere paragraphs, footnotes or parentheses. Where the fate of the Jews was treated, the message conveyed was that some bad people, almost alien people, called Nazis somehow invaded Weimar Germany, seized power, wrought both evil and havoc and were destroyed or brought to justice at Nuremberg.

However, genocide must, and does, have context. In slightly different wording, Yehuda Bauer and Richard Dekmejian have pinpointed the prerequisites of both the Jewish and Armenian genocides. Among others, they insist on an ancient hatred, or an ideological imperative. In the case of the Jews, antisemitism was the fuel; without it, there could have been no Holocaust. Argument has raged among scholars as to whether German antisemitism was always 'exterminatory' (as Daniel Goldhagen (1996) insists) or only became so at opportune moments during the war. So when did it begin? Or rather, when did Jew-hatred begin to look 'serious', become institutionalised rather than merely a matter of individual 'prejudice', and to assume near-homicidal or even genocidal proportions?

GERMAN ANTISEMITISM BEFORE HITLER

I thought scholars had finally done with the 'Hitler-arrived-from-outer-space-in-1933' explanation of German antisemitism. Yet William Rubinstein (formerly of Deakin University in Geelong, Victoria and now at Aberystwyth in Wales) has revisited this mischief (*Australian Jewish News*, 31 May 1996). It is 'simply wrong', Rubinstein declared, to say 'that Germany was pervasively antisemitic before Hitler came to power'. There was a 'golden age of Jewish achievement', typified by Berlin giving Albert Einstein 'a princely official residence' in 1930. Jews, he contends, were 'universally accepted in Weimar Germany'; most had good, 'even excellent relations with their Gentile neighbours until 1938' – in fact, he writes, most didn't perceive Germany as 'murderously anti-Jewish even after 1933', and 'most [German Jews] remained where they were until after *Kristallnacht*'.

Rubinstein deplores the 'ahistoricity which bedevils so many works on the Holocaust'. My serious concern is with his *un*historicity. What can and should be said about the position of German Jews from the end of the nineteenth century, or even from Weimar in 1919, until 1933, in the cultural, political, academic, scientific, social and even sporting fields?

Modern German antisemitism may well have its wellspring in the peasant riots of 1819, seventy years before Hitler was born. And while there were different antisemitisms at work, much of the content shows a continuity. From the middle of the nineteenth century, the Jew was depicted in German literature as being without soul, without the traditional humble German virtues, uprooted, troublesome, malevolent, shiftless. Much of the literature followed Gustav Freytag's character, Veitel Itzig, who was ugly, grasping, without a shred of humanity. Hermann Gödsche's novels 'revealed' the Jews as conspirators against the Gentile world.

Wilhelm Marr, who founded the Anti-Semite League in 1879, placed great store on these literary pieces. Through his works and those of Eugen Dühring, Otto Boeckel and Heinrich von Treitschke, the stereotype of the dangerous Jew was integrated into the dynamics of the *völkisch* struggle against a state that did not represent, for them, the true will of the German people.

As early as 1895, Hermann Ahlwardt introduced a *Reichstag* bill to close Germany's borders to 'Israelites who are not citizens of the Reich'. Teutons wanted no more Jews, people of a different race and culture, people who would, as 'cholera bacilli', cause the death of Germanness. Mixing the metaphor, he saw them as beasts of prey who had best be exterminated. But tramps, beggars and social nuisances were different: they were 'Germans like us', something the Jew could never be. The bill was defeated then by 167 votes to 51, but succeeded in 1906. Some historians like to talk about 'a generalised xenophobia' in such contexts, but if anything was highly 'Jew-specific', it was these legislative forays.

Wistrich points out that while these 'rabble-rousers' were ultimately unsuccessful, and while ephemeral anti-Jewish political parties came and went with the vagaries of the economy, there were, indeed, powerful and more enduring forces at work (Wistrich, 1992: 60–62). Right-wing lobbies, imperialist lobbies, the *Akademischer Turnerbund* (a gymnastics club) and the *Verein Deutscher Studenten* (an antisemitic students' movement), helped transform German antisemitism 'into a formidable political force'.

The German, rather than the Nazi, state had a view of the Jews as a biologically determined race. Frenchman Comte Arthur de Gobineau's work on 'the essential inequality of the human races' postulated that mixed and mongrel man had finally come together in a 'pure blood type' and that Jews, as 'baneful germ plasms', were the omnipresent danger to that purity. De Gobineau societies spread throughout Germany, aided greatly by Richard Wagner and his son-in-law, Houston Stewart Chamberlain. They spearheaded an antisemitism which, while not yet physically murderous, was homicidal in language, spirit and intent. From then on, journals and university departments of 'racial hygiene' flourished – well before Hitler. *Völkisch* belief, now substantiated by 'science', owed nothing to Hitler, but much to Imperial and Weimar Germany.

Legally, Jews received little justice and almost no satisfaction from the Weimar courts. The *Centralverein für deutsche Staatsbürger jüdischen Glaubens*, founded in 1893, spent decades fighting attacks, calumnies and libels on Jews, using Paragraph 130 of the Criminal Code (on what amounted to incitement to racial violence) and then, despairing of the courts finding in favour of Jews, using Paragraph 166 on crimes against religion.

The chief defamer was, of course, Julius Streicher and his *Der Stürmer*. In the 'Great Nuremberg Ritual Murder Trial' of 1929, Streicher was charged with suggesting that some unsolved deaths were Jewish ritual murders. He was given two months in prison, but nearly every other case brought against him resulted in acquittal because he argued, successfully, that he was attacking not the Jewish religion but the separate Jewish race! In 1924, a judge came to the aid of a newspaper editor charged with incitement against Jews. This was 'far from incitement', he ruled: 'even the best men of our nation share this view [antisemitism]'. A Berlin court rejected a Jewish landlord's claim of defamation against an evicted foreign tenant who called him 'a German swine'. The startling judgment was that 'despite his German citizenship, the plaintiff does not fall into the category of persons popularly connoted by the word "German"'. *Und so weiter*, in the pre-Hitlerian courts.

The German youth movement, the *Wandervögel*, was based on the concept of *Volk*, that is, German faith, heroism, tradition, lore and all the Nordic virtues. By 1914, 92 per cent of the local chapters reported that they had no Jewish members; in fact, 84 per cent had specific constitutional clauses banning Jews. *Blau Weiss*, Blue and White, the Jewish youth movement, was founded in 1916 in self-recognition of Jews as being separate from the mainstream.

How comfortable could Jews have been in such environments? German students were swept up by *völkisch* ideology, their fraternities embracing virulent hostility to all things Jewish. The Jews were 'the enemy within', a belief the students expressed violently. *Die Mitteilungsblätter*, the major Jewish journal devoted to combating antisemitism, had much to report. When a distinguished legal professor told his class to read the works of two Jewish legal theorists, he was jeered and decried. In 1920, Berlin University students threatened riot if the university went ahead with a memorial service to the assassinated Foreign Minister, the Jewish Walter Rathenau.

As ever, the only protection for Jews was to form their own fraternities, starting as early as 1896. As ever, they were ostracised by university authorities and closed down at every opportunity. Heidelberg University decreed that 'the very existence of a Jewish fraternity is sufficient to endanger peace among the students'.

The highest form of social interaction among students was duelling – for sport and for honour. Early on, German students barred Jews from this significant activity. The message from noisy students and silent, acquiescent professors was smash the Jewish conspiracy and the *Volk* will flourish.

Jews were excluded from the socially important student gymnastic organisations and had to form their own *Turnerschaften* (gymnastics associations). Gershom Scholem (1966) has written poignantly about the assimilating, German-loving, German-craving Jews. The German liberals castigated a culture or 'race' that surrendered so readily; the Jew-haters wanted to know what kind of 'bacillus' this was that invaded them, purporting to be German when it so patently was not and could not be. Torn by this dilemma, German Jewish male youth resorted to suicide in great numbers between the wars. Suicide – much of it rational, conscious, political suicide – was, indeed, a litmus of the German–Jewish relationship within pre-Hitlerian Germany. In a farewell letter, Fritz Rosenfelder said he was 'unable to go on living with the knowledge that the movement to which national Germany is looking for salvation considers [him] a traitor to the fatherland . . . I leave without hate or anger . . . and so I have chosen a voluntary death in order to shock my Christian friends into awareness' (Kwiet, 1984: 147).

Einstein, his 'princely official residence' notwithstanding, was hated by many. Philipp Lenard and Johannes Stark, both Nobel laureates, did their best to discredit Einstein, as Jew rather than as scientist. As one Nobel laureate observed: 'A Jew conspicuously lacks understanding for the truth, in contrast to the Aryan research scientist.' Long before *'Kristallnacht'* the Nazis 'persuaded' or forced the cream of German scientists, especially physicists, to leave their posts and their Fatherland: no less than nine Nobel prize-winners had to leave Germany. Hitler's gift to the West, in the end, was a total of 1,500 scientists, who between them had achieved twenty Nobel prizes by the 1960s (Medawar and Pyke, 2000: 1–31).

Rubinstein's 'golden age' of achievement really began with the creation, in September 1933, of the Jewish umbrella organisation, the *Reichsvertretung der Juden in Deutschland*, under Rabbi Leo Baeck. Under the direction of Martin Buber, Jewish adult education programmes led to Schocken Books publishing 5,000 titles between 1933 and 1938. A great achievement – but how 'golden' were the dynamics that gave rise to it, especially in the years 1933 to 1938? There are many accounts of this so-called 'golden' era, but even a glance at Saul Friedländer's chapter on 'The Spirit of Laws' would show Rubinstein just how grim life was for German Jews in the 1930s (Friedländer, 1997: 147–73).

So what did the majority of German Jews perceive about their world? How comfortable were they in a society in which they believed they were integrated and accepted, in which they pursued Germanness rather than Jewishness, but which degraded them in special laws, denied them judicial fairness, banned their kosher dietary rituals, excluded them from the social and sporting life of universities, despised them in mainstream literature, excoriated them as racially different, as inferior and dangerous?

What they did was to leave, in great numbers. To the best of anyone's knowledge, there were 566,602 Jews in Germany in 1933, a mere 0.86 per cent of the population. By 1941, 347,103, or 61 per cent, had left. More significant is that 252,400, or just on 45 per cent, had left before 'Kristallnacht', and before the forced emigration policy got fully under way. Most German Jews assuredly did not stay.

Hitler wasn't the first to present a package called antisemitism. There were already several antisemitisms in Germany, and Hitler radicalised the traditional forms of that mindset. Rubinstein asserts that Jews were comfortable with the Weimar brand and 'enjoyed excellent relations' with their despisers and detractors. If that statement contains any truth, it tells us something about some German Jews and their perceptions, or their absence of perceptions. To say that they were 'happy' is not to say that there was no objectively visible and provable danger intrinsic to their past and their present. (I grew up among 'happy South Africans', surrounded as they were by virulent and violent physical attacks on persons and property. In today's crime and violence-ridden South Africa, there are still many who claim 'happiness'.)

Imperial and Weimar antisemitism was cruel, unkind, demeaning. It singled out the most loyal and devoted of all Jewish communities, the one that tried so hard to be German above all else. It caricatured Jews in literature, art and music, it excluded Jews as migrants, penalised Jews in courts, and ostracised its Jewish students. It made Jews, with Gypsies, the especial target of racial hygiene policies. None of this was yet fatal to Jewish suburban, business or actual life. But the antisemitic fuel tanks were full enough, historical enough, institutionalised enough to make the genocidal engine ready for its radical driver.

'KRISTALLNACHT': THE DEFINING MOMENT

The 'Night of Broken Glass', the official and intentional euphemism for the NSDAP pogrom on 9–10 November 1938, confronts us with several major questions. First, was it an aberration in the German–Jewish relationship or an extension of continuous German antisemitism? Second, was this planned pogrom the turning point in German–Jewish history, the first shot in the war against the Jews, shots which, in Herbert Strauss's words, signalled that this November night saw Jews as 'the first victims of World War II' (Strauss, 1980)? Third, did German Jews stay when they could have left? Fourth, does this pogrom help us resolve the debate about whether the Holocaust was intended from the start, or whether it happened, functionally, as a result of happenstance, of chance; or, rather, whether it resulted from a series of opportunities that were neither expected nor predictable?

To address these questions, I invite readers to consider the table below, and then to follow the brief annual accounts which follow.

Migration of German Jews, 1933 to 1945

Total Jewish population in Germany in January 1933: 566,602
Numbers who left (from Jewish sources given to the Nazis):

1933	63,400
1934	45,000
1935	35,500
1936	34,000
1937	25,500
Sub-total	203,400
1938	49,000
1939	68,000
1940	20,996

(It has been argued that 'Kristallnacht' greatly increased emigration, that 35 per cent of emigration between 1933 and the end of 1939 was in the fourteen months after the pogrom.)

1941–45	8,500
Total	**349,896 (or 61.7 per cent)**

Where they went:

	German Jews only	German, Austrian, Moldavian and Bohemian Jews
North America (particularly US)	57,000	approx. 90,000
Central America	9,728	13,428
South America	53,472	68,028
Asia	16,374	40,336
Palestine	53,000	64,000
Africa	14,000	17,500
Australia	4,015★	5,962★
Total	207,589	299,254
'Third Reich' countries, like Holland, Belgium, France		153,000
Total		**360,589**

Note: Given the difficulty of finding precise figures, there is a good correlation here between the figure of 350,000 Jews who left Germany and the 360,000 believed to have found haven in various countries.

★ Konrad Kwiet lists a total of 9,000 Jews (from all sources) from 1933 to 1945: 1,500 until 'Kristallnacht', a total of 7,200 before the war began, plus 1,500 (German, Austrian, Czech) aliens transported by Britain to Australia on the Dunera, plus 500 from Singapore, Hong Kong and Iran during the war.

Let us now look at each year from 1933 until 1945.[1]

1933

63,400 Jews left because of panic at the Nazi arrival in government. Regrettably, in the belief that Hitler was a short-term aberration and that return would soon be possible, they went mainly to neighbouring countries like Belgium, Holland and France. Usually husbands stayed and sent their wives and children.

Article 9 of the Weimar Constitution was a barrier to Nazi action against Jews: it proclaimed that all citizens were equal before the law. In March 1933, the Nazis passed the 'Enabling Law' which cleared the way for persecution.

Those Jews who were considered 'politicals' left, as did those who became unemployed as a result of the April 1933 'Law for the Restoration of the Professional Public Service' which aimed at 'de-Judaising' the public service. In the same month, the short-lived boycott of Jewish shops, goods, lawyers and doctors began. Measures were taken to reduce Jewish activity in many professions: Jewish doctors and dentists couldn't participate in the state health insurance plans. Kosher food rituals were outlawed.

In September, after years of internal bickering and disunity, the new Jewish umbrella organisation, the *Reichsvertretung der Juden in Deutschland* (National Representation of German Jews), was established under Rabbi Leo Baeck and Otto Hirsch. The opening statement of this organisation was one of 'hope for the understanding assistance of the Authorities, and the respect of our gentile fellow citizens, whom we join in love and loyalty to Germany'. People who went to Palestine could take out property: they lost around 20 per cent of its value.

1934

45,000 left, for two reasons: first, the continuing panic about Hitler; second, the now omnipresent and enduring antisemitism in which there was no clear political line. In short, there was a high degree of ambiguity, and much unease and uncertainty. Jews were no longer allowed to be licensed as pharmacists. The 1933 law to establish a Reich Culture Chamber specifically excluded non-Aryan membership. But in this year they were allowed a cultural association (*Kulturbund deutscher Juden*), albeit one supervised by the State Police and other Nazi organs.

The *Hilfsverein der deutschen Juden* (Aid Association of German Jews) now had an additional task, that of giving advice and assistance to those wanting or needing to emigrate. Even in this climate, the *Hilfsverein* could talk about 'feeling an inner bond with their Fatherland', but if 'emigration becomes economically and politically necessary', they would assist such emigration. Desecration of buildings, attacks on synagogues and arbitrary arrests were commonplace, but there was no killing of Jews. There was a policy of curbed violence, a moderated violence, that could easily become murderous.

1935

A decreasing number, 35,500, left. This was not because countries were closing their doors, but because there was greater physical and economic security as a result of the Nuremberg Laws. The first act to reduce Jews' citizenship rights was the March 1935 law to reconstruct the German army, the Wehrmacht: it banned Jews, 100,000 of whom had enlisted and 12,000 of whom had died for Germany in World War I. (Unofficially, so to speak, it did allow well over 100,000 Jews of 'mixed-blood' descent to serve.) The Nuremberg Law for the Protection of German Blood and German Honour, passed on 15 September 1935, deprived Jews of German citizenship. Henceforth, marriages and sex between Jews and 'subjects of the state of German or related blood' (which no longer included Jews) were forbidden. Jews could no longer employ such 'German blood' women under the age of forty-five as servants, and Jews could no longer fly the national flag but could display their own. As non-citizens, Jews no longer had the right to vote in elections and they could no longer hold any public office. The sale of Jewish newspapers in the streets was prohibited.

Earlier, I mentioned Emil Fackenheim's contention that these Laws signalled a fatal change for Jews. He says these Laws were the second great catastrophe in Jewish history: the first was the destruction of the Temple in 70 CE; the second was the enactment of the Nuremberg Laws. They removed citizenship not because of what Jews did, or preached, or practised, but simply *because they were*. He stands in strong contrast to the responses of the Jewish representative body, the *Reichsvertretung*, on 24 September 1935:

> The Laws decided upon by the Reichstag in Nuremberg have come as the heaviest of blows for the Jews in Germany. But they must create a basis on which a tolerable relationship becomes possible between the German and the Jewish people. The *Reichsvertretung der Juden in Deutschland* is willing to contribute to this end with all its powers. A precondition for such a tolerable relationship is the hope that the Jews and the Jewish communities of Germany will be enabled to keep a moral and economic means of existence by the halting of defamation and boycott.

They believed that there were limits to Nazi antisemitism, that they could rely on people like bank managers to stop any murder of Jews. They believed, erroneously, that the SA, the Storm Detachment or Storm

Troopers, had been destroyed in 1934 and that, as a result, a second emancipation was possible and a *modus vivendi* was attainable. In short, they saw the Nuremberg Laws as something they could cope with, if that was indeed the worst that was to befall them, and they believed that an accommodation of sorts was possible. Hitler, too, depicted these Laws as 'the only possibility of achieving a tolerable relationship with the Jews living in Germany'.

There was an internal Jewish struggle: let's wait another winter, said the optimists, but even they did not foresee a return to the days of Weimar. From a Nazi perspective, the Laws were essentially a bone thrown to the SA to appease their desire for greater action against the Jews. The idea had first been floated in 1933, but rejected. So here we have two sharply conflicting perspectives: Fackenheim's notion of a 'semi-final' prelude to the end of German Jewry as opposed to the shallow and superficial Nazi use of these Laws merely as a sop to appease their extreme wings.

1936

34,000 left. Again, this was a lower number because of a belief in some kind of accommodation. It was a relatively quiet year, mainly because of the winter and summer Olympic Games. A Yugoslav medical student, David Frankfurter, killed the Nazi Party representative in Switzerland, Wilhelm Gustloff, yet Hitler ordered no action. It was important at that time for Nazis to present an image of calm and moderation. There were a few days of controlled press indignation, a state funeral, followed by the important business at hand, the Olympics. It is interesting to compare that response to an assassination with the event that was to trigger *'Kristallnacht'*.

Jews had already lost their right to vote in *Reichstag* elections. Despite the 'quietness' of the year, a significant book was published by Victor Gollancz in England in February 1936. The *Yellow Spot*, probably written by Gollancz, and based on many intelligence reports to him in England, was sub-titled 'The outlawing of half a million human beings'. From the text, and the tenor of his sub-title, it was clear that he and his colleagues knew, as few others seemed to know, that something more serious was afoot than banning Jews from flying the German flag, from playing in orchestras, or from owning theatres and large stores.

1937

25,500 left. Figures were down as part of this accommodation. The number in concentration camps was low, about 7,000. What we don't know is how many *émigré* Jews returned, from Poland (because of pogroms), from France and even from Palestine. Limitations were placed on the numbers of Jewish pupils in schools and universities. However, relatively speaking, there were no major legislative or administrative actions against Jews in this year.

1938

49,000 left. This high figure was not related to '*Kristallnacht*' which, as we know, occurred at the end of the year. The year began badly. It saw a revitalisation of Nazidom, a re-Nazification. It also saw the economic destruction of German Jews. Something radically new was happening in Nazi politics and antisemitism was becoming more strident, more vigorous. In March, Jewish community organisations were prohibited from being legally registered as incorporations under public law. Jews had to hand over their property, and as of 1 January 1939, all Jews would be obliged to carry special identity cards. All Jewish physicians were obliged to call themselves *Krankenbehandler*, caretakers of the sick. All Jewish street names were changed.

In July, at Evian in France, the international community met to discuss the plight of Jewry, but did nothing practical to achieve any positive outcomes. In August, all Jews were required to take an additional name, adding 'Israel' and 'Sarah' to the given names of each and every male and female. In the same month, Eichmann took complete control of Austrian Jewry, now in a state of great confusion and flux, establishing the Central Office for Jewish Immigration in Vienna. By October, Eichmann insisted on people signing to leave as part of the now full-scale forced emigration phase. 'If the Jews have no passports', he wrote, 'then they will be pushed over the Czech border to Prague without a passport.' Vienna's Jews were subjected to unspeakable acts of spite and brutality.

There was pressure for more antisemitic activity. Jews could no longer keep their drivers' licences and students could no longer attend universities. The fantasies of an accommodation were fast disappearing. The SS newspaper, *Das Schwarze Korps*, was now openly talking of an extermination policy. On 24 November 1938, it was advocating that all Jews be driven out of their dwelling places, marked and segregated from the rest of society.

They would soon 'sink down into a criminal existence' and there was no way the German people would put up with 'hundreds of thousands of criminals' who 'crumble away from the edge of our own nation as the result of a process of natural elimination . . . We shall therefore now take the Jewish Question towards its total solution.' By 1938, Jews who left could take nothing in the way of money or property.

1939

68,000 left. The year began with Hitler's infamous *Reichstag* speech on 30 January:

> Today I will once more be a prophet: If the international Jewish financiers in and outside Europe should succeed in plunging the nations once more into a world war, then the result will not be the bolshevisation of the earth, and thus the victory of Jewry, but the annihilation of the Jewish race in Europe!

The 1939 exodus was due directly to economic destruction and to the impact of '*Kristallnacht*' the previous November. So, what is '*Kristallnacht*' (always in inverted commas)? We need to remember that it was '*Reichs-Kristallnacht*', a sarcastic term used in Berlin to remind Nazis that this was not, as Goebbels insisted it was, 'a spontaneous public response' to vom Rath's death, but a *Reich*-organised pogrom.[2]

In essence, this event was the most violent public display of antisemitism in German history. The codified verbal menace of the Nuremberg Laws had ended. There was to be no more masking of the underlying violence towards the Jews. It was also the most aberrant behaviour, given that the Nazis had achieved in Germany what they had promised in 1933, then a time of agitation, street fights and selective violence, namely, *Ordnung*, *Ruhe*, and *Recht*, public order, peace and law. German historian Martin Broszat saw this pogrom as transforming Jews from a stigmatised group into a '*minorité fatale*' (in Kwiet, 1986: 59).

The details of the events themselves are well rehearsed and documented elsewhere. It will suffice simply to record here two quotations, the first from the American Consul in Leipzig, David Buffum:

> At 3 a.m. on 10 November 1938 was unleashed a barrage of Nazi ferocity as had had no equal hitherto in Germany, or very likely anywhere else in

the world since savagery began. Jewish buildings were smashed into and contents demolished or looted . . . Jewish shop windows by the hundreds were systematically and wantonly smashed throughout the entire city at a loss estimated at several millions of marks . . . Three synagogues in Leipzig were fired simultaneously by incendiary bombs and all sacred objects and records desecrated or destroyed, in most cases hurled through the windows and burned in the streets. No attempts were made to quench the fires, the activity of the fire brigade being confined to playing water on adjoining buildings . . . Ferocious as was the violation of property, the most hideous phase of the so-called 'spontaneous' action has been the wholesale arrest and transportation to concentration camps of male German Jews between the ages of sixteen and sixty, as well as Jewish men without citizenship. This has been taking place daily since the night of horror. This office has no way of accurately checking the numbers of such arrests, but there is very little question that they have run to several thousands in Leipzig alone. Having demolished dwellings and hurled most of the movable effects into the streets, the insatiably sadistic perpetrators threw many of the trembling inmates into the small stream that flows through the Zoological Park, commanding horrified spectators to spit at them, defile them with mud and jeer at their plight . . . These tactics were carried out the entire morning of 10 November without police intervention and they were applied to men, women, and children . . . It has been reported that three Aryan professors at the University of Jena have been arrested and taken off to concentration camps because they had voiced disapproval of this insidious drive against mankind.

Buffum, 1946: 1037–41

And, from a fifteen-year-old Jewish boy, Arno Hamburger, who was a witness in Nuremberg:

Many of the 'spontaneous' avengers were equipped with pistols and knives, while each group brought along axes, large hammers, and iron bars to force entry into Jewish homes. Several SS men had bags for collecting money, jewelry, paintings, and other valuables which they hauled off. The apartments were supposedly being searched for weapons because of a new law enacted the day before that forbade Jews to possess such items. Glass doors, mirrors, and pictures were broken. Paintings were cut with knives, and beds, shoes, and clothes were cut apart. Everything was broken into small pieces, and so, on the morning of November 10th, the victimised families had nothing left. Most had no coffee cups, no spoons, no knives, nothing at all . . .

in Wollenberg, 1996: 11–14

At a meeting on 12 November, the same day on which he issued the decree 'Regulation for the Elimination of the Jews from the Economic Life of Germany', Göring made this significant statement:

Gentlemen! Today's meeting is of a decisive character. I have received a letter written on the Führer's orders by Bormann, the chief of staff of the Fuhrer's deputy, requesting that the Jewish question be now, once and for all, coordinated and solved *one way or another* . . .

in Arad, 1981: 108–15

That last phrase, Hitlerian wording used at least two years earlier, '*so oder so*', 'one way or another', is the key to the fate of the Jews. Henceforth, with all that organised violence behind them, there was, in a sense, no turning back.

The pogrom signalled that the Jews had finally been stigmatised as never before as an unwanted people. Jews who had reasonable relations with Germans were now removed from the ranks of society. Seven weeks after '*Kristallnacht*', a health insurance agency wrote to a member, saying that 'as a Jewish member, your continued membership is highly undesirable due to your race'. Jews were now outside the social network, outside the society of human beings. Within two years, Jews were not permitted in Aryan insane asylums, they had lost their driving licences because their presence on the roads offended 'the German traffic community', there was a tobacco ban on Jews, and then the decree to wear the yellow Star of David, and so on.

'*Kristallnacht*' was not a pre-ordained, pre-planned step in the systematic plan for Jews. But it did hasten emigration, which was Nazi policy at that time. Emigration, however, was also something of a negation of another, conflicting policy, namely, to keep Jews and exploit them financially. The result? A radicalisation of everything: *Gauleiters* of cities like Berlin, Frankfurt and Vienna began competing as to which would be the first to be free of Jews. '*Kristallnacht*' produced new demands for more radical means of solving the 'Jewish question'. It was also, in Herbert Strauss's analysis, the precursor to war, that is, a war against the Jews within, or alongside, another kind of conventional war.

After World War I, Germans had become fixated with the belief that they had lost that war because the Jews and their lackeys – the socialists, the pacifists, the trade unions – had stabbed the undefeated German army in the back. In the paranoia of Hitler, combined with these *völkisch* beliefs, we can see what became the strategy: in order to pre-empt a second stab in the back, you get the Jews first. You remove Jews from German society, lest they again fulfil the fantasies of yesteryear. Hitler's famous, or rather, infamous *Reichstag* speech of 30 January 1939 is to be seen in this context. '*Kristallnacht*' was indeed the first *Aktion* in the elimination of Jews.

In July 1939, the Jewish *Reichsvertretung*, a mere six years old, was recreated, by law, as the *Reichsvereinigung der Juden in Deutschland*, now primarily responsible 'to further the emigration of Jews'. It was also directly responsible to the *Reich* Minister of the Interior.

1940

20,996 left. The war had started and so had the first deportations of German Jews. Jews couldn't get visas and couldn't reach ports. The way out was to cross into France, cross the Pyrenees into Spain and then try to find some way of eventually reaching the Trans-Siberian rail system.

1941–45

Astonishing as it may seem, some 8,000 got out in these years. This figure includes women with Turkish citizenship who were sent to the Ravens-brück camp and exchanged; those fortunate enough to have Palestine residence certificates who were sent to the Lauffen camp in Bavaria and later to France where they were exchanged; and property owners who could afford to buy their freedom and were sent to Sweden in 1944. Some bribed their way out of Theresienstadt. Despite the enactment of a law banning the emigration of Jews from the *Reich* in October 1941, in that year Eichmann was assisting Jews to get to Palestine. After all, his job was to facilitate the forced emigration of Jews.

THE SILENCE OF THE CHURCHES

On 29 July 1999, His Excellency, the Honourable Sir William Deane, AC, KBE, then Governor-General of Australia, chaired an evening at the

Wesley Institute, Sydney. The occasion was the presentation by His Eminence, Edward Idris, Cardinal Cassidy, of the Vatican's document *We Remember: a Reflection on the Shoah*. In 1987, the Vatican Commission for Religious Relations with the Jews began preparation of an official Catholic statement on the Church and the *Shoah*. By 1999, this short document was ready for presentation around the globe.

My response to the Cardinal that evening is transcribed below, with some later comments added in square brackets. The Vatican has since denied further access to its wartime archives by its own Commission for Religious Relations with the Jews. To date (2003) it has allowed access to only eleven volumes of the Acts and Documents of the Holy See during World War II, a fraction of the total. The Vatican no longer insists on enforcing its policy that papal papers may not be opened for seventy-five years from the date of any pontiff's death. After much outcry, there has been some relenting. The war years of Pacelli (Pope Pius XII) will begin to be exposed to the world possibly as early as 2006 and no later than 2009. This was a result of the direct intervention of the present Pope, John Paul II.

My address

His Excellency, the Governor-General, has opened the way for a response to the Vatican's *We Remember* document. Sir William Deane suggests a tone of 'polite frankness'. Let me then be both polite and frank.

One has to surrender the idea that the Catholic Church is a monolithic structure, at least in the Holocaust years. There was not one Catholic church during this era, but dozens of Catholic churches and thousands of churchmen: some saved Jews, others defended Jews, some killed Jews, and some betrayed Jews. On one hand, Father Jozef Tiso, a priest, headed a Nazi puppet state in Slovakia, from where Jews were deported to Auschwitz; on another, Carmelite nuns in Vilna ran guns for the Jewish underground. Holocaust history has taught me that one cannot view the Church as a singularity, and therefore this important Vatican document, while talking about Catholic differences, does the Church something of a disservice by talking about a single, indivisible Church.

The Vatican document inadvertently poses a problem for all churches, all faiths, including Judaism: that nationalism and ethnic fire often transcend religious adherence. Catholics and Protestants alike have a duty to uphold and venerate life: yet 43 per cent of Germans were Catholics, and a much greater percentage were Catholic in the 'Independent State of Croatia' that saw fit not only to kill Jews *en masse*, but also to annihilate (at least) 500,000 Serbs under the Ustasa leader, Ante Pavelic.

Cardinal Cassidy talks of the sons and daughters of the Church 'who fostered long-standing sentiments of mistrust and hostility which the Vatican calls anti-Judaism'. If only it had been merely mistrust and hostility. Jews could have lived with that, as they have done for two millennia, and longer. But they had to live with, and die from, things infinitely greater than mere mistrust and hostility.

What motivated people to behave the way they did? The Cardinal says: 'Many Christians did in fact fail to give every possible assistance to those being persecuted.' He talks of people 'who failed to give the witness that might have been expected of them as Christ's followers'. The tenor of this is that, at worst, the Catholic Church was merely one third of what we call the Holocaust triangle, whose corners comprise perpetrators, victims and bystanders. The latter were those who by their indifference, or even by what Professor Yehuda Bauer calls their 'hostile indifference', allowed it to happen. Many churches, and churchmen, were very much more than bystanders. The document also makes several references to the Church, or its adherents, as co-equal victims. There is a near-blasphemy involved in equating the fate of the Jews of Europe with the fate of the Catholic Church, or even several hundred of its servants.

There are, literally, innumerable examples of Catholic perpetrators, whether in Germany or among her satellite allies. We don't have time for them here. But we do have to address some aspects of Church involvement.

The essential thrust of *We Remember* is that there was a 'them' and 'us' dichotomy: 'us' were the anti-Jewish Church leaders and ideology-makers who taught and preached a doctrine of contempt, now regarded as morally and ethically wrong; 'them' were an aberrant group of pagan Nazis whose roots lay outside of Catholic Christianity and who murdered in the name of blood and race. This, I regret to say, is deflection that does not become the Vatican. It is reminiscent of the famous German historian, Ernst Nolte, who talks about 'us' Germans, the good people, the anti-Nazis, and the 'them' Germans, Nazis who seemingly descended from some alien planet ship in 1933 and who were vanquished by the forces of good in 1945.

Not only were 43 per cent of Germans Catholics, but 22.7 per cent of the SS were adherents, Catholic Christians, attendees at mass, seeking rites and rituals. Only twenty-three SS officers were ever court-martialled for refusing to obey orders or carry out 'Final Solution' policy. It is certainly true that Hitler was a radical figure, the one who put the extermination engine into operation. But the engine, and most of its parts, were well assembled before Hitler came to power. The radicalism of Hitler was that he threw off the brakes or reins that had always held back the Church, namely, the injunction of St Augustine in the fourth century that Jews could be, should be, demeaned, brought low, expelled, harassed, deported, reviled, but not killed.

Inevitably, there will always be a major focus on Pope Pius XII, and whether or not his personality was responsible for the inaction of the Vatican. But before touching on that issue, we need to see the context of his all-important constituency, which was German Catholicism.

In the Weimar period in the 1920s, bishops spoke out against the glorification of race and blood, but said nothing about anti-Jewish propaganda. They did, however, talk strongly about 'the destructive influence of the Jews'. The main protagonists were Franciscan Father Erhard Schlund, Jesuit Gustav Gundlach and Bishop Buchberger.[3]

In the post-Weimar period, Hitler had intense dialogue with the Catholic leadership, who in turn began an appreciation of the values of racial purity. Archbishop Konrad Gröber, heavily involved in persuading the German bishops to sign a concordat with the *Reich*, stated:

> Every people bears itself the responsibility for its successful existence, and the intake of entirely foreign blood will always represent a risk for a nationality that has proven its historical worth. Hence, no people may be denied the right to maintain undisturbed their previous racial stock and to enact safeguards for this purpose. The Christian religion merely demands that the means used do not offend against the moral law and natural justice.

The famous Advent sermons of 1933 by Cardinal Michael Faulhaber have been misinterpreted: he said he didn't object to the attempt to keep national characteristics 'pure and unadulterated' but he objected to placing loyalty to race above loyalty to the Church. This was misinterpreted as Catholic condemnation of Nazi ideology. It wasn't. He went on to say that he was 'not concerned with defending the Jews of our time'. In fact, despite condemning the euthanasia programme, he never once uttered a word about the persecution and extermination of the Jews.

In 1939, Bishop Hilfrich of Limburg conceded the Jewishness of Jesus 'but the Christian religion has not grown out of the nature of this people and is not influenced by their racial characteristics'. Rather, he said, the Church 'has to make its way against this people'.

The Church agreed to the Nuremberg Laws which prohibited marriages between Jews and Aryans: in short, the Church agreed to an inadmissible infringement of her spiritual jurisdiction to give sacraments to a baptised Jew. While many Catholic leaders abroad condemned these Laws, Bishop Hudal, head of the German Church in Rome, said the Nuremberg Laws were 'essential as a measure of self-defence against the influx of foreign elements'.

A pastoral letter from the German bishops was read on the first Sunday in January 1937. It agreed with Hitler's perception of the Bolshevik danger:

> The German Bishops consider it their duty to support the head of the German Reich by all those means which the Church has at its disposal. Cooperation in repelling this threat is a religious task.

In effect, the bishops were at one with Hitler in perceiving Jews as the chief engineers, carriers and exploiters of Bolshevism.

The appalling pogrom of 9 November 1938, known as 'Kristallnacht', went uncommented upon by Catholic churchmen, apart from Provost Bernhard Lichtenberg of Berlin. Lichtenberg commented: 'What took place yesterday, we know; what will be tomorrow, we do not know; but what happens today, that we have witnessed; outside this church the synagogue is burning, and that is also a house of God.' He was taken to Dachau, and died en route, of causes unknown.

One other churchman, a Protestant minister in the small town of Wurttemberg, asked: 'Who would have thought that one single crime in Paris would have resulted in so many crimes being committed in Germany?' [Dietrich Bonhoeffer and Pastor Niemöller, founders of the Lutheran Confessing Church, may be lauded for their opposition to the 'Aryan Paragraph' in its constitution, but they and their 6,000 adherents were as silent as the Catholic churches on the events of 'Kristallnacht'. Both men, now folk heroes, remained deeply ambivalent about Jews, the 'Chosen People who nailed the saviour of the world to the cross'. Otto

Dibelius, the Church's general superintendent, sermonised that 'one cannot ignore the fact that Judaism is taking a leading role in all of the destructive manifestations of modern civilisation' (Wolfgang Gerlach in Wollenberg, 1996: 68–71).]

The Church in Germany also supplied lists of birth certificates of those not considered Aryan, and was therefore directly complicit in assisting the deportation processes. The Church in Germany also rejected, from service and sacraments, those ordered to wear yellow armbands. They were fellow Catholics, but they were Jews.

The Church in Germany certainly protested against the euthanasia programmes and Cardinal-Archbishop of Munster, Clemens Galen, has rightly been honoured as a heroic figure. But he, like Gröber and Faulhaber, never protested against Jewish treatment. That was left to the lonely figure of Provost Bernhard Lichtenberg of Berlin.

By the end of 1942, the German episcopate was well informed of what was happening. Colonel Kurt Gerstein had joined the SS to 'take a look into Hitler's kitchen', to see for himself what was happening to Jews. After witnessing a gassing near Lublin, he tried to inform Cesare Orsenigo, the Papal Nuncio. The Monsignor refused to see him. [Gerstein also informed about one hundred members of the Confessing Church about the gas chambers, but no one wanted to believe him.]

In February 1943, the German bishops were most upset at the forced annulment of mixed marriages. They made no statements about the fate of Jews in Dachau or in other camps, but expressed concern solely at the intrusion into the indissolubility of Christian marriages. Archbishop Bertram and others expressed concern about Jewish converts in the camps, but not about Jews in general. What is so astonishing is that in all their pleas and pleadings about the right to life and liberty, these men could not bring themselves to utter the word 'Jew'. What is also astonishing is that these men opposed the euthanasia programme to the extent that it at least stopped, officially, though it continued in private until the last day of the war. But they could not find it within their Christianness to oppose the Jewish programmes. It was these self-same men who were ordered to deny the sacraments to Catholics who engaged in duelling or who sought cremation rather than burial, but did not deny such rites to men who killed Jews.

We need to look briefly at the roles of Pius XI and Pius XII. On 14 March 1937, Achille Ratti, Pope Pius XI, wrote the first ever encyclical in

German, addressed to the German bishops. It ran to twelve pages and was taken by courier to Berlin. On 21 March it was read from every pulpit. He declared: 'Whoever exalts race or nation or the State to the highest norm and worships them like idols perverts and distorts the divine order of things . . . True Christianity proves itself in the love of God and in the active love of one's neighbour.' He added that 'human laws which run counter to natural laws are not obligatory in conscience'. The encyclical was entitled *Mit brennender Sorge*, 'With serious [or burning] concern'.

In 1938, he asked the renowned American Jesuit writer on black–white relations, John LaFarge, to help him pen another encyclical, *Humani Generis Unitas*, a document which some historians have suggested quite seriously might have averted the Holocaust. Conor Cruise O'Brien, probably with some hyperbole, calls it 'one of the greatest and most tragically missed opportunities of history'. Unlike *Mit brennender Sorge*, it mentioned Jews and antisemitism:

> People who fought so valiantly for their countries are treated as traitors; children of those who fell on the field of battle become outlaws, by the sole fact of their parentage . . . This flagrant denial of elementary justice to the Jews leads to the expulsion of thousands into the hazards of exile, without any resources. Wandering from country to country, they are a burden to themselves and to humanity.

But even in this there was no denunciation of Nazi policies, no condemnation of anti-Jewish programmes. The draft, regrettably, was still very much in traditional Catholic mould: it repeats the theological nonsense about the historic curse on Jews for their rejection of Christ. LaFarge was assisted by Gustav Gundlach, who earlier had written an encyclopaedia article defending a 'permissible anti-Semitism'. The hundred-page draft didn't go any further and the Church waited till 1965, to the most significant *Nostra Aetate* of the Second Vatican Council, to declare a total break with the centuries of contempt.

When Pius XI died in February 1939, Bernard Joseph, on behalf of the Executive of the Jewish Agency, wrote to the Patriarch in Jerusalem:

> In common with the whole civilised community, the Jewish people mourns the loss of one of the greatest exponents of the cause of international peace and goodwill . . . More than once did we have occasion to be deeply

grateful for the attitude which he took up against the persecution of racial minorities and in particular for the deep concern which he expressed for the fate of the persecuted Jews of Central Europe. His noble efforts on their behalf will ensure for him for all time a warm place in the memories of Jewish people wherever they live.

These are not words that Jews will ever come to use of his successor, Eugenio Pacelli, Pope Pius XII. It is not only Jews but many Catholic thinkers who despaired then, and now, of this man's failure to do certain things that were within his powers to do.

Pacelli failed to promulgate an explicit and direct condemnation of the war of aggression. He failed to speak out against the acts of violence against Jews and others under Nazi occupation. He had full knowledge of the facts from early on, and his sin, if I may use the term, was not to use his influence. He continued to remain silent, despite ceaseless appeals from his own adherents, from Jews and from governments, to speak out. In April 1943, he wrote to Bishop Konrad Preysing in Berlin, saying he wouldn't speak out against the genocide that was the 'Final Solution' 'in order to avoid greater evils'. What could possibly have been a greater evil? He condoned the Vichy Government's 'Jewish Statutes'. The French bishops protested, but Léon Bérard, the Vichy Ambassador to the Holy See, reported to Marshal Pétain that the Vatican did not consider such laws to be in conflict with Catholic teaching.

As Bishop of Rome, Pius XII did act, after a fashion, after much imploring from his cousin, a *contessa*, who phoned him in the middle of the night to urge action as Jews were being deported from literally under the Vatican balcony. One thousand Rome Jews went to Auschwitz, and only fifteen returned. Another 7,000 were hidden by Italian citizens. The Pope's orders to give sanctuary to Roman Jews saved the lives of 4,000 – and, as Jews say, he who saves one life may well have saved the world. [It seems that I, too, have been the victim of much Pacelli myth. Susan Zuccotti, a renowned and respected scholar, has researched this matter in great detail. In her book, poignantly titled *Under His Very Windows*, published in 2000, she concludes that Pacelli never gave any written or oral order to save Jews (Zuccotti, 2000). She observes that the Vatican has never done anything to dispel this story. More important, she writes, were the efforts of ordinary Italians, including nuns and priests, to save Roman

Jews, unprompted by any directives from anyone. There is no way, she claims, that the saved can be quantified.]

In the eyes of many leaders of the Catholic Church, as Saul Friedländer would say, the 'Jew was less than whatever other consideration he was weighed against'. The Jew was assuredly less than Catholic property in many instances, less than Church self-interest, less than the very principles of Christianity that command help to brothers and sisters in need.

There is a point to all of this: everyone should welcome the Church's admissions, regrets, the Church's remembering and the Church's call for *teshuvah*, Hebrew for repentance, something the Cardinal rightly describes as beyond apology. But there is something else that is needed following the Cardinal's promise that this document is not the last Vatican word on the subject: that remembering must be full memory, not partial memory, not selective memory. There was, and is, good, bad and ugly. We all need to look at all three behaviours, face them and come to terms with what they are.

It doesn't help to suggest that the Church was a co-equal victim. It doesn't help when this and other churches seek to appropriate the Holocaust, to Christianise it in a variety of ways, such as, recently, the building of a convent at the gates of Auschwitz or the sanctification of Dr Edith Stein as a Catholic martyr who died in Auschwitz (because she was a Jew rather than because of her activities as a professing Catholic).

Hopefully, these are the first words of the repentant Vatican. Hopefully, all future dialogue should proceed from where we are tonight, and avoid going back to an elementary ABC.

I conclude with an appeal to the Church. We must remember that Hitler's war against the Jews resulted in thirty-five million dead. That war, and its dead, was and is a world problem, not a mystical, sacralised Jewish problem, not a sacralised Catholic or Protestant problem. Its roots lay in traditional Christian antisemitism and its radicalisation in Germany. Without antisemitism there is no Auschwitz. And since Jews alone cannot ever combat anti-Judaism, the world needs to enlist the world's greatest single institution, the Catholic Church of Rome, in Rome, to influence the hundreds of thousands of little Catholic churches across the globe.

4

AUSTRALIA: DEFINING AND INTERPRETING GENOCIDE

No one in his right senses believes that the Commonwealth of Australia will be called before the bar of public opinion, if there is such a thing, and asked to answer for any of the things which are enumerated in this convention.

Archie Cameron, Liberal Member for Barker, in the parliamentary debate on Australia's ratification of the *Convention on the Prevention and Punishment of the Crime of Genocide*, June 1949 (Hansard, 1949: 1871)

... the horrible crime of genocide is unthinkable in Australia ... That we detest all forms of genocide ... arises from the fact that we are a moral people.

Leslie Haylen, Labor Member for Parkes, in the same parliamentary session

In the current climate of heat in Aboriginal affairs, which I will describe later, very few people use the word genocide. Nearly all who hear it abjure it. Almost all (white) historians of the Aboriginal experience avoid it, as I also discuss later. They write about pacifying, killing, cleansing, excluding, exterminating, starving, poisoning, shooting, beheading, sterilising, exiling, removing, but avoid 'genociding'. Are they ignorant of genocide theory and practice? Or simply reluctant to taint 'the land of the fair go', the 'lucky country', with so heinous and disgracing a label? Australians appreciate only the filmic scenes, the by-now conventional scenes, of historical and present-day slaughter, where genocide means bulldozed corpses at

Belsen or serried rows of Cambodian skulls, or panga-wielding Hutu in pursuit of Tutsi victims, or 'ethnic cleansing' in the former Yugoslavia. As Australians see it, we can't be connected to, or with, the stereotypes of Swastika-wearing SS psychopaths, or crazed black tribal Africans. Apart from Australia's physical killing era, there *are* clear differences between what those perpetrators did and what we did in assimilating people and removing their children. But, images notwithstanding, we are connected by virtue of what Raimond Gaita (1998) calls 'the inexpungable moral dimension' inherent in genocide, whatever its forms or actions.

DEFINING GENOCIDE

There are three ways of approaching the issue of definition: to follow the legal path, to use the social science perspectives, or to adopt the common or general approach to what is or isn't genocide.

The legal path

The pragmatic path is to use the yardstick of the only extant international legal definition of genocide, namely Article II(a) to (e) of the United Nations Convention on the Prevention and Punishment of the Crime of Genocide, 1948, as set out at the beginning of this book.

There are flaws, perhaps grievous ones, in the Convention. Nowhere is there mention of the role of the state as a perpetrator, yet it is the signatory state that is required to report (itself?) to the United Nations. To obtain the Soviet Union's support for the Convention, political groups were omitted, thus ensuring no possible reference to the Soviet genocide of the land-owning peasants, the *kulaks*, or to Stalin's elimination of those whom he defined as 'enemies of the people'. Physical killing usually occurs in a compact time period, as with the Jews, but not always, as for example with the Tasmanian and Queensland Aborigines. Sterilisation and removal of children imply a much more enduring time frame, over generations perhaps. We know what constitutes serious bodily harm, but how do we calculate mental harm? The Convention equated in seriousness, and over vastly different time spans, the act of physical killing and the act of forcibly removing children, an equivalence not easy to grasp.

Certainly there are differing motives, different orders and levels of intent, scale, method and outcome. The physical killing specified in II(a) is seen by most Australians as wholesale killing within a short or definable time frame and in a localised geography, such as in death camps. Clearly there has been no Australian Auschwitz or Srebrenica. Clearly, if there was no Auschwitz here, then no genocide occurred here. Since 1997, however, II(e) on forcible removal of children, has, instead, moved into sharp focus. Certainly, the quantum leap, within the meaning of one word, genocide, from images of Auschwitz to those of sad and ragged Aboriginal children clustered in old sepia photographs is beyond most Australians. Critics can rail at the presence of II(e), but it is there, in a legal treaty ratified by Australia in 1949, albeit with some remarkable protests.

It is instructive to read the *Hansard* record of debate on this ratification. In some nineteen pages, the fate of Jews occupied four or five lines. Aborigines were not mentioned. The bulk of discussion was devoted to possible or probable Cold War 'genocides' in communist-controlled or communist-occupied Europe. Adair Blain, the Member for the Northern Territory, objected to the ratification bill: it was a slur on Australia because 'it deals with a crime of which no Anglo-Saxon could be guilty'. The Liberal Member for Henty, H.B. (Joe) Gullett, was eloquent in defence of events in Germany: 'It is a wretched spectacle to see many German generals, now old men, who, during the war, rendered good service to their country according to their lights, being subjected to every possible kind of degradation simply because in accordance with the ethics of their profession and acting under instructions from their government they carried out their duties as best they could' (Hansard, 1949: 1864–81).

Overlooked by many people, including genocide scholars, are clauses II(b), (c) and (d) of the Genocide Convention. Overlooked by almost everyone is Article III of the Convention: not only is genocide a crime, but so too are 'conspiracy to commit genocide', the 'attempt to commit genocide' and 'complicity in genocide'.

Genocide is said to have three parties: the perpetrators, the victims and the bystanders, those without whom the perpetrators cannot effect their purposes. (In chapter 6, I suggest five parties: these three plus the beneficiaries of genocide and the denialists.) Within the bystander category, there are those who are simply indifferent, those who are hostilely indifferent, those who are, in some degree, complicit, and those who are, for want of a clearer or better term, companions to events. In chapter 1, I discussed the notion that one can be a companion to something even in the act of opposing it. It seems never to occur to those who deny involvement, or legal or moral guilt, or who distance themselves from past events, that they were, and are, indeed companions, and therefore in some degree complicit.

The social science approach

Another measuring rod of genocide is to be found in the perspectives of the social sciences. A much broader conceptualisation has been suggested by Christian Pross, the Berlin Director of the Centre for the Treatment of Torture Victims. He speculates that nineteenth-century race theory led, in effect, to genocide by providing the ideological tools for a biological solution to a social (or political) problem (Aly *et al.*, 1994: 1). His less forensic concept helps us to better appreciate the justifications, ideologies, race theories, motives and moral defences. However much I prefer this approach, it strays from the wording of the international law by seeking either proof or disproof in the definitions of historians and social scientists. Robert Manne says he wrestles with Hannah Arendt's formulation following the trial of Adolf Eichmann in Jerusalem – that genocide is the desire (by Nazis) that certain distinct people (Jews) 'disappear from the earth' (Manne, 1999: 15–45). Certainly Arendt was trying to find words for that which was then (relatively) new in our moral (and physical) experience – a monstrous attack upon human status and human diversity. Perhaps if she had delved into that much overlooked half-brother to the Holocaust, the killing of 1.5 million Armenians by the Turks in 1915–16, she might have been less surprised and bewildered by Nazi behaviour. Manne believes, with Raimond Gaita, that genocide can be committed by non-murderous means, such as the biological assimilation of Aborigines. He is less certain about socio-cultural assimilation.

There are many more, and better, definitions of genocide than Arendt's. Social science definitions may well assist in the analysis of causes and in conceptualising events (see the evolution of ideas in Definitions of Genocide, at pages ix–xi). There is much discussion of the definition dilemma in Charny's excellent *Encyclopedia of Genocide* (1999).[1] Whereas Chalk and Jonassohn (1990) take the narrow view that 'genocide is a form of one-sided mass killing' by the state or by some other authority, Charny's much broader view sees genocide, in the generic sense, as the 'mass killing of substantial numbers of human beings, when not in the course of military action . . . under conditions of the essential defencelessness and helplessness of the victims' (Charny, 1994: 75–94). He emphasises the victim status of essentially 'defenceless and helpless' people, but he insists on mass killing of substantial numbers, which applies well to Australia's nineteenth-century private settlers' killing of Aborigines but not to the 'sophisticated' state removal of children. However, many cannot share his vision that the accident at the Chernobyl nuclear reactor was 'genocide resulting from ecological destruction and abuse'. Charny is a passionate defender of his view, while some critics, like Henry Huttenbach (2002), argue that while 'emotionally he is correct, academically, he is wrong'. The broadest view comes from Huttenbach, who defines genocide as 'any act that puts the very existence of a group in jeopardy'. Courts, I believe, would find it impossible to pinpoint 'any act', the meaning of 'existence' and what constitutes 'jeopardy'. He may be academically correct, but legally (and practically) he is wrong.

The commission of genocide with impunity is now an enormous issue: the wider the concept the less likely that any court will be able to arrive at conviction and punishment. At the International Association of Genocide Scholars conference in Minneapolis in June 2001, Henry Theriault argued for a narrower definition than the one in the Convention, thus enabling a sharper focus on both prevention and punishment. My argument here is that Articles II(b) and (c) are, indeed, very broad, but no one has yet seen fit to indict crimes because of the acts described therein. If we venture into this realm of improved definitions, we will have no universally accepted yardstick, certainly no justiciable basis for trials of genocidal practice or for civil suits for restitution by victims. Some theorists will seek to narrow the definition and others will expand the genocidal universe to the point of meaninglessness. It is significant that the 1998 Rome conference, establishing the new International Criminal Court (in July 2002), had no hesitation in incorporating verbatim the United Nations' 1948 definition into Article 6 of the Court's statute.

The common view

The lexicographers are often overlooked, and not always rightly so. The *Shorter Oxford* (1973) has four (much shorter) words of definition: 'annihilation of a race'. This, of course, captures the popular or general conception. *The Macquarie Dictionary* is little better: 'extermination of a national or racial group as a planned move'. However, it is left to the incomparable Noah Webster to provide us with what could be the most comprehensive, sensible and workable definition of them all:

> genocide: 1. the use of deliberate systematic measures (as killing, bodily or mental injury, unlivable conditions, prevention of births) calculated to bring about the extermination of a racial, political, or cultural group or to destroy the language, religion or culture of a group; 2. one who advocates or practices genocide.

There are some obvious weaknesses here, but at least the compilers have taken on board the Convention, and the important, but at times convoluted, ingredients identified by Raphael Lemkin (see p. x); they have addressed the issue of political and cultural groups, and they have paid attention to the destruction of religion, language and culture.

Australian political leaders would, I'm sure, plump for *Oxford*: Aborigines exist, in growing numbers, *ergo*, there was and is no annihilation. In July 2002, Australia decided, by a slim majority within the Coalition (Liberal Party and National Party) government, to ratify the Court. John Anderson, the leader of the National Party, and many Liberal Party members, were (and are) 'worried about the broad definition of genocide' – precisely because Article II(e) is included. (Webster might suit because child removal is omitted, but then again, the rest of the wording fits the Australian case all too neatly.) Curious, indeed, that contemporary politicians feel 'worried' about a court that can only deal with contemporary crimes, that is, those committed after the commencement of the Court, not retrospective ones. Does John Anderson fear that present-day bureaucrats would still consider removing, or would actually remove, Aboriginal children, or would unilaterally sterilise Aboriginal women?

Debate about better definitions will continue, but endless talk about revision and reform has proven pointless. In 1978, and again in 1985, the Special Rapporteur (to the UN) on genocide concluded that the Convention had not deterred or prevented genocide, that stronger measures were needed to stop the crime, and that issues of domestic jurisdiction and state sovereignty shouldn't take precedence over protection against genocide. No changes were made and we are now most likely saddled with the 1948 wording for yet another fifty years. I do believe that the wording in Article II is broad enough to encompass most of the crimes that academics envision in their perception of genocide.

Misconstruing the nature of genocide, and failure to pay due attention to the partly precise, partly broad and elusive language of Article II, can lead to some startling cases. One such was the application to the Australian Capital Territory Supreme Court by four Aborigines for the arrest of the Prime Minister and Deputy Prime Minister on the grounds that, by securing the Wik ten-point plan legislation in 1998,[2] they committed specified and unspecified acts of genocide, and that all members of federal parliament have committed genocide by, *inter alia*, failing to enact an Australian offence of genocide.[3] Many worse things have befallen Aborigines in their history than the extinguishment of those native title rights which the High Court ruled could and should co-exist with pastoral rights on leasehold properties.

We need a firm basis for both discussion and action. The only solid (and universal) definition, however flawed, is the one set out in international law. Even so, we have to look to the philosophy inherent in the legal wording of Article II, namely, that genocide is, as Lemkin argued, the systematic attempt to destroy, by various means, a defined group's essential foundations. In both the legal and broader 'philosophical' senses, the senses in which Raphael Lemkin coined the word *genocide*, Australia is guilty of at least three, or possibly four, acts of genocide: first, the essentially private genocide, the physical killing committed by settlers and rogue police officers in the nineteenth century, while the state, in the form of the colonial authorities, stood silently by (for the most part); second, the twentieth-century attempts to achieve the biological disappearance of those deemed 'half-caste' Aborigines, both by intermarriage and by the official state policy and practice of forcibly transferring children from one group to another with the express intention that they cease being Aboriginal; third, a *prima facie* case that Australia's actions to protect Aborigines in fact caused them serious bodily and/or mental harm.

THE HISTORICAL CASE

Aborigines – and first contact

Aborigines probably landed on Cape York, in northern Australia, between – and this is hotly contested among prehistorians at present – 24,000 and 60,000 years ago, forming about 500 tribes with different languages and customs, and numbering between 250,000 and 750,000 at the time of the British arrival, or invasion, in 1788.[4]

Hunters and food-gatherers in an inhospitable land of low rainfall, they had no animals that could be domesticated. Semi-nomadic, they roamed within set areas, in domains they called (and still call) their 'country'. Their way of life precluded a rich material culture, yet it wasn't 'primitive' in the disparaging sense in which so many observers noted, and still note, their 'lack of alphabet' and alleged 'lack of arts, science and invention'. Their stone-tool technology predates European and Asian usage by thousands of years. Aboriginal social organisation was highly complicated, their religion deep and complex, their art and myths rich and varied. Of note was their strong and foolproof system of incest prohibition, their system of kinship, reciprocity and child-rearing. United by religious and totemic ties, Aborigines held their land in trust, collectively and in perpetuity. Within the various social units, kinship implied certain behaviour and reciprocal responsibilities. Patterns of social interaction were tightly prescribed, co-operation within each group was high, and group sanctions, by way of punishment for breach of rules, were harsh.

There was no formal political organisation, but there was a strong sense of adjudication of disputes. They had a reign of social law. It was their lack of outwardly visible political organisation – the absence of what Western society sees as the prerequisites of governance, namely, a system resembling a state, or organs akin to a legislature, a judiciary, an executive – that placed Aborigines at a huge disadvantage in confrontation with white settlement. That handicap was nowhere greater than in the centuries-long doctrine that, in 1788, Australia was *terra nullius*, a land empty but for fauna and flora. *That* legal (and political) fallacy was finally put to rest in 1992 in the monumental decision of the High Court in *Mabo v the State of Queensland* (Number 2). John Locke's seventeenth-century doctrine that property in land originally came from tilling the soil – 'mixing labour and land' – took a long time to die. As recently as 1993, members of the Samuel Griffiths Society in Melbourne argued that the Murray Island people (Eddie Mabo's country), but not the Aborigines, should have land title, because the former were Melanesians who are 'millennia ahead of the Palaeolithics [Stone Age people] in terms of social organisation' and because, unlike the 'palaeos', they farmed (*Australian*, 27 October 1993).[5]

Botany Bay was the site of Britain's new convict colony. On 28 January 1788 the First Fleet took possession of Australia in the name of King George III. From the outset, relations between black and white were well intentioned at the official level, but rent with strife in practice. Whether 'empty' or inhabited, whether there was an extant state*less* or state*ful* society, official instructions to Governor Arthur Phillip were 'to endeavour by every means in his power to open an intercourse with the natives and to conciliate their goodwill, requiring all persons under his Government to live in amity and kindness with them'. The Letters Patent establishing the colony of South Australia in 1836 similarly contained a proviso that 'nothing should affect the rights of the natives in regard to their enjoyment or occupation of the land'.

The Letters Patent and instructions to governors in the eighteenth and nineteenth centuries were really benign utterances of far-away governments. The hard clashes of interest on the spot were of a different order. Land was seized by the white settlers as their only means of support. Aborigines retaliated by taking stock and provisions – for which they developed a taste. Reprisals followed, with the advantage always heavily on the white side. As the settlers spread out from the centres of administration, government control lessened, newly introduced diseases spread among the Aborigines, the birth rate dropped, the Aboriginal population declined markedly, and law and order became impossible to maintain.

Near-extermination

Over 130 years ago, the English novelist Anthony Trollope visited Australia. 'There has been some rough work', he wrote:

> We have taken away their land, have destroyed their food, made them subject to our laws, which are antagonistic to their habits and traditions,

have endeavoured to make them subject to our tastes, which they hate, have massacred them when they defended themselves and their possessions after their own fashion, and have taught them by hard warfare to acknowledge us to be their master.

Trollope, 1966 [1873]: 134–42

By 1911, 123 years after settlement, the 'rough work' had reduced the Aboriginal population to 31,000. Much of this section examines and explains that catastrophic reduction, under headings which borrow from the Convention's definition.

Disease as genocide

The 'disease-as-genocide' argument needs brief assessment, first because it must be challenged and second because of the strong tendency among some historians to inculpate smallpox, and exculpate settlers, as the major factor in mass Aboriginal deaths. To date, no one has refuted the hypothesis of the late Professor Noel Butlin, an eminent economic historian, of introduced disease as an intentional weapon of extermination. He concluded – albeit in a book he described as 'explicitly speculative and hypothetical' – that the single most effective killer of Aborigines was smallpox (Butlin, 1983: 175). More to the point, while the origins of 'the main killer' are obscure, 'it is possible and, in 1789, *likely that infection of the Aborigines was a deliberate exterminating act*' [my emphasis]. Butlin was much influenced by his reading about the fate of Native Americans; he, in turn, has influenced others on this issue, including the Australian scholar Jan Kociumbas.

Stannard, in an account of the horrendous, willed death of native peoples in the Americas, has a section entitled 'Pestilence and Genocide' (1992: 109). The key is *and*, not pestilence *as* genocide. Even though elementary forms of inoculation were already known – for example, Lady Mary Wortley Montagu introduced inoculation practice, which she learned in Turkey, into England in 1721 – I find it difficult to believe that barely literate colonists understood (or even intuited) germ theory well enough to knowingly use pestilence as a weapon of mass destruction. Could a group of settlers, themselves dying of the disease, have the knowledge, and the will, to implement a germ warfare genocide a mere year after their arrival, as Butlin suggests? We began to understand that these diseases were spread by communicable bacteria and viruses only 120 years ago.[6] Why, then, the specific assertion about this one and only disease – among the myriad in the catalogue of infectious death – as part of the genocidal armoury? (And how much more indictable would Australian behaviour have been if it had been deliberate?)

The first major smallpox epidemic among Aborigines was in April 1789, fifteen months after first settlement. The second was in 1829–31, its origin never determined, according to Frank Fenner in his monumental work on the disease (Fenner *et al.*, 1988: 240–41). The third major epidemic occurred between 1865 and 1869, generated almost certainly by the visits of Malayan trepang fishermen. Goldsmid has posited three possibilities about the 1789 epidemic: first, that it was spread deliberately, as in America where, as American scholars assert, smallpox–infected blankets were introduced to 'extirpate this execrable race'; second, that Aborigines stole bottles of 'variolous matter' brought by the surgeons of the First Fleet, and subsequently became infected; third, that Aborigines were accidentally infected from a local 'variolate' colonist (Goldsmid, 1988: 29–31).

That there is no evidence whatsoever of premeditation is also the opinion of Watkin Tench, a captain in the First Fleet, who suggested at the time that this was 'a supposition so wild as to be unworthy of consideration'. Stephen Kunitz has looked carefully at the impact of European settlement on the health of Aborigines (1994: 83–5, 178). He cites the massacres by that hideous creature of colonial administration, the Native (or Black) Police,[7] as the major cause of Aboriginal death, followed by the 'hunting propensities' of the settlers and the poisoning of flour issued as rations. It wasn't, he contends, exotic disease that produced a 25 per cent decline in the Queensland population, but rather 'the savagery of the settlers and their calculated slaughter of the indigenous population'. 'Not all natives dropped dead whenever they got downwind of a European', he concludes. Pueblo Indians, perhaps, is his caustic response, but not Aborigines. Jan Kociumbas (2001) is convinced that there is a document, somewhere, that will substantiate deliberate use of smallpox: several important diaries, notably those of Surgeon White, have been heavily edited, and others have been lost. I remain unconvinced of both Butlin's thesis and the assertion that any of the huge numbers of deaths during the colonial period in North America and Africa was achieved by deliberately introduced disease. The gun and the sword have been 'outstanding' facilitators of death these past three centuries: why resort to the much slower, less certain though lethal, likely self-harming instrument of small-pox-smeared blankets? There is simply no explanation offered by any researcher as to how Aborigines boarded the fleet and stole the vials; nor is there diary, memoir or other material to suggest that Australian settlers (or convicts) conceptualised 'germ warfare' against the natives while they were simultaneously battling against a disease they couldn't comprehend.

'Killing members of the group'

While it is true that the diseases introduced by convicts and settlers – smallpox, typhoid, tuberculosis, diphtheria, whooping cough, influenza, pneumonia, measles and venereal disease – had an undeniably devastating impact and seriously depleted Aboriginal numbers, it was contingent on the 'accident' of white settlement, not something deliberate. It is to the intentional genocidal impulses and actions of the settlers that we must turn for evidence of Australia's treatment of the Aboriginal peoples.

In the context of Article II(a), we know something about the physical killing of Aborigines, as a definable group, particularly in the latter half of the nineteenth and the early part of the twentieth century. The first white settlers came to Tasmania in 1803, and by 1806 the serious killing had begun (see Ryan, 1981). In retaliation for the spearing of livestock, Aboriginal children were abducted for use as forced labour, women were raped and tortured and given poisoned flour, and men were shot. They were systematically disposed of in ones, twos and threes, or in dozens, rather than in one massacre.

They were at risk from predatory sealers and settlers. In 1824, settlers were authorised to shoot Aborigines. In 1828, the Governor declared martial law. Soldiers and settlers arrested, or shot, any blacks found in settled districts. Vigilante groups avenged Aboriginal retaliation by whole-sale slaughter of men, women and children. Between 1829 and 1834, an appointed conciliator, George Robinson, collected the surviving remnants: 123 people, who were then settled on Flinders Island. By 1835, between 3,000 and 4,000 Aborigines had been killed. This wasn't simply a murder-ous outbreak of racial hatred. They were *killed*, not solely because of their spearing of cattle or their 'nuisance' value, but rather *because they were*

Aborigines. The Genocide Convention is very specific on this point: the victim group must be at risk because they *are* that group.

Henry Reynolds (2001a, 2001b) believes many writers are ignorant of Tasmania's history. There was, he concedes, much public and open discussion about 'wars of extermination'. But the reality was, he argues, that this talk of extermination and the ensuing attempts to kill were concerned with perhaps two tribes, and certainly not all Tasmanian Aborigines. What began as a genocidal intent, he insists, ended in failure, and in Governor Arthur's efforts to save the remnants. In sum, what happened in Tasmania 'comes within the range of genocide without its being genocide'. What Reynolds fails to see is something he has consistently failed to see in all his writings: that the attempted destruction of 'part' of a people is enough for the commission of the crime, and that genocide doesn't have to be successful in order to be genocide. (In law, there is no lower or upper limit to the destruction of a 'part' of a people.) Furthermore, he ignores one essential difference between one particular criminal law and this particular international law: in the former, attempted murder *is not* murder but another crime, but in the latter, attempted genocide *is* genocide. He also ignores the Convention's injunction that criminality is inherent in conspiracy, incitement *and* complicity in genocide.

White settlers killed some 10,000 blacks in Queensland between 1824 and 1908 (Evans *et al.*, 1975: 75–8). Considered 'wild animals', 'vermin', 'scarcely human', 'hideous to humanity', 'loathsome' and a 'nuisance', they were fair game for white 'sportsmen'. In 1883, the British High Commissioner, Arthur Hamilton Gordon, wrote privately to his friend William Gladstone, Prime Minister of England:

> The habit of regarding the natives as vermin, to be cleared off the face of the earth, has given the average Queenslander a tone of brutality and cruelty in dealing with 'blacks' which it is very difficult to anyone who does not *know* it, as I do, to realise. I have heard men of culture and refinement, of the greatest humanity and kindness to their fellow whites, and who when you meet them here at home you would pronounce to be incapable of such deeds, talk, not only of the *wholesale* butchery (for the iniquity of that may sometimes be disguised from themselves) but of the *individual* murder of natives, exactly as they would talk of a day's sport, or having to kill some troublesome animal.

In 1896, Archibald Meston was appointed as Royal Commissioner to investigate the slaughter. In the same year, he produced his *Report on the Aborigines of North Queensland* (Queensland Parliament, 1896). The treatment of the Cape York people, he wrote, was 'a shame to our common humanity'; their 'manifest joy at assurances of safety and protection is pathetic beyond expression. God knows they were in need of it.' Aboriginal people met him 'like hunted wild beasts, having lived for years in a state of absolute terror'. He was convinced their only salvation lay in strict and absolute isolation from all whites, from predators who, in no particular order, wanted to kill them, take their women, sell them grog or opium. The Aboriginals Protection and Restriction of the Sale of Opium Act 1897 followed. Apart from some changes to its wording, this remained in force until 1985. In 1939, the statute was amended slightly and renamed as the Aboriginals Preservation and Protection Act. In our age of environmentalism we are used to the notion of 'protected species' in the context of, for example, exotic eagles or rare marsupials. 'Protected Aborigines' meant just that: a sub-species which had to be saved from the murderous impulses and practices of settler Australians.

The history of Aborigines in Western Australia was little different (see, *inter alia*, Haebich, 1988; for material on the Pinjarra massacres of the 1830s see Grose, 1927: 30–35, Fletcher, 1984: 1–16 and Green, 1984). There were hundreds of massacres between settlement and the 1920s, with the last of them, the Forrest River killings, as late as 1926. This was the only episode to result in a Royal Commission – yet another such judicial inquiry resulting in the acquittal, and then promotion, of the two police officers involved in the shooting, and then burning, of perhaps a hundred people. One massacre or mass murder is not genocide, but given the pattern and propensity of such actions, one must conclude that Raphael Lemkin was correct when, in 1944, he coined the word *genocide* to mean co-ordinated or systematic actions aimed at destroying a racial, ethnic or religious group's essential foundations. He didn't say the killing had to be wholesale, or in a compacted time frame, or in specified killing fields. Nor did the Genocide Convention which followed his work.

The history of Aborigines in South Australia was rather different. The early whalers and sealers at the start of the nineteenth century were brutal: they killed and kidnapped. But from 1836, when permanent settlement began, the colonists forged a more independent line, on all matters, than their colonial brothers and sisters elsewhere. Despite dispossession of land and abrogation of Aboriginal culture and customs, there was less shooting and poisoning than in other colonies. (Aborigines argue that this was because there were fewer to shoot following the smallpox epidemic that came with settlement.)

There was a massive population loss in central Australia – particularly in the region of what is now Alice Springs – between 1860 and 1895. Richard Kimber speculates that 20 per cent may have died from influenza, typhoid and diseases which they had not previously encountered. But some 1,750, or 40 per cent, of the Aboriginal population, were (mostly) shot in what was euphemistically called 'dispersal' (Kimber, 1997: 33–65). A Native Police lieutenant, giving evidence in 1861, was asked what was meant by 'dispersing'. 'Firing at them', was his reply, but 'I gave strict orders not to shoot any gins [Aboriginal women]'. Another euphemism was that troopers were out shooting 'kangaroos'. An early observer, E.M. Curr, writing in *The Australian Race* in 1886, concluded: 'The White race seems destined, not to absorb, but to exterminate the Blacks of Australia.'

'Causing serious bodily or mental harm to members of the group'

Courts hold trials, that is, efforts to examine and determine causes or issues. In this section, I do not bring the charge that Australia, in the name of protecting people from physical killing, initially instituted intentional policies and practices that led to 'serious bodily or mental harm' to Aborigines (Article II(b)). But there is certainly room for exploration of an argument that protection, however well intentioned, resulted in disaster of a most harmful kind.

Protection legislation began in an elementary way in the 1840s: by 1843, five of the colonies had appointed Protectors. Protection, in earnest and in great legislative detail, began in Victoria in 1869 and 1886, in Western Australia in 1886, in New South Wales in 1909, in South Australia in 1911, in the Northern Territory in 1910 and 1911, and in Tasmania in 1912.[8] Most of these laws were predicated on the philosophy of 'smoothing the pillow' of a race near extinction. Given that there was a widespread assumption that Aborigines were dying out, settlers fulfilled the prophecy by acting to ensure that such was indeed the outcome.

There were to be two protective fences against genocide in most of

Australia: the legal one, which was soon found to be insufficient, followed by the geographic one of gross isolation, the additional barrier against white predators. Law would keep whites out and Aborigines in protective custody. Geographic location would see to it that no one could get in, or out. Government-run settlements and Christian-run missions were established in inaccessible places to protect the people from their predators; to encourage, sometimes to coerce, Aborigines away from the 'centres of evil'; to allow for the Christianising and civilising process in private and away from temptations; to enable better ministration – in the quiet of a hospice, so to speak – to a doomed, remnant people.

Catherine deMayo has explained why 'mission' Aborigines came to be where many still are. A Lutheran pastor visiting Bloomfield River in Cape York in 1898 said: 'All the mission can really achieve for them is a kind of Christian burial service.' Another concluded that 'the Christian Church and the Government can but play the part of physicians and nurses in a hospital for incurables'. These 'children of darkness' needed places like Yarrabah, near Cairns, described as 'splendidly secluded'. Some Christian views of Aborigines were no better than those of the squatters and 'sportsmen'. In the 1870s, a clergyman in Queensland wrote:

> If our instincts are true we must loathe the aborigines as they are now, less estimable than the mongrels that prowl like them in the offal of a station. By the ashes of their fire . . . they are crouched with their knees up to their chin and with a half idiotic and wholly cunning leer on their faces, their hair matted in filth . . .
>
> quoted in deMayo, 1990

The missionaries did not simply supply a nursing service for 'incurables' or a burial service: they became active agents of various governmental policies, such as protection-segregation, assimilation, so-called integration and some of the latter-day notions like self-determination and self-management. More than agents, they were delegated an astonishing array of unchallengeable powers. Uniquely – in terms of modern missionary activity in colonised societies – mission boards became the sole *civil* authority in their domains. They ran schools, infirmaries, farms and gardens, provided water, sewerage and similar public utility services, established dormitories, built jails, prosecuted 'wrongdoers', jailed them, counselled them, controlled their incomes, forbade their customs and acted as sole legal guardians of every adult and every child. Almost incidentally, they also tried to Christianise the inmates according to their varying dogmas and doctrines, with little success. The eighteenth-century English radical philosopher Jeremy Bentham has bequeathed us a succinct definition of such 'penitentiary homes': places of 'safe custody, confinement, solitude, forced labour and instructions' (Bozovic, 1995: 34).

Mission societies and government departments of Native or Aboriginal Affairs set about the business of protecting the people. But in what spirit? As a student of 'native administration' in South Africa, Australia, Canada and New Zealand, I find one facet of Australian practice noteworthy for its absence. Baron Lugard of Abinger, the doyen of British colonial policymakers from 1888 to 1945, always held that successful administration was contingent on officials having a sense of love for the administered people – and if not love, then at least a liking, and if not a liking, at least a respect for them. By and large, Australian officials, lay and clerical, protected in a spirit of *dis*like, in what Minogue would rightly call (if he were writing in this particular context) a configuration of contempt.

Reminiscent of the manner in which Jews have been held in contempt by church, state and science, we have clerical disdain not only in the 1880s but also a century later. In the early 1980s, the Roman Catholic Bishop of the North-West (of Western Australia) was pressed to remove Father Seraphim Sanz as the no longer acceptable superintendent of Kalumburu Mission. He also dispensed with the philosophies of the general Catholic mission policy-maker, Father Eugene Perez. In his book, Perez entitled a chapter, 'East Kimberley Primitives'; he described Aborigines as corresponding to the Palaeolithic Age, 'primitives dwarfed to the bare essentials of human existence', people with 'inborn cunning', 'lacking interest and ambition', with 'undeniable immaturity', forever seeking 'the unattainable EL DORADO, coming to them on a silver tray', people 'with no sense of balance or proportion', people who 'want "today" what cannot be given till tomorrow', people to whom physical goods are 'like the toy given to a child, which will soon be reduced to bits, and thrown into the rubbish dump' (Perez, 1979: 346–8). And so on.

Contempt also came in 'scientific' guise. In 1913, we had the views of Professor W. Baldwin Spencer, the man who was to become a significant and powerful figure in Aboriginal affairs, as author, theorist and administrator:

The aboriginal is, indeed, a very curious mixture: mentally, about the level of a child who has little control over his feelings and is liable to give way to violent fits of temper . . . He has no sense of responsibility and, except in rare cases, no initiative.

Commonwealth, 1913

The revered professor of biology was dismayed: Aborigines didn't even realise that they could make clothes out of kangaroo skins, and they didn't cultivate crops or domesticate animals. 'Their customs are revolting to us', and they were 'far lower than the Papuan, the New Zealander or the usual African native'. While Chief Protector of Aborigines in 1911–12, he declared that 'no half-caste children should be allowed in any native camp', after which he established the Kahlin Compound in Darwin. Assuredly, neither Perez nor Spencer was an Alfred Rosenberg or a Richard-Walther Darré – two of several key race theorists in the Nazi firmament – but in their own way, in our especial Anglo-Saxon, white, Australian way, they were accomplished enough in 'scientific' race theory and, more importantly, in its practice.

The special laws show that the 'protections' which parliaments had in mind were as much from outside intruders as from the Aborigines themselves. In Queensland, protection in theory quickly became discrimination in practice. Stopping the predators from coming in resulted in Aborigines being incarcerated for life, even for generations, on the remotest of places, like Yarrabah, Palm Island, Mornington Island, Doomadgee, Bamaga, Edward River, Weipa, Bloomfield River and Woorabinda. Protection of Aboriginal morality came to mean control of their movements, labour, marriages, private lives, reading matter, leisure and sports activities, even cultural and religious rituals. Protection of their income came to mean police constables – as official Protectors of Aborigines – controlling their wages, their withdrawals from compulsory savings bank accounts, rights to enter contracts of labour and of purchase and sale.

In the Northern Territory, from 1911 to 1957 and again from 1957 to 1964, when all 'full-blood' Aborigines were declared 'wards', protection included the need for permits to leave reserves and the Territory, prohibition on alcohol, prohibition on inter-racial sex, prohibition on inter-racial marriage unless with official permission, inability to vote or to receive social service benefits, employment at specified, statutory Aboriginal rates of pay (well below the famous basic wage, which Australia innovated in 1907), exclusion from industrial awards, and so on (Tatz, 1964).

In Queensland, protection included banishment from one part of the state to another, for periods ranging from twelve months to life ('During the Director's Pleasure' was the official phrase), for offences such as 'disorderly conduct', being 'uncontrollable', a 'menace to young girls', and 'on discharge from [urban] prison'. It also involved imprisonment on the settlement or mission, for a maximum of three weeks per offence, for offences only Aborigines could commit: 'being cheeky', 'refusing to work', 'calling the hygiene officer a "big-eyed bastard"', 'leaving a horse and dray in the yard whereby a person might have been injured', 'committing adultery', 'playing cards', 'arranging to receive a male person during the night', 'being untidy at the recreation hall', 'refusing to provide a sample of faeces required by the hygiene officer and further, wilfully destroying the bottle provided for the purpose, the property of the department' (Tatz, 1963; also Nettheim, 1973, 1981). Often charges were not laid concurrently: an 'offender' would get three weeks for one offence, then on discharge be 'charged' with a separate offence, albeit one arising from the same initial circumstance. The legal maximum of three weeks became a continuum of six, nine, twelve weeks. In Western Australia there was 'protective' punishment for anyone who didn't 'conduct themselves in a respectable manner at all times', used 'obscene language', drank alcohol, didn't keep dwellings 'clean and tidy', 'cut down trees', wasted water, didn't keep their dogs under control and who didn't 'empty and clean' troughs and coppers in the laundry.

The era of protection–segregation didn't end with the formal adoption of assimilation policies by the national conferences of officials in 1937, and again in 1951 and 1961. Despite proclamations of equality in those two latter decades, the old policies and practices persisted. This was because the lay and clerical bureaucrats who remained as guardians couldn't or wouldn't accept the 'elevation' of 'their' wards to the status (of power, goodness, correctness, civility) they enjoyed. The settlements and missions continued as before, with draconian powers vested in officials – or 'inspectors' as Bentham would have called them (Bozovic, 1995: 8, 29) – who maintained a regimen of work, instruction, discipline, good order and hygiene. These bogey men, especially in Western Australia and Queensland, were real enough. 'The welfare', to use the Aboriginal idiom, remains indelible in the contemporary Aboriginal psyche.

It was only after the Labor Party won federal office at the end of 1972 that these institutions began to be dismantled: the 'inmates' stayed and became citizens (in legal theory), but the 'inspectors' of the draconian rules 'for the good order and discipline of the settlements' – the guards and the gatekeepers – disappeared, at least in the flesh. Their spectres remained. What has also endured is the myth, and the euphemism, that all of this treatment – over nearly three-quarters of a century, at least – was simply and mundanely *nothing more* than 'the era of handouts'.

In an ironic sense it was the removal of the draconian structures that created, in my view, the present climate of violence and disorder in population centres. All commentators, analysts and scholars attribute the present breakdowns, including the propensity for suicide, to colonialism, racism, oppression, landlessness, population relocations, and destruction of cultures and environments. The Royal Commission into Aboriginal Deaths in Custody has an excellent summary of all of this, which explains the underlying causes of the disproportionate numbers of Aborigines in custody (Johnston, 1991: 3–47).

All true, in the broad sense and sweep. But there is an identifiable set of actions which has been largely responsible for the present. These 'asylums' or 'total institutions', as Goffman calls them,[9] these settlements and missions, became 'communities', regardless of whether or not there was a *communitas*. In the protection–segregation and wardship eras, settlements and missions were designed as 'institutions', with the residents termed 'inmates'. There were locks and keys of a legal, administrative and physical kind. With the changes that came shortly before and after 1972, these nineteenth- and early twentieth-century institutions were euphemistically re-named 'communities', and superintendents and managers were transformed by administrative pen into 'community development officers'.

No one ever tried to understand or define the characteristics of community, no one trained the officers in 'development', and no one ever consulted the black populations about their notions of a civil order, an organised society, a polity. Born out of sheer political expedience, and a laziness about doing any homework on these groupings and their common or uncommon character, bureaucrats eventually gave these prison-like 'total institutions' 'freedom', a budget and autonomy of a limited kind. Nobody gave thought to how one de-institutionalised institutions of such penitentiary flavour; no one gave lessons in autonomy; and, importantly, nobody remembered, or wanted to remember, that the inmates-turned-citizens were often people moved or exiled to these places, people who had to be disciplined or punished, or people rounded up by desert patrols and simply placed there for the great 'social engineering' experiment of 'assimilation' – the official policy slogan of the time – in the deserts and monsoon lands. Most places were not peopled by a *communitas*, by groups in a voluntary association, with a common tribal or linguistic membership and fellowship, a common historical, or political or cultural heritage, communalistic in their membership, integrated and socially coherent.

Infrastructure in the institutions was artificial. It was the omnipresence of the 'inspector' (usually the director), the authoritarian laws and regulations under special legislation, and the associated powers, together with mission evangelism, which gave these institutions 'viability' – of a kind. The struts and pillars propping up the institutions began to be removed only in the 1970s and, in Queensland, even later. Thus there is, in effect, a vacuum in many of these places, an absence of an overarching or binding philosophy (however bad or misguided), a lack of system, without any goals beyond mere survival. The rallying call for land rights, especially since 1969, and the protracted legal hearings, have filled only a very small part of that vacuum. Lacking structure, many 'communities' lack order, and have become disordered societies. The much respected Aboriginal values of affection, reverence for family and kin, reciprocity, care of the young and aged, veneration for law, lore and religion, are foundering or have been displaced for now. What began as protection against genocide has ended, for the present, in a legacy of chronic distress.

I must stress that there is no suggestion whatever in these observations that we return to the nightmare that was the wardship and welfare era. That call is now the province of the Bennelong Society, chaired by the former Minister for Aboriginal Affairs, John Herron. He, former cabinet minister Peter Howson and a group of like-minded denialists of Aboriginal history, profess concern for the Aboriginal present and future, yet call for a return to the era I have just described. They have never delved into the 'Hasluck era', looked at the gulf between his (often ambiguous and ambivalent) policy and practice, to see what devastation it wrought and brought to body and soul. The Bennelong mob utter 'the Hasluck era' as a magical incantation, without any notion of the appalling spell it cast, and left behind. It is hardly a claim I enjoy or would wish to make, but many professionals who work in the Territory tell me that, apart from a few statistical, legal and administrative changes, most of what I wrote in my 'dissection' of the Hasluck era some forty years ago remains valid today.

Forced assimilation

An important contradiction occurred during the era of protection–segregation: while Aborigines in some domains had to be protected and given shelter from genocidal depredations, in others they had to be 'dispersed' into mainstream society. Thus, while physical killing was a feature of Tasmania, Queensland, Western Australia and the Northern Territory, a different facet of genocide was under way in Victoria and New South Wales. As early as 1858, in Victoria, there was a call for treating 'half-castes' differently from 'full-bloods'. The (first) Protection Board said, in relation to 'half-castes', that it had a duty to 'interfere at once to prevent their growing up amongst us with the habits of the savage, as they possess the instincts, powers of mind and altogether different constitution of the white man'. By 1886, forced assimilation was in full swing: the Aborigines Protection Act 1886 (Victoria) declared that only 'full-bloods' and 'half-castes' over the age of thirty-four were entitled to aid. In other words, all non-'full-bloods' under thirty-four were forcibly expelled from missions and reserves, irrespective of marital or sibling status, of need, of ability to cope in the mainstream, or whether they had anywhere to go in the outside world. The penalty for returning was a £20 fine – the equivalent of perhaps $10,000 in today's currency. Here the statute and the practice overrode normally enforceable civil contracts, such as marriage.

Forced assimilation also meant the forcible removal of children from parents and family and 'relocation' to white foster parents, white adoptive parents, or to special 'half-caste' or 'assimilation' homes. In 1905, W.E. Roth, the Chief Protector of Aborigines in Queensland, ruled that the 'social status of half-caste children' had to be raised: 'In the future, all such infants taken from the camps should be brought up as white children.' In his view, 'if left to themselves', the 'half-caste girls became prostitutes and the boys cattle thieves' (Roth, 1905: 13). In 1909, C.F. Gale, the Chief Protector in Western Australia, wrote:

> I would not hesitate for one moment to separate any half-caste from its Aboriginal mother, no matter how frantic her momentary grief might be at the time. They soon forget their offspring.
>
> Gale, 1909: 9[10]

O.A. Neville, Chief Protector in the West from 1915 to 1940, was of identical mind. He could do nothing for Aborigines, who were dying out, but he could absorb the 'half-castes':

> The native must be helped in spite of himself! Even if a measure of discipline is necessary it must be applied, but it can be applied in such a way as to appear to be gentle persuasion . . . the end in view will justify the means employed.
>
> Haebich, 1988: 156

Neville had a 'three-point' plan: first, the 'full-bloods' would die out; second, take 'half-castes' away from their mothers; third, control marriages among 'half-castes' and so encourage intermarriage with the white community. The 'young half-blood maiden is a pleasant, placid, complacent person as a rule, while the quadroon [one-quarter Aboriginal] is often strikingly attractive, with her oftimes auburn hair, rosy freckled colouring, and good figure . . .' These were the sort of people who should be elevated 'to our own plane'. In this way, it would be possible to 'eventually forget that there were ever any Aborigines in Australia' (Beresford and Omaji, 1998: 47–8). Here, in unmistakable language and intent, was ideology justifying why biology should solve this 'social problem'. And so Neville established Sister Kate's Orphanage in 1933, on the guiding principle that the good Sister took in those whose 'lightness of colour' could lead them to assimilation and intermarriage.

Neville's legacy – his mishmash of nineteenth-century race theory, twentieth-century eugenics, his own brand of assimilationism and illogic – is to be found in the quite astonishing Natives (Citizenship Rights) Act 1944 (Western Australia). A 'native' could apply to a magistrate for 'citizenship' – something never really lost to Aborigines, since they were always regarded as 'subjects' of the monarch, especially in their susceptibility to the criminal law. To become 'white', in effect, the applicant had to show a magistrate that he or she had 'dissolved tribal and native associations', had served in the Commonwealth armed forces and had received an honourable discharge, or was 'otherwise a fit and proper person to obtain a Certificate of Citizenship'. But much more than that, the magistrate was required to be satisfied of many things before an applicant was no longer 'deemed to be a native or Aborigine': first, that for two years before the application, the applicant had 'adopted the manner and habits of civilised life'; second, that full citizenship rights were conducive to his or her welfare; third, that the applicant could 'speak and understand the English language'; fourth, that the applicant was 'not suffering from active leprosy, syphilis, granuloma, or yaws';[11] fifth, that the applicant was of 'industrious habits' and 'of good behaviour and reputation'; and finally, that the applicant was 'reasonably capable of managing his own affairs'. There was, of course, a catch – one unequalled, I believe, in 'native administration' anywhere in the world: that if the Native Affairs Commissioner, 'or any other person', made complaint, a magistrate could revoke the certificate and the person became a native or Aborigine once more. The grounds of complaint? The citizen wasn't 'adopting the manner and habits of civilised life'; or that he or she had two convictions under the Native Administration Act 1905–41 (Western Australia) for the normally non-criminal offences discussed above, like cutting down trees, being untidy, or leaving the laundry in a mess, or was a habitual drunkard; or had, in the non-Aboriginal phase of their Aboriginal lives, 'contracted leprosy, syphilis, granuloma or yaws'! This statute was not repealed until 1971.

In 1928, J.W. Bleakley, then Queensland Protector of Aborigines, was asked by the federal government to report on Aboriginal policy – including the future of 'half-castes' – in the Northern Territory (Bleakley, 1929: 17, 28). Those of 50 per cent or more Aboriginal 'blood', 'no matter how carefully brought up and educated', will 'drift back' to the black, he declared. But those with less than 50 per cent 'Aboriginal blood' should be segregated so that they could 'avoid the dangers of the blood call'. Thus there should be 'complete separation of half-castes from the Aboriginals with a view to their absorption by the white race'; further, there should be complete segregation of blacks and whites 'in colonies of their own' and 'to marry amongst themselves'. Thereafter 'half-castes' were sent to specified institutions around the country, to be 'salvaged' because their 'white blood' was their springboard to civilisation and Christendom. It is indeed strange that many of these assimilation homes were located in places of great isolation, for example, Croker Island, Garden Point (now Pularumpi) on Melville Island, the Bungalow in Alice Springs, Cootamundra Girls' Home and Kinchela Boys' Home in rural New South Wales. The St Francis Home in Adelaide, Sister Kate's Orphanage in Perth and Kahlin Compound and the Retta Dixon Home in Darwin were among the few institutions located in white urban domains.

In the biological footsteps of Professor Baldwin Spencer, Dr Cecil Cook, Chief Protector of Aborigines in the Northern Territory, believed that 'the preponderance of coloured races, the preponderance of coloured alien blood and the scarcity of white females to mate with the white male population' would create 'a position of incalculable future menace to the purity of race in tropical Australia'. What was worse was that a large population of blacks 'may drive out the whites' (Beresford and Omaji, 1998: 47–8). I met Dr Cook several times in the early 1960s: having just emigrated from South Africa, I had a terrible presentiment, when talking with this man, that I hadn't left behind that not so beloved country.

The Neville–Bleakley–Cook philosophies became official policy in the Territory in the early 1930s. The Administrator's Report of 1933 had this to say, in the plainest of eugenicist language:

> In the Territory the mating of an Aboriginal with any person other than an Aboriginal is prohibited. The mating of coloured aliens with any female of part Aboriginal blood is also forbidden. Every endeavour is being made to breed out the colour by elevating female half-castes to the white standard with a view to their absorption by mating into the white population.
>
> Northern Territories Administrator's Report, 1933: 7

State and Commonwealth administrations met in Canberra in 1937 to discuss possible federal control over Aborigines and to adopt, if possible, some national and overarching policies. Neville's ideas were very persuasive. In the end, each regional authority held on to its domain, but the unanimous conclusion was that 'the destiny of the natives of Aboriginal origin, but not of full blood, lies in their ultimate absorption by the people of the Commonwealth, and it therefore recommends that all efforts be directed to this end'. Efforts were very much directed to such biological solutions. This wasn't killing but it was assuredly practice directed at child removal, 'breeding them white', and 'transforming to white' everyone who was regarded as less than 'full-blood'. All of this was very much more than a 'sentiment' of 'unease', 'contempt' or 'rejection' about a people who were different.

Eugenics, as a science of animal pedigree, can only work in controlled stud and stock farms. Fortunately, societies can't be regulated in the veterinary sense, but Neville, Bleakley and Cook certainly intended the disappearance of the 'part-Aboriginal' population by 'eugenicising' many of them through encouraging or discouraging various forms of 'mating'. This was a clearly articulated intent to commit what would come to be called genocide. The Convention talks about the 'intent to destroy, in whole or in part': it doesn't say that the crime requires successful completion.

'Forcibly transferring children of the group to another group'

In 1983, historian Peter Read published a short monograph on the 'stolen generations' in New South Wales. The annual reports of the Aborigines Protection (later Welfare) Board were always explicit: 'This policy of dissociating the children from [native] camp life must eventually solve the Aboriginal problem.' By placing children in 'first-class private homes', the superior standard of life would 'pave the way for the absorption of these people into the general population'. Further, 'to allow these children to remain on the reserve to grow up in comparative idleness in the midst of more or less vicious surroundings would be, to say the least, an injustice to the children themselves, and a positive menace to the State'. The committal notices prescribed by law required a column to be completed under the heading 'Reason for Board taking control of the child'. The great majority of responses were penned in one standard phrase: 'For being Aboriginal'!

Read's estimate of the number of children removed in New South Wales between 1883 and 1969 is 5,625, allowing (as he notes) that there is a distinct 'lack of records'. My assessment is a much higher figure, perhaps 35,000. I have not examined such Board or child welfare records as remain, but base my higher figure on an extrapolation of the numbers of forced removals and institutionalisation among the 1,200 Aboriginal sports people recorded in my own book on the history of the Aboriginal experience as seen through sport (Tatz, 1995). (One example: of the 129 men and women in the initial Aboriginal and Islander Sports Hall of Fame, twelve were stolen, another six, possibly seven, were adopted by white families, while another twenty-two grew up in institutions.) The National Inquiry into the 'separation' of Aboriginal and Torres Strait Islander children from their families, published in 1997 under the title *Bringing them Home*, summarises the situation: 'We can conclude with confidence that between one in three and one in ten indigenous children were forcibly removed from their families and communities in the period from approximately 1910 until 1970' (Human Rights and Equal Opportunities Commission, 1997).

In July 1995, journalist Stuart Rintoul met Colin Macleod, a former patrol officer with the Department of Territories, the agency responsible for Aboriginal welfare in the Northern Territory from 1945 until the mid-1960s. Macleod, now a Melbourne magistrate, believes that the policy was indeed dictated by the notion that 'half-castes' were 'salvageable', whereas 'full-bloods' were not. While he disagrees (now) with the removal of children for purely assimilationist or 'experimentalist' reasons, he maintains that some removals were 'for their own good' and 'not done heartlessly'. Girls, he says, were at risk of being made sexual chattels, either by the pastoralists who employed them or by the old men to whom they were promised by tribal custom. In his book, Macleod talks about young girls 'becoming mothers way before they were old enough to be good mothers, in conditions of unspeakable squalor and cruelty, often inflicted by the child's father' (Macleod, 1997: 166). Agreeing that he was one of the 'benevolent dictators', he is strongly supported today by a Catholic brother who insists that 'our belief was that we were doing something wonderful for these children by providing them with a home'.

In sharp contrast are the memories of the 'salvaged' ones: there was little that was wonderful in the experience; there was much to remember about physical brutality and sexual abuse; and, for the majority, the homes were scarcely homes, especially in the light of the then healthy Aboriginal practices of kinship, family reciprocity and child-rearing in extended families. 'We were locked up in the dormitories . . . We were more less like slaves, I think'; 'Gone to pieces. Anxiety attacks. I've passed this on to my kids'; 'How do you sit down and go through all those years of abuse?'; 'I feel I have been total denied a childhood'; 'That's another thing that we find hard – giving our children love. Because we never had it.' And so on, from just several of the witnesses to the National Inquiry. There is considerably more recorded and substantiated evidence of abuse in the 'safe homes' than Macleod claims was occurring in Aboriginal environments. In some forty years of involvement in Aboriginal affairs, I have met perhaps half a dozen men who liked Sister Kate's or Kinchela Boys' Home. I have yet to meet an Aboriginal woman who liked Cootamundra Girls' Home or Colebrook. No one failed to mention the incessant sexual abuse, or the destruction of family life. The late Professor W.E.H. Stanner believed, following a one-day visit, that places like Sister Kate's gave children 'a prospect of a better life'. In the end, the views of the inmates remain better testimony, certainly better than the clamours of Australian denialists that 'nothing happened' or 'nothing but good happened' in these institutions.

AUSTRALIA: A GENOCIDAL SOCIETY?

Has genocide ever occurred in this land which dedicates itself to the Olympic ideals? Can we measure what was, or wasn't, genocidal practice? Let us ask a set of questions.

- Did Australians ever kill Aborigines with the intent of destroying them, 'in whole or in part', because they were Aborigines?
- If much of this early killing was done privately, by squatters and settlers, were the colonial authorities complicit by countenancing these events?
- Were Aborigines simply in the way of the economic progress of the cattle and mining industries?
- Did Australian governments, and their agents of policy, the mission societies and the pastoralists, ever introduce or condone practices that caused serious bodily or mental harm to Aborigines *qua* Aborigines?
- Did any official policies or practices inflict conditions of life calculated to bring about the total or even partial physical destruction of Aborigines?
- Did the Native Police 'disperse kangaroos' (Kimber, 1997: 33–65) or shoot Aborigines?
- Has any government agency ever tried to prevent Aboriginal births?
- Has any government 'forcibly transferred' Aboriginal children to another, non-Aboriginal, group?
- Even if none of the above occurred, or if none are provable, has any

government conspired, or incited, or attempted to do these things, or been complicit in their having occurred, each of which is a punishable offence under the Convention?

In addition to the unambiguously positive responses with which most of these questions must be answered, and in fact have been answered by some politicians, church people and academics in recent years, there is the template of international law: Aborigines were killed, were the victims of bodily and mental harm, had birth-control measures imposed upon them and had their children forbibly transferred *because of who they were*. It does not matter that the killing or the harming did not always succeed: 'success' is not a factor in adjudging the commission of the crime.

What if we reject the formalism and legalism of the Genocide Convention and consider genocide in the broader sense in which some historians and social scientists want us to conceive of this phenomenon? Is there more, or less, evidence, more or less of a case, to be made about Australia? More: we killed, we maimed, removed, relocated, separated, generally dispossessed, incarcerated and engaged in all manner of Trollope's 'rough work'. We wanted Aborigines to 'go away': and many people still harbour that feeling. In Henry Huttenbach's 'stretched' version of genocide, have we committed 'any acts' that placed the existence of Aborigines in any kind of 'jeopardy'? Indeed. Raphael Lemkin would have asked whether we had 'destroyed the essential foundations of the life' of Aborigines, 'their personal security, liberty, health, dignity'? We did, with both good and bad intent. The wider we go, the worse the indictment; the narrower the framework, the more evidence is needed to sustain specific acts of guilt.

AUSTRALIAN RESPONSES TO THE GENOCIDE QUESTION

Public awareness of genocide began to dawn with the realisation that child removal was one of the acts specified in the Genocide Convention. Peter Read brought the stolen generations to the attention of mainstream Australia in the early 1980s and by 1990 the issue had come to the top of the Aboriginal agenda.

Bureaucratic responses

In 1990, the Secretariat of the National Aboriginal and Islander Child Care (SNAICC) organisation demanded an inquiry into child removal. In August 1991, an Aboriginal media release mentioned this 'blank spot' in Australian history:

> The damage and trauma these policies caused are felt every day by Aboriginal people. They internalise their grief, guilt and confusion, inflicting further pain on themselves and others around them . . . We want an enquiry to determine how many of our children were taken away and how this occurred . . . We also want to consider whether these policies fall within the definition of genocide in Article II(e) of the United Nations Convention . . .

In May 1995, the federal Labor government responded to Aboriginal and media pressure by establishing the 'National Inquiry into the Separation of Aboriginal and Torres Strait Islander Children from their Families'. The terms of reference were reasonable and admirable. The Inquiry had to trace past laws, policies and practices and their consequences, investigate ways of assisting in location of family, and 'examine the principles relevant to determining the justification for compensation for persons or communities affected by such separations'.

There were, however, some troubling aspects. First, the constant use of 'separation' in the terms of reference – a fairly anodyne word, implying some degree of mutuality in the severing of these parent–child relationships, as well as keeping open a door to a reuniting. Neither mutuality nor uniting was ever intended, or involved, in practices which began in Victoria in the 1880s and ended in New South Wales in the 1980s (not the early 1970s, as the National Inquiry states). The 'removal' bureaucrats envisaged absolute *finality*. Second, there was always the possibility that 'principles to determine justification for compensation' could, if they eventuated, become prescriptive and therefore the *only* legal mechanisms for compensation. Third, the reality of the 'stolen generations' didn't need further proof, since the history and the consequences were well enough known, especially to the victims. Nevertheless, the final report is a monumental document and a pivotal point in contemporary race relations.

In 1993–94, the Australian Archives presented an exhibition in Sydney,

Adelaide, Canberra and the Northern Territory entitled *Between Two Worlds*, a study of the federal government's removal of Aboriginal 'half-caste' children in the Territory from 1918 to the 1960s (MacDonald, 1995). It was a brilliant depiction of one facet of genocide, without using the word. Throughout this entire history, there were exceptionally few men and women who heard whispers in their hearts that anything was awry or amiss.[12] But among many exhibits were letters from the late E.C. (Ted) Evans, then Chief Welfare Officer (and Macleod's boss), to the Administrator, urging that removals cease: because, he wrote, they were intrinsically evil and because the world would never understand either the motives or the practices. (Evans, a devout Catholic, often said as much to me in our long association in the Territory.) This exhibition was to be yet another impetus to the movement initiated by Aborigines – the Link-Up project – to discover and recover this peculiar form of Argentina's 'disappeared ones', Australia's *desaparecidos*.

By 1994, Aborigines at the 'Going Home' conference in Darwin felt sufficiently confident to begin planning civil lawsuits against governments and missions for the forced removal of children, the break-up of family life and the physical placement of people outside the ambit of areas now available (or claimable) under land rights legislation. The late Joy Williams twice prosecuted her civil suit, claiming abuse by the state as a removed child: she was both ill and ill-prepared and lost her claims against New South Wales. So too did six Aboriginal plaintiffs from the Northern Territory in what is known as the *Kruger* case.[13] They argued that the Aboriginals Ordinance was, in effect, an unconstitutional law, one which gave powers to commit genocide, specifically by removing children so that their religious practices could not be sustained. In what I believe was a poorly constructed case – in part because the legal team tended to ignore Article II(b) and (e) of the Genocide Convention, concentrated on the constitutionality of the offending ordinance (rather than the powers exercised under that ordinance), and depicted genocide as deprivation of religious rights – the High Court (in 1997) found the ordinance valid because it was enacted 'in the interests of Aborigines generally'. The *Gunner* and *Cubillo* cases, lost in Darwin in 2001, are discussed briefly later.

Is it possible to have a law, asks genocide scholar Barbara Harff (1984: 67), 'that can, through a perverted collective morality, become a murderous weapon'? Yes, indeed. That sentence is a reasonable verdict on nearly all

pre-1970 special legislation for Aborigines, statutes which began, or pur-
ported to begin, as protection, but which became their value opposites in
practice. Most scholars and lawyers look to parliamentary debates and the
legal language of statutes as evidence of 'policy'. What has been so signally
missing in Australia is analyses of the administrations which sought to
realise policies. My research has always tried to examine, and to explain,
the gaps, often the gulfs, between policy aspirations and their translations
into practice. The results are of interest: the administrative machinery has
stopped most policies of inequality from coming to fruition but has ensured
that most policies of equality emerge as true inequality, often beyond the
letter of the law.

The National Inquiry reported in April 1997. Of the 118 official
investigations – judicial inquiries, parliamentary committee reports and
royal commissions – into aspects of Aboriginal affairs in the last century,
this was by far the starkest and strongest indictment, concluding that
Australia has knowingly committed genocide through the forcible transfer
of children, as a matter of official policy, not just yesteryear but as recently
as the 1970s. A finding of genocide was presented: the essence of the
crime, it was stated, was acting with the intention of destroying the group,
not the extent to which that intention was achieved. The forcible removals
were intended to 'absorb', 'merge', 'assimilate' the children, 'so that
Aborigines as a distinct group would disappear'. That such actions by
perpetrators were in their eyes 'in the best interests of the children is
irrelevant to a finding that their actions were genocidal'. Here the inquiry
posited, without stating it plainly, an important theme about intent, which
is the key phrase in the legal definition of genocide.

We need careful examination of the applicability of the word 'destroy'
in the legal definition. 'Destroy' was clearly used in the immediate
aftermath of World War II with its tally of thirty-five million dead across
the globe. Destroy is a negative, pejorative verb, resonant of evil, wanton-
ness, violence. With hindsight and lapse of time, that is what can now be
read into it. But, as with all statutes, we are obliged to look at the ordinary
or plain meaning of the word(s), not at what we think the framers intended,
or felt, at the time.

'Destroy' brings to light an issue current in the debate about the stolen
generations, namely, that whatever was done in this country was done
with good intent and therefore could not, by definition, be genocidal. We

always assume that 'with intent to destroy' means intent with *male fides*, bad faith, 'with evil intent'. Nowhere does the Convention implicitly or explicitly rule out intent with *bona fides*, good faith, 'for their own good' or 'in their best interests'. Elazar Barkan (2000: 247) asks whether there can be genocide 'despite ostensibly good intentions'. In Starkman's opinion, 'The illegitimacy of the white man's burden may suggest that indeed the answer is affirmative.' Starkman's is one of several opinions that the reasons for the crime, or the ultimate purpose of the deeds, are irrelevant: 'The crime of genocide is committed whenever the intentional destruction of a protected group takes place' (Starkman, 1984: 1). Matthew Storey (1997: 11–14) points out that 'genocide does not require malice; it can be (misguidedly) committed "in the interests" of a protected population'. Gaita (1997: 21) contends that 'the concept of good intention cannot be relativised indefinitely to an agent's perception of it as good'. If we could, he writes, then we must say that Nazi murderers had good, but radically benighted intentions, because most of them believed they had a sacred duty to the world to rid the planet of the race that polluted it. This, incidentally, is what the senior Liberal MP Joe Gullett was arguing during the debate on ratification of the Convention in 1949. Further, the defenders of removal always maintain, illogically in my view, that anything and everything done by way of solution to a 'problem' must, by definition, be worthy or brave or well meant, rather than unworthy. Not so. Nor do they examine the extent of the 'problem' that justified removals, or the disproportion of the 'solution' to the 'problem'.

Throughout 1996, the National Inquiry pressed the new federal Conservative government to make a formal submission, as state governments had done. The government baulked, stalled and eventually presented an anonymous, last-minute submission.[14] Doubtless written hurriedly by bureaucrats from one or two federal agencies, the thrust of the submission was a 'shotgun scatter' of exonerations, mitigations and plain refusals to become involved. It declared that 'the Government can see no equitable or practical way of paying special compensation to these persons, if compensation were considered to be warranted'. Further, restitution will 'produce new injustices and inequities', 'create serious difficulties', and cause 'adverse social and economic effects'. It will be 'very difficult to identify persons', it's all 'problematic' and, rather ominously for existing programmes, it will 'divert resources in mounting or defending cases'.

The Coalition federal government, in short, will not compensate for child removal, though it was most generous in restitution for the buy-back of now illegal guns. The government also takes the view that, in judging these practices, 'it is appropriate to have regard to the standards and values prevailing at the time of their enactment and implementation, rather than to the standards and values prevailing today'. The document ends with this remarkable rationalisation: 'There is no existing objective methodology for attaching a monetary value to the loss suffered by victims.' Yet Germany has (twice) given us a reparations model, and, as of 1998, found the will to compensate the surviving slave labourers of over half a century ago. In 2001, the Swiss government and banks gave us another model. There is no insuperable problem identifying the majority of those removed, or those who had children removed. Restitution, according to the federal government, will cause 'intolerable inequities'. To whom? What could be more intolerable than the removals themselves?

The Conservative government under John Howard was elected to its first term in March 1996. When *Bringing Them Home* was released, media attention focused very heavily on the need for acknowledgement and apology. When pressed about apology, the then Minister for Aboriginal Affairs (Senator John Herron) and the Prime Minister immediately locked themselves into the exact wording of the bureaucracy's submission to the Inquiry: restitution was not possible, there was no methodology for it, it would create 'new injustices', formal apology could open the way for lawsuits, all this happened yesteryear and, in a new version of 'for their own good', removal was akin to white Anglo children being sent to boarding school. Furthermore, some very successful Aborigines had come through these assimilation homes. Finally, in the words of the Minister for Aboriginal Affairs, 'I don't believe we ever attempted genocide . . . This practice could not be described as genocide as it did not involve an intentional elimination of a race' (*Australian*, 27 May 1997). Not one of these responses incorporated, let alone appreciated, the overwhelming sense of grief, pain, confusion and loss felt by the removed people who testified.

Academics

On my arrival in Australia from South Africa in 1961, Sir Keith Hancock, then professor of history at the Australian National University, gave me a copy of the 1961 edition of his *Australia*. Within its 282 pages, he discussed Aborigines in twenty-three lines. 'Pathetically helpless when assailed by the acquisitive society of Europe', the invading British did their 'wreckers' work with 'the unnecessary brutality of stupid children'. 'From time to time [Australia] remembers the primitive people it has dispossessed, and sheds over their predestined passing an economical tear' (Hancock, 1961). That summarised his Aboriginal 'treatment'. As I was about to start my doctoral study of contemporary Aboriginal life in northern Australia, my perception of the past was, in a phrase, 'unnecessary brutality' – by the brutish British, not by past or present Australians. As I read in preparation for my study, I certainly derived no notion, let alone any framework, for genocide.

A decade later, Charles Rowley discussed the way in which Aborigines, and their physical killing, had been ignored by practically every historian to date. Rowley was always polite. Australian historians 'tended to play down' the history, consigning 'the moral and political issues to the past'. The 'mental block [had] by no means disappeared' when he was writing in the early 1970s: there was a 'majority sentiment that raking up the misdeeds of the past serves no good purpose'. He quietly lamented the catchphrase that 'what is done is done and should now be forgotten', but he was encouraged by the knowledge that 'a few young historians are beginning to work in the field of Aboriginal affairs' (Rowley, 1970: 1–9).

Soon enough the works of Raymond Evans, Kay Saunders and Kathryn Cronin in 1975, Lyndall Ryan and Henry Reynolds in 1981, Noel Loos in 1982, and Noel Butlin in 1983, began to percolate, and then to trickle rather than bubble over, into school and university curricula. Here was physical killing, but, because it occurred over long periods, in sporadic and episodic rather than in (seemingly) systematic ways, and because the killings were in twos, threes, dozens and sometimes hundreds at a time, it never entered the mind that this was genocide in any Armenian and Jewish sense. It seemed to be murder, mass murder at times, massacre often enough, bush pogrom perhaps, but nothing that could be equated with those appalling European and Near Eastern events.

Several ventured the word extermination. Butlin (1983), who speculated that disease may have been 'a deliberate exterminating act' against Aborigines, did not conceive of that alleged 'action' in the language of genocide studies. No one, except Michael Cannon (1990), used the term genocide. Andrew Markus (1990) shied away from the word, and Ann McGrath

(1995) was prepared to talk about attempted genocide in Tasmania, but not on the mainland. Henry Reynolds still admits to a reluctance about, even an avoidance of, talking about that crime; his recent thinking is that some Tasmanian events 'came within the range of genocide while not being genocide'. Robert Manne (1999, 2001) and Raimond Gaita (1997, 1998), in the forefront of the literature on removed children, wish that a more appropriate nomenclature, or a better or more flexible formal definition, could be found for what has happened in Australia.

In the 1980s and 1990s, the developing preoccupation was with massacre. Myall Creek, Waterloo Creek, Forrest River, Bathurst, Orara River, Gippsland, Palmer River, Pinjarra and Alice Springs became more familiar as sites of killing. But nobody was studying genocide theory and practice and no one was examining the Convention outlawing its attempt or its implementation. Up until at least 2001, when a Raphael Lemkin quotation appeared on the cover of the journal *Aboriginal History,* no one was reading the Polish international jurist who coined the word for the destruction of a genus of people. No scholar was looking at the fine print, or at the fact that the United Nations had created an international law which equated physical killing with such acts as imposing birth-control measures and forcibly transferring children. We were all steeped in Auschwitz, Treblinka, Sobibor and Belzec, in monstrous SS men, in Himmler, Heydrich, Hoess and their henchmen. Who needed to look further than these men and their doings for an understanding of genocide? Who could look any further?

Tony Barta, a historian at La Trobe University, was the first to penetrate the membrane that locked or blocked out the 'unthinkable' notion of genocide having occurred in this 'moral' country. In 1985, at 'The German-Jewish Experience' symposium in Sydney, he gave a paper entitled 'After the Holocaust: consciousness of genocide in Australia' (Barta, 1985: 154–61). My paper, on the same day, reflected movement towards recognition of some parallel themes or echoes: it was called 'Racism, responsibility and reparation: South Africa, Germany, and Australia' (Tatz, 1985: 162–72). The editors of the proceedings asked me, with some disquiet and scepticism, whether Barta's 'surrealistic' vision should be included in the conference publication. I have a memory of momentary shame because I hesitated before saying 'yes'. Why this hesitation? I think I was still unwilling to believe that 'our' Australian behaviour could, in any way, be analogous to this kind of German criminality. (In 2001, Barta resumed work on Australian and German parallels.)

Peter Read's seminal essay, *The Stolen Generations*, was written in the early 1980s. It coincided with the work of Richard Chisholm, who wrote about the policy that pervaded the Aborigines Welfare Board, certainly from 1912: the 'socialisation of children away from their Aboriginality' (Chisholm, 1985: 18). Read and Chisholm triggered a memory of a research visit I had made to the Retta Dixon Home in Darwin in 1962. While inspecting the place with Miss Amelia Shankleton, she asked my wife to hold an infant boy. At the tour's end, she asked my clearly doting spouse if we'd 'like to have him'. 'What do we have to do?' we asked. 'A donation of 25 guineas will be acceptable', replied the amiable servant of the Australian Inland Mission. Incredibly, we didn't blanch at the prospective 'sale'. There was no mention of maternal release of the child. We drove around for an hour, contemplating, debating, and in the end decided no: to raise a child as both Aboriginal and Jewish would truly be a double cross. This was the first of many first-hand experiences of the trafficking in Aboriginal children.

Periodic lectures at Yad Vashem in Jerusalem made fleeting mention of Gypsy children removed from parents in Switzerland, of some 200,000 Polish children considered as looking 'Aryan' enough to be stolen and taken to Germany as future soldiers of the Thousand Year *Reich*. I can't and don't speak for others, but, in my case, the synapses finally connected a variety of concepts and realities: irrational prejudice acted upon; scientific racism; nationalism; physical killing; Native Police 'dispersing' Aborigines; the eugenics movement; doctrines of racial 'purity'; obsession with degrees of 'bloodness'; all that Australian legal and administrative language – mixed-blood, half-caste, quadroon and octoroon; forced assimilation; systematic destruction of the essential institutions and foundations of particular societies; causing serious mental and bodily harm to particular groups; transfer of children and their 'socialisation away from their Aboriginality'; official policies which aimed at 'eventually forgetting that there were ever any Aborigines in Australia', and so on. As I added together each of these factors, the answer came out not as the discovery of new facts but as a recognition that there was, in law, a term for an aggregation of such established acts – genocide.

What has happened with the word genocide in the Australian context?

A younger, fresher cohort of historians, social scientists and lawyers now actively seek out the Aboriginal experience. They, too, have begun to find the words, the models, the templates for analysis and evaluation of the historical record. Have they, as the denialists assert, contrived to find, or squeeze, or even manufacture ingredients to support a 'new-fangled' crime? Is this use of the ultimate word in our lexicon merely a 'fit-up', a contrived calumny, for such vague reasons as hating Australia or wanting to see Australia squirm on the hook of guilt and shame? Is the use of this word simply political correctness and moral blackmail? Or is it, rather, a case of some Australians finally catching up with an Australian version of a reality that has been with the world for some thousands of years, although only formally defined and criminalised a mere fifty years ago?

As we know it today, the sub-discipline of Aboriginal history is barely thirty-five years old, baptised by the journal *Aboriginal History*. The serious analysis of some of Australia's history as constituting genocide is less than half that age. The youth of both may help explain why a few dozen 'moral' democrats and humanists – a coterie of conservative politicians, a half-dozen broadsheet and tabloid journalists, a barrister, a pair of retired senior bureaucrats and a quartet of freelance academics – feel emboldened enough to want to snuff out any notion of an Australian genocide.

They want not only to expunge the word genocide, but also the very acts which have come to earn that label. There are many questions, mostly unarguable, which they won't address, let alone concede.

THE CASE FOR REDRESS

Even though the 2001 census indicated a tenfold increase in the Aboriginal population on that appalling figure of 1911 (from 31,000 to 410,003, this latter reflecting 2.2 per cent of the total population), Aborigines ended the twentieth century at the very top, or bottom, of every social indicator available: top of the medical statistics for diseases they didn't exhibit as recently as thirty years ago – coronary disease, cancer, diabetes,[15] respiratory infections; bottom of the life expectancy table, at 50–55 years or less for males and around 55 years for females; with much greater rates of unemployment, much lower home ownership and considerably lower annual *per capita* income;[16] an arrest and imprisonment rate grossly out of proportion to their numbers; the highest rate of suspension from schools; the highest rate of institutionalisation; with crimes now prevalent which were rare as recently as the 1960s, namely, homicide, rape, child molestation, burglary, physical assaults, drug-peddling and drug-taking; and, sadly, youth suicide, no longer a criminal act, at a rate among the highest on this planet (Tatz, 2001a).

There is now a high degree of personal violence within groups; widespread child neglect, including an insufficient supply of food and general care; a marked increase in deaths from non-natural causes; much destruction of property, whether supplied by agencies or self-acquired; increasing attacks on white staff and visiting professionals who work with groups; and a vast quantity of alcohol and drug abuse, commonly offered as the sole 'explanation' of the above.[17]

A major underpinning, almost an article of faith, of Australian race relations history has been a Social Darwinist notion that the unfittest don't survive: thus Aborigines, or especially those known by the term 'full-blood', were destined to disappear in the face of white civilisation. That they were succumbing to disease was all too evident. That they were perishing through the premeditated actions of settlers was less so, but was part of a mindset that beheld extinction as inevitable. We need to open our eyes to just how much premeditation has been at work in the 215 years since the British arrived, to set the present predicament of Aborigines and Islanders into context, and to recognise just how much of the past underlies, even suffuses, the present-day Aboriginal life and the responses of Aborigines to today's circumstances.

In the matter of redress by governments, Australia lags last, at least among Western nations. Questions arise. Do Aborigines have a claim for civil redress? If they do, what have governments done in response? Mari Matsuda (in Brooks, 1999: 7) posits five prerequisites for a meritorious claim for redress: a 'human injustice' must have been committed; it must be well documented; the victims must be identifiable as a distinct group; the current members of the group must continue to suffer harm; and such harm must be causally connected to the past injustice.

The catalogue of disrespect for Aboriginal human rights has already been dealt with, and for the purposes of this discussion I define Australia's 'human injustice' as the genocidal acts committed against Aborigines because of who they were. A claim for civil redress is usually based on both the nature of the injustice and the degree of injustice which can be related to a quantifiable reparation. Civil redress is obviously contingent on the perception of just what injustice has been done to Aborigines. The assessment of the greatest injustice is a subjective perception, both for the victims and for the commentators: for me, it is those genocidal acts, and attempted genocidal acts, over and above what is usually meant by the abuse of the fundamental freedoms and human rights of the individual victim.

If we accept Matsuda's model, does the Aboriginal case fit the prerequisites? The answer is yes, in all five respects. The fifth prerequisite is the one which many Australians contest, namely, that there is any privity, that is, any legally recognisable connection between 'what our forefathers did' and the contemporary ills besetting Aboriginal society. There are, indeed, powerful, even overpowering, connections, including the testimony of the living witnesses of child removal and of their children, notwithstanding the view of one journalist, P.P. McGuinness (2001), that 'all of that' is only 'false memory syndrome'. My book on Aboriginal suicide is a serious examination of such connected harm (Tatz, 2001a).

As the new century begins, the stolen generations issue is the most serious matter in the lives of the majority of Aborigines. Acknowledgement and apology, they contend, constitute the key to any kind of reconciliation. (In this sense, Australia is lucky: nearly all other victim communities believe that 'sorry' isn't enough.) We now have a public politics of apology, simultaneously eliciting acknowledgement, admissions and regrets – of which more in chapter 6 – but not (yet) compensation.

5

SOUTH AFRICA: GENOCIDE OR NOT?

South Africa always sounded and looked as though it ought to be on the list of genocidal states. Richard Goldstone, former chief prosecutor of the UN Tribunals for the former Yugoslavia and Rwanda, laments the 'highly questionable omission' of apartheid from Israel Charny's *Encyclopedia of Genocide* (Goldstone, 2002: 261–5). South Africa has a dreadful history, and a reputation to match. Nazi Germany apart, it was both the yardstick and the bogeyman of twentieth-century racism and its consequences. It proclaimed separateness in every sphere of life, from bus stops to blood transfusions. It claimed equalness with separateness, yet never managed that distribution of rights, goods and services in any single sphere of human endeavour: not in wages, pensions, political rights, prisons, the administration of justice, health, education, church services or sport.

It killed, kidnapped, murdered and maimed in the name and process of telling the world it was *the* model for a multi-racial society. It subverted, perverted and inverted all the rights that fall under the rubric of 'the rule of law'. It denied freedom of the press, speech, movement and domicile, and the rights to public assembly, open and fair trial, legal representation and to compensation for expropriation of land. It even made freedom of religion difficult, as I will explain below.

South Africa had several of the prerequisites for genocide noted by Yehuda Bauer (in lectures) and Richard Dekmejian (1980). There was an 'ancient hatred' or rather, an ideological imperative; there was, for blacks, an authoritarian regime, if not a dictatorship; there was an ever-compliant bureaucracy; and, since 1652, a great many people, mostly black, have, one way or another, been killed. Goldstone, now a Justice of the Constitutional Court of South Africa, reminds us that in 1973 the UN General Assembly deemed apartheid both a crime in itself and a crime against humanity. So what is missing, and why have Charny and I, quite separately, excluded apartheid from the panoply and plethora of genocides?

'RACE-CIVILISATION'[1]

'We complain of severe losses which we have been forced to sustain by the emancipation of our slaves.' That was the grievance in 1837 of Boer leader Piet Retief, in his 'Manifesto of the Emigrant Farmers'. He was explaining why the Afrikaners (*Boers*) began their Great Trek north after Britain abolished slavery in 1833. But that wasn't the real reason. His daughter, Anna Steenkamp, elaborated: 'It is not so much their freedom that drove us to such lengths as their being placed on an equal footing with Christians.' 'They were', she said, '*schepsels*', creatures, other than human (Tatz, 1962: 3).

From the start, Afrikaners were impelled and propelled by their Dutch Reformed Church (DRC) credo, a fundamentalist, Calvinist Christianity which treats the Bible as literal truth. One such 'truth' is God's curse on Ham, the black son of Noah. Because Ham saw his father both drunk and naked, the affliction on his progeny was that they were to be forever 'the hewers of wood and drawers of water', the perpetual servant class. But servanthood wasn't the real curse. Rather, it was that no matter how much black people moved up the social and economic scale, they could never achieve true spirituality, as could the 'white race'. In sum, it is God's will that they are eternally 'other' – other than 'us'.

Such was, and is, the religious ideology of Dutch Reformed Afrikaner-dom. There was also a secular version of this imperative, one which went back into the nineteenth century and was expressed in a variety of colonial constitutions and laws. Thus, the 1858 *Grondwet* (constitution) of the South African Republic (later the Transvaal) stipulated that 'the people desire to permit no equality between Coloured people and the White inhabitants, in either Church or State'. Nor was there to be any form of equality in three of the four colonies, except for Cape Coloured people and Cape Africans in the matter of the franchise.

In 1926, almost a century after the Great Trek, Prime Minister General J.B.M. Hertzog announced his 'Solution to the Native Question' (Tatz, 1962: 38–54). In 1926, he explained that there were differences, not simply between races, but in and between 'race-civilisations'. Hertzog was not a DRC Calvinist, and so he preached in secular language:

> As against the European the Native stands as an eight year old child next to a man of greying experience – a child in religion, a child in moral conviction; without art and without science; with the most primitive requirements and a most rudimentary knowledge of how to supply these needs . . .

There was, he said, a difference in national characteristics and habits. There would, therefore, always be a difference in racial needs 'and for that reason separate treatment shall be meted out not only as regards legislation, but also in regard to the administration of the law'. The gist of the matter was that the African had 'an aptitude to surrender himself to the abuse of strong drink' and had 'a lack of power in resisting evil'. In short, the African was 'still in his nonage' and in need of a guardian. Hertzog's racial philosophy, and practice, came to be called, officially, 'Christian Trusteeship'.

This was the ideological imperative, writ large in both politics and law. These religious and secular political belief systems segregated the races in all things: one group was clearly civilised and human, the other was clearly not. Thus Hertzog was able to lay down, *inter alia*, his 'civilised labour policy' – and all the economic and social policies that flowed and followed from it – a policy in force until the early 1990s:

> Civilised labour: the labour rendered by persons whose standard of living conforms to the standard generally recognised as tolerable from the European standpoint.

> Uncivilised labour: that rendered by persons whose aim is restricted to the bare requirements of the necessities of life as understood among barbarians and undeveloped peoples.

Here we see one of the clearest expositions of what political theory calls an 'ethnic nationalism', one based on the inherent superiority of 'white civilisation'.

THE RIVERS OF APARTHEID

There were to be three consistent streams irrigating apartheid throughout the twentieth century, beginning with union of South Africa in 1910 and ending, in theory only, in 1994. Most of these flows had begun in the previous century, a fact which has been singularly misunderstood, both in South Africa and abroad, one which has left a widespread myth that the evil in race relations began only with the election of the Nationalist Party in 1948, and would end when that Party lost power. (I vividly remember meeting the former Australian Prime Minister, Sir Robert Menzies and two of his cabinet colleagues in the mid-1960s: they were looking forward to the days when the United Party returned, signalling the end of apartheid!)

Removal of political rights

The first ideological *leitmotif* was white determination to remove the political rights of 'non-whites' in the Cape Province, a franchise first granted for municipal elections as early as 1836. The South African Native Affairs Commission of 1903–5, a predominantly English-speaking (that is, not Afrikaner) body, pushed for territorial segregation of the races. It insisted that the Cape Native franchise was a danger to the imminent union of the Transvaal, Orange Free State, Cape and Natal. Blacks should be disfranchised and given their own lands where they could live and develop along their own lines, with their own political structures, and so on. The land *versus* franchise battle was to last from the time of the National Convention in 1909 until the last vestiges of African political rights were removed by a later Prime Minister, Hendrik Verwoerd, in 1954 and 1959.

In the intervening fifty years, Africans were forbidden to purchase land by the Native Land Act 1913, and in 1936, as a trade for the loss of the Cape African (but not Cape Coloured) vote – this surrender of what the government called 'the shadow of the vote for the substance of the land' – the government promised to provide land for Africans up to a maximum of 13 per cent of the country's total acreage. It took until the 1980s for that 'quota' to be achieved.

This was the small-v 'vision' of the Native Affairs Commission in 1905 as it produced its race relations blueprint for the future South Africa (Tatz, 1962: chapter II).

This became Hertzog's obsessive mission from 1930 onwards. From the mid-1950s, it became the Grand Vision of Verwoerd: 'Bantustans', reserves totalling 13 per cent of the land, where, in theory, 80 per cent of the population would develop into separate nation states, forming a Commonwealth with (white) Mother South Africa.

Re-tribalisation

A second stream in South African history was the unique attempt to re-tribalise a fast-detribalising society. By the time of World War I, it was apparent to Smuts, Hertzog and other leaders that there was a beginning of an African middle class, a lower division perhaps, but one that was Christian, urban, bi- and tri-lingual, aspiring to homes, wireless sets, refrigerators and Western medicine and some form of wage justice. Simultaneously, there was a recognition of the plight of nearly a quarter of the Afrikaner population, some 500,000 people, ill-educated and unskilled, constituting the particular problem of 'the poor whites'. How could they reconcile any notion of radical (and racial) difference between two very similar population groups, peoples often living literally on opposite sides of the road in several Johannesburg suburbs, as in Brixton and Newclare?

Even in those days, skin colour alone was not considered a sufficient political (or moral) justification for differences in law, wages, facilities. (The DRC *predikants* could justify all manner of things from their pulpits, but none of the first three prime ministers – Botha, Hertzog and Smuts – who spanned thirty-eight years in that office, was a believer.) But if one could establish tribalism as a differential, then all manner of separate programmes would be justifiable. Hertzog would then be able to say, indeed, that here was visible evidence of a difference in 'race-civilisation'. The 'tribal native', clad in traditional blanket, bangled, polygamous, payer of *lobolo* (bride price), *kraal* (hut or village) dweller, had his own rich culture, but one radically different from that of 'the men of greying experience'. And so, from 1917 onwards, laws were passed to restore the powers of tribal chiefs, to allow criminal and civil jurisdiction to these men, men now much paler and weaker relics of the once mighty Chaka Zulu.

The Native Affairs Act 1920 and the Native Administration Act 1927 were, in the language of General Jan Smuts, an attempt 'to be just and fair to the Native' by 'taking the right step ... in setting up the proper institutions in which his legitimate desires and aspirations can be satisfied'. The Bantu Authorities Act 1951 was yet another extension of the system of establishing African infrastructure of a tribal nature – as proof of their 'primitiveness'. This was to become a feature of the 1950s and 1960s, leading to separate school syllabuses for African and white children and separate university education. The Bantu Education Act 1953 and the Extension of University Education Act 1959 tried, in vain of course, to teach through mother-tongue 'ethnic' languages, to provide syllabuses appropriate to 'the black station in life', to make the blacks realise that 'they could never graze in European pastures'. Only in their Bantustans, replete with 'tribal colleges', could they fulfil 'their ethnic souls', learning physics, chemistry, even theology through the medium of Tswana, Zulu, Xhosa, Venda and Sotho. If African youth in the urban centres wished to matriculate to universities, they had to return to their 'homelands' where they could re-discover the richness of their own cultures.

Migratory labour

The third, and continuing, stream running through South African history is that of the migratory labour system: exploitative, manipulative, destructive and oppressive, it comes as close as is possible to grounds for accusing South Africa of approximating Articles II(b) and (c) of the Genocide Convention.

The notorious 'pass laws' had a long history. They established a system of population control, 'influx control', which regulated the movement of Africans (not Cape Coloureds, Indians or whites). It enabled movement of (initially) black males only to parts of the country where their cheap labour was needed. A 'pass' was, literally, a set of documents – at one point as many as eleven before they were consolidated into one largish booklet – which said the bearer could pass from one place to another for legitimate work reasons. Failure to produce the pass on demand resulted in a heavy fine, £10, or in default, six months in jail, for a technical, not a criminal offence. Pass prisoners were regularly sold to private citizens – to clear weeds, to mow lawns, or to work on white farms – at a rate of 10 cents a day per prisoner. Arrest rates reached 1,000 a day, until the police finally persuaded the government they had far more serious problems to attend to than these technical breaches, even if it meant the loss of what amounted to slave labour.

(I have a vivid memory, as a ten-year-old, of being asked by my mother, then busy with something else, to write a 'special' for the 'houseboy' whom she wished to send on an errand. In schoolboy 'running writing', I penned a 'to whom it may concern': 'This is to certify that Solomon [none of us ever knew servants' surnames] has permission to be on the streets between 2 and 4 p.m. this afternoon. He may go to the shops to buy milk for the Madam.' (The wording was close enough.) Later, the Central News Agency, a huge stationery chain, printed little tear-off books, with the *pro forma* wording. All one had to do was fill in the name of the 'boy', date it, specify the hours of 'freedom to be abroad' and sign it. From memory, our 'boy' was in his late fifties. The 'special' was in addition to the set of passes he was obliged to carry at all times.)

Labour bureaux also had a long history. There were recruitment agencies to procure sufficient workers for manufacturing, farming, mining and domestic servant needs. Much of this history was appalling. For example, the notorious Mozambique Convention of 1909 provided for one of the world's most bizarre modern slavery 'contracts': Mozambique, then a Portuguese colony, would provide 100,000 male labourers at the Johannesburg railhead each year in exchange for the Transvaal exporting 55 per cent of its goods via the railway line to Lourenço Marques (now Maputo) rather than through South Africa's own port of Durban. The Convention was re-negotiated in a new, secret treaty in 1971 and was formally modified a decade later.

These bureaux also recruited heavily in the reserves, the areas destined to become Bantustans, for work in the diamond, coal and gold-mining industries. In 1936, these lands comprised ten million *morgen*, a pitifully small acreage for what was then a probable population of three million. (A *morgen* was a measure equal to two and one-ninth acres, or 0.9 hectares.) In addition to these three million people, a further three million Africans lived in the cities and the remaining four million resided on white-owned farms, as labourers working on the 'ploughing-by-halves' system. In return for their labour, the workers could keep a portion of the crops they ploughed for their subsistence. The reserves were in a dreadful state. The Native Economic Commission of 1930–32 talked of 'overstocking [of cattle] as an evil of the first magnitude'. Unless this was stopped, 'the very existence of large numbers of Natives in the Reserves will, in the near future, be impossible'. The practices in the Ciskei region would soon spread to other reserves: 'Denudation, *donga*-erosion, deleterious plant-succession, destruction of woods, drying up of springs, robbing the soil of its reproductive properties, in short, the creation of desert conditions.' (A *donga* is a gully formed by land and soil erosion.) The Commission concluded:

> The magnitude of the problem is appalling. But the problem which will present itself, if the reserves continue at their present rapid pace towards desert conditions, will be even greater and more appalling.

Governments kept these reserves at these levels of poverty to ensure that adult males were more than ready to export themselves to other rural areas and to the cities to work in agriculture and mining. And so the migratory labour system became an institution, part of 'the South African way of life'. It came to mean that every adult male, between 15 and 65, exported himself, on average, for three three-year terms during his lifetime.

Were they slave labourers? No. Were they well fed? Yes, the mines wanted healthy labour. Were they well paid? Not by comparison with white workers. The 'civilised labour' policy saw to it that, no matter the level of skill, a black worker above and below ground was paid roughly one-tenth of the rate of his white counterpart. Could they live with their wives and children? Assuredly not. All of this was maintained under the guise of a philosophical precept of apartheid, namely, that blacks had their areas, whites had theirs, but blacks could be allowed into white areas only 'to render their services' and 'to supply the white man's needs' – always on a temporary basis. Blacks could have no rights in these domains: they were, perpetually, 'temporary work seekers'. Could they have conjugal rights? No, but yes when they went 'home'.

Miners were housed in all-male compounds, some as many as 10,000 strong, for three-year terms. These places became the world's most singular source of 'forced' or 'environmentally determined' homosexuality. A 'day off' was confined to about two half-days per month. Most of those days were spent in urban *shebeens*, cat-houses and illegal grog shops. The rate of venereal infection was alarming. The reserves, denuded of able-bodied males, were tilled and shepherded by old men and young, husbandless wives. On the return of the men, the reserves were in an even worse condition. These men also infected their wives. Here was the start of the destruction of African family life – and the setting of the scene for South Africa's now astronomic AIDS epidemic.

When Kwame Nkrumah became Prime Minister of Ghana in 1952, he was asked about his first action for the newly independent state. His answer was that he would do everything possible to persuade all African states to stop exporting labourers to South Africa. If they didn't, he said, African family life would be destroyed, irreparably. This was an interesting priority from the head of a country that was not exporting labour to South Africa. Considering how many sub-Saharan African countries exported their labour, on a temporary basis, to South Africa through this (and even the present) era, the spread of HIV infection throughout the region should come as no surprise.

In the allegedly 'softer' life of domestic service, male and female servants, quartered in outhouses of white homes, or on the roof-gardens of apartment blocks, were not allowed, by law, to have spouses reside with them. Children were usually cared for by grannies living in the reserves or on the edges of small country towns. Here, too, was destruction of family life, with legions of men and women in twentieth-century history growing up deprived of spouses, mothers, fathers, children.

Were they coerced by government, by law? Coerced by 'the system' is the answer, by economic necessity, by a need to sustain not life and limb but a slightly better state of life for their families. There has always been a difference between what Westerners call a poverty datum line and that which pertained in South Africa, namely, a 'subsistence' (or existence) level for most Africans. Whites could be poor, but blacks had to find ways to subsist. Given that the average annual cash (as opposed to barter) income of families in areas like the Transkei was less than £20 a year, the choices were somewhat Hobsonian.

'A LANDSCAPE OF DEATH'

That phrase comes from one of South Africa's foremost Afrikaner poets, Breyten Breytenbach. He used it when addressing my students at Macquarie University in the 1980s, and in praise of Alan Paton's ironic novel *Ah, But Your Land is Beautiful* (published in 1981). Beautiful, indeed, said

Breytenbach, those Kruger National Park lion and hippo scenes, all those marvellous Drakensberg valleys, Dutch Cape farmsteads and wineries, Table Mountain, those beautiful neck-bangled Ndebele women, but a landscape of death nonetheless.

South Africa has always been a place of daily violence, from the earliest frontier days to its unenviable reputation of today for being the world record-holder for daily rapes and murders. There were tribal wars and brutal mass murders in forging the Zulu empire; there were frontier wars between Boer and black, guns versus *assegais* (short spears), cosmic clashes as at Blood River. Many rebellions were put down by force. From Union onwards, there were riots almost annually. Many were episodic or spontaneous eruptions of African grievances, such as the attempt to impose the pass laws on women after World War I and again at Zeerust in 1958.

Several of these riots and rebellions stand out as milestones (or gravestones) of infamy. After the passing of the Native Land Act in 1913, black anguish at becoming 'pariahs in their own land' led to a proliferation of independent Christian churches and sects. In 1921, Enoch Mgijima formed the Israelite sect on a commonage at Bullhoek, near Queenstown, in the Cape. Inspired by some divinity in Halley's comet, his group was heavily imitative of Jewish history. They defied all government attempts to move them, but at one point pleaded to be allowed to stay until the Passover festival had ended. Attacking the police, they were bombed in return.

In the same year, the grievances of the inhabitants of Bondelswarts in the mandated territory of South West Africa (now Namibia) were roused by several events.[2] Tribal leader Jacobus Christian was arrested without proper cause as he was reporting to police about his return from exile. Further, whites had been encroaching on their land and the Administrator had imposed a heavy dog tax that they simply couldn't pay. The dogs were hunting animals, for subsistence food. Abraham Morris, a leader who had led the Bondelswarts people to rebellion against their (earlier pre-war) German colonisers, returned from sanctuary in South Africa with a group of armed supporters. They agreed to surrender when confronted by the Administrator, G.R. Hofmeyr, but miscommunication about the surrender led Hofmeyr, backed clearly by Prime Minister Jan Smuts, to call in aircraft to bomb the tax-evaders. Women and children were killed; the men fled to the mountains to maintain their rebellion; and the Union again sent in troops and aircraft.

This was 'enforcing the law', South African style. It led one of South Africa's greatest poets, the self-exiled Roy Campbell, to pen this quatrain about General Smuts, politician, statesman, renowned philosopher (particularly of holism), eminent botanist, and a major crafter of the Covenant of the League of Nations and the Charter of the United Nations:

Holism

The love of Nature burning in his heart,
Our new Saint Francis offers us his book –
The saint who fed the birds at Bondelswaart
And fattened up the vultures at Bull Hoek.

There was to be more, much more, but without the aerial bombing. In 1957, there was serious rioting in the vicinity of Dube Hostel, Johannesburg. The Riots Commission found that 'ethnic grouping' of blacks, now firm government policy, was the cause. The Johannesburg Non-European Affairs Department stated that the segregation of various tribes on a racial or tribal basis 'was conducive to racial strife'. The reality was that Verwoerd was busy building a divide-and-rule system among blacks, emphasising tribal differences, exploiting old animosities. 'Tribalism', said the Prime Minister, 'was engraved on their ethnic souls.' Much of the violence in Natal, from the 1960s to the present, has resulted from these earlier policies of evoking, nurturing and fomenting the dormant centuries-old enmities.

Much rioting occurred as a result of the imposition of a Bantu Authorities system in rural areas. Sekhukhuneland in the Transvaal, Tembuland and eastern Pondoland erupted between 1957 and 1961, all ruthlessly suppressed by police. It is likely that 1,000 people died in riots at Cato Manor in Durban in 1949. Sharpeville is a word that remains in the international vocabulary of violent politics: the 1960 debacle in which the police, using dumdum bullets, killed sixty-nine and wounded another 180 pass law protesters. Soweto is another name in the South African hall of infamy: 176 people, many of them schoolchildren, died and over 1,200 were wounded by police. The issue was the children's rejection of Bantu education, and of a new attempt to force the Afrikaans language upon them. They rejected a separate system of schooling designed to confine them to a social system of servitude. They threw rocks and died for their efforts.

There is no need to list more of these events. The point is that each of them saw inter-racial violence and most of them ended in police violence resulting in multiple deaths. There were, at times, mass murders and certainly there were massacres, but there were never genocidal killings as defined in the Genocide Convention.

'THE SOUTH AFRICAN WAY OF LIFE'

Whether it was called segregation, territorial separation, 'Christian Trustee-ship', separate development, or plain apartheid (apart-ness, apart-ship), the South African way of life – an admirable concept in white eyes – amounted to a tyrannical system of exploitation and oppression. It was a system kept in place by custom and convention, and later buttressed and 'invigorated' by law. A way of life became an official ideology, maintained by fear through a terroristic police force, an inner army of dirty tricksters who killed, kidnapped, tortured and maimed 'the enemies of the state'. The rule of law, albeit always in favour of the white population, was totally subverted: the onus of proof of guilt by the state was, in the case of political offences, shifted to an onus of innocence to be shown by the accused, or by the 'deemed'. 'Deeming' people communists, saboteurs or traitors became the order of the day. In many instances, legal counsel were precluded from defending accused persons by being themselves banned or deemed.

Political organisations were banned, blacks and other 'non-whites' were precluded and excluded from democratic politics, race politics as a 'topic' was banned for all but the white parties. Individuals like Winnie Mandela, among thousands of others, were 'exiled' within their own country, ordered into a form of house arrest for indefinite periods. People were 'house arrested' for ninety, then 180 days, recurring. People were banned from practising their professions. Gatherings of more than three people for 'political purposes' were forbidden. Banned people needed permits to attend gatherings of more than three at funerals or weddings, or to have more than two home visitors. Famous people, outspoken people, like Alan Paton, had their passports withdrawn, and were unable to go abroad to receive prizes, accolades or further education.

Movies were banned in ludicrous fashion. I recall seeing the 1958 film

St Louis Blues. Listed at 93 minutes, it ran in Johannesburg for 41. The cuts were necessary because the law forbade any display of racial intermixing, which meant one could only see solos, or solos with black bands, as we tried to hear the story of W.C. Handy and his music, sung by Nat King Cole, Eartha Kitt, Pearl Bailey, Cab Calloway, Mahalia Jackson and Ella Fitzgerald. Book banning became a cause for world hilarity: one could comprehend the fear of Marx's *Das Kapital* but when the censor banned the famous children's horse story *Black Beauty* we were left incredulous.

The 'civilised labour' policy saw to it that in every sphere of life, the white wage in an occupation was highest, followed by the Cape Coloured wage, then the Indian, then the African. A black doctor's highest possible salary in public service ended below the starting salary of a white doctor, despite both having graduated from the same medical school. So, too, with school teachers, nurses, dentists and all manner of technicians.

The fear of racial mixing led to an increased set of penalties for inter-racial sex. The Immorality Act 1927 prohibited sex between whites and 'non-whites'; believing that to be too general, the government passed the Immorality Act 1957 which banned sex between a member of any one racial group with a member of another. The Prohibition of Mixed Marriages Act 1949 did just what its name says, despite the fact that in any one year prior to that date, there had never been more than forty-four such inter-racial marriages.

The same fears led to separate entrances, exits, elevators, trams, trains, queues at public facilities, benches in parks, and (naturally) toilets. There was no law preventing inter-racial sport – only custom. There was no shame or chagrin when a visiting Japanese swimming team was given the status of 'honorary whites' rather than risk a break in imminent trade relations. Nor was there a moment of shame when Papwa Sewgolum, an Indian golfer, won a Natal Open at Pietermaritzburg Country Club (where I had been a student member) and had to receive his cheque in the rain, outdoors, because he couldn't enter the clubhouse.

Throughout all this assault on human dignity, 'we remained a decent people', intoned the vast majority of white South Africans, almost but not quite in Himmler's vein. There was pride in living in a democracy, where whites, the real South Africans, had the vote. There was a glow that we had a Westminster system of government, including an opposition, even though for almost a decade the only opposition came from one woman,

Helen Suzman, whom it would have been necessary to invent if she hadn't been there to help live out the lie about the nature of 'Westminster'.

SOUTH AFRICA: A GENOCIDAL SOCIETY?

Within the three streams of South African race policy and practice referred to earlier – removal of political rights and land, re-tribalisation, and what was virtually indentured, migratory labour – was there anything that could be said to constitute genocide in its legal sense? Goldstone says he is wedded to the Convention definition and is 'uneasy about this [social science] kind of scholarly dilution of the definition of genocide' (Goldstone, 2002: 261). The land and franchise issues offered a pipedream of territorial segregation or racial separation, an each-to-his-own policy, even though the groups were hardly equal in shares and domains. That land had to be allocated was a given. A franchise could be denied, but it had to be compensated for by way of further land, three white representatives in the House of Assembly and four white Senators, and a Natives Representative Council, an advisory body to government. A raw deal and, by and large, a bad deal, but hardly comparable with the removal of Jews' citizenship by the Nuremberg and ensuing laws.

The re-tribalisation of people turned out to be, for the wrong initial reasons, a boon to black African nationalism. When Steve Biko began the Black Consciousness Movement, Africans were united only in, and by, their struggle for rights denied them by a common enemy. A more binding and cohering force was needed, and so Biko promoted the notion of pride in African worthiness, as a way of breaking the psychological yoke of the master–servant relationship that had been there for centuries. Ironically, perhaps, this 'negritude' philosophy had a tailor-made foundation for new programmes: pride in linguistic and nationalistic heritage, pride in Africanism and Africanness, promoted and often provided by the white system for the wrong reasons. Biko, it should be said, didn't start his movement because of anything that white society had insisted upon. His cue came from the Black Power movement in the United States and its roots in Marcus Garvey and others long before.

It is only in migratory labour that there is a glimmer of genocidal practice, one wrought and brought about without intent and without foresight, or insight, that the system would produce dire consequences. The system still operates, but the social and economic barriers to marital and parenting relationships have ended.

A vicious society, a race-riven and race-divided society, a land where laws were used to subvert the very notion of law, where democracy, after a fashion, was only in question for one group in four of the total population. This was a land of fury and violence, anger, rage and great frustration – a land rarely given to grace or generosity. David Bankier (1996) has observed that throughout Germany's period of radical antisemitism, even though there were pockets of misgiving by some of the populace, there was 'scarcely a trace of humanitarianism' when it came to Jews. In like vein, I recall but one such episode in my twenty-six years in South Africa. In the late 1950s, a tornado hit an African township just outside Johannesburg. The SABC broadcast an appeal for blood. I rushed to Hospital Hill, site of the Red Cross Blood Bank – to find the queue, of whites, nearly a mile long. But that was before they started putting white circles on white bottles of red blood and refusing, legally, to allow lifesaving inter-racial transfusions.

In so many respects, black South Africans resembled the Jews of Nazi Germany. But South Africa never wanted to expel them – they only wanted more of them. They didn't 'mercy-kill' or sterilise them, they wanted them to produce more of themselves. They would harass them, arrest them, imprison them and sell them, beat them, relocate them, control their movements and regulate their lives, including their bedroom lives, but they always wanted more of them, not fewer of them. They wanted them healthy and compliant, not dead.

Was South Africa guilty of crimes against humanity? Assuredly. But the charge of genocide against white South African governments doesn't stand up to critical evaluation. Only one of the Genocide Convention's five criteria comes close to being met, but even so there was never any *intent to destroy* – even at the height of apartheid's most infamous excesses.

REFLECTING ON GENOCIDE: DENIALISM, MEMORY AND THE POLITICS OF APOLOGY

There have been antithetical reponses to the genocides of the twentieth century. On one hand, admission of the events, trials of those responsible, punishment or reparations by the perpetrators, a momentum of memory and memorials and, more recently, national apology to the victims; on the other, denialism, ranging from the relatively benign and insignificant to aggressive diplomatic strategies. Memory has moved from personal and collective recollection and remembrance to state-sponsored programmes, including mandatory school courses, national and international museums, even package tours to the sites where genocide occurred. Trials followed events, then lapsed as societies insisted on 'moving on', then returned with some vigour. By century's end, truth commissions, with either justice or reconciliation (but not both) as the spur, flourished in pursuit of 'what happened'.

DENIALISM

I have some critical reflections on this consequence of genocide. My two main concerns are: first, the motives of those who deny the genocides of the Jews, the Armenians and the Australian Aborigines; second, their power and, by contrast, their impotence. The outpourings and 'products' of the Holocaust and Turkish denialists are known well enough, the Australian variety less so. My focus is on their political rather than their psychological motives. Exploration of what propels these people might help develop more effective strategies to deal with, or perhaps even nullify, their activities. Because the Australian case is less known abroad, I treat it more fully. The motives of those who deny – including Prime Minister John Howard, two ex-state premiers, several retired senior bureaucrats, a small grouping of senior journalists and a quartet of academics with scholastic credentials – have little in common with Holocaust denialists but they do strongly echo and parallel the Turkish denial industry.

Power

In Terrence des Pres's anatomy of life in Nazi death camps, he reports on a Dachau survivor who was told by an SS guard 'that we had no chance of coming out alive', but even if they did 'the rest of the world would not believe what happened . . . people would conclude that evil on such a scale was just not possible' (des Pres, 1976: 35). Later, Stanley Cohen said much the same thing about ethnic Albanian women driven from Kosovo: 'They look like figures from their own dreams. This sensation only heightens their fear that even if they do survive to testify, others will not believe what happened' (Cohen, 2001: 142).

Denial stories are much more believable than Holocaust stories. Imagine a class of teenagers in 1960, 1970, 1980, 2003 (and, even more so, in the remoter years of 2013 or 2023) trying to decide which is more credible:

- that refugee or displaced louse-infested Jews were disinfected in showers before going to work camps, or that mere handfuls of Germans, with local helpers, were 'processing 12,000 *stukke*', that is, they were murdering, on average, 10,000 to 12,000 people (*pieces*) per day in specially built Polish death factories?
- that more Turks than Armenians died in a civil war, one in which armed, rebellious, fifth-columnist Armenians suffered some unavoidable casualties, or that in the middle of World War I, Turks systematically killed Armenian children in early-model gas chambers in a military hospital, shot men, blinded young girls in hospital theatres, and death-marched women and children all the way to Syria as a way of eliminating at least half of the people they viewed as 'microbes' in their body politic?
- that Aboriginal children, especially girls, were removed from cruel environs where they were promised in marriage to old men, or that officials meeting in Canberra in 1937 were engaging in some

eugenicist fantasy to breed Aborigines for ever out of the Australian landscape?

In all or any of this, which would the students prefer to hear? Which history would they find more manageable? With which would they feel more comfortable?

We are told often enough that genocide consists of a triangle: the perpetrators (or the immolators, as the Israeli scholar Yair Auron calls them) constitute one side, the victims a second, and the bystanders the third. In some cases, there is a fourth dimension: the beneficiaries. Now we must add a fifth: the denialists. The goal of the denialists, the rationalisers, relativisers and trivialisers, according to Richard Hovannisian, is 'to deceive and to confuse' (Hovannisian, 1997: 53). As each genocide recedes, at least in the public memory, so denialism grows. Denialism certainly doesn't perpetrate the original crime, but its potential to sanitise, even to obliterate the deeds, and its ability to disfigure the survivors' own memories of what happened to them, makes it worthy of our attention. By attention, I mean our focusing on the motives of the denialists rather than solely on their activities.[1]

Time, energy and a growing literature have been devoted to the outpourings of Holocaust denialists like Rassinier, Faurisson, Thion, Garaudy, Hogan, Harwood (Verrall), Christophersen, Frey, Staeglich, App, Butz, Carto, Leuchter, Zundel, Irving, Nolte, Hillgruber and, here in Australia, Bennett and Toben; and to the agitations, machinations and fabrications of the Turkish denial industry, and to the writings of its acolytes, the two Shaws, McCarthy, Lowry and, somewhat sadly, the otherwise admirable Bernard Lewis. The Australian press no longer mentions John Bennett and his outpourings in his widely distributed 'Your Rights' publication. Tucked into an otherwise useful-looking booklet on one's rights as a tenant or as a customer buying on hire-purchase, Bennett inserts his poison-pen material. He does so under the rubric of what sounds like a respected and respectable organisation, 'The Council for Civil Liberties'. He was once a member of the well-known Victorian Council for Civil Liberties in Melbourne, from which he was expelled, only to re-surface as head of his own 'Council'. From time to time, the comings and goings of Frederick Toben are covered, his jailings in Germany and the lawsuits mounted against or by him in Australia, culminating in the banning of his hate website by an Australian federal court in September 2002.

Now the spotlight is, instead, on a coven of Australian newspaper and journal critics who similarly peddle denials of Aboriginal history. We are well aware of the 'product' of such writers and often of their intentions and goals. But goals, masked or stated, are not motives. Where or what were, and are, their mainsprings? Can they simply be dismissed as the 'Lunar Right'? Does their 'work' arise out of paranoia, obsession or possibly from nihilism, or from profound ethnic sectarianism, or perhaps, from an acute, misguided patriotism?

Two important works were published in 2001: Robert Manne's essay *In Denial – The Stolen Generations and the Right* and Stanley Cohen's book, *States of Denial*. Both are excellent, yet both disappoint me in failing to elicit motivation. They explain and expand, dissect and demolish what denialists do, yet they don't, other than fleetingly, discuss political motivation. Cohen gives a masterly insight into three kinds of denial: literal denial, maintaining that nothing happened; interpretative denial, claiming that what happened was really something else; and implicatory denial, alleging that what happened was justified. A sociologist, he nevertheless chooses to use the language of psychology: 'Someone else', he writes, 'will have to write a political economy of denial.' Neither work comes to grips with what Noam Chomsky would call, and what I call, political denial, that is 'the blatant lies, the double messages and the averted gazes' that are 'conscious, intentional denial informed by geopolitical [or] local political interests only' (Cohen, 2001: 163).

My essay into this area isn't an exercise in psychopolitics (for that perspective, see Charny, 1992, 2001). I have no interest in explanations of the psyches of the denialists, the role played by their childhoods or by the traumas these men may have experienced. But I would like help in eliciting their motives. This would enable me (and others) to find more effective ways of dealing with their political and, therefore, accountable behaviour. Chomsky, although not my favourite author, is compelling in this context: 'The intellectual responsibility of the writer as a moral agent is obvious: to try to find out and tell the truth as best one can about matters of human significance to the right audience – that is, an audience that can do something about them' (quoted in Cohen, 2001: 286). Trading insults and injuries in a contest of 'truths' is not cost-effective: at worst, and it is very much a worst, it bestows on these people an equal status as debaters and as participants in judging 'the verdicts of history'. For example, Michael

Shermer and Alex Grobman have sought an explanation of Holocaust denialists and conclude that many of them believe what they say (Shermer *et al.*, 2000). Accordingly, they include a long chapter trying to convince these denialists of the wrongness of their beliefs.

Most denialists have a political history behind their exercise of propaganda. Exposing who and what they really represent in today's open society is more effective by far than trying to counter them, or to score points off them, let alone persuade and re-educate them or their audiences. Their ability, in a free society, to utilise the print and mass media to get to 'our audiences' is the hurdle we have to overcome.

Holocaust denialism

Lucy Dawidowicz, Deborah Lipstadt and Pierre Vidal-Naquet, among others, have analysed the works of those who contend, or who may even believe, that the Holocaust was and is, in Arthur Butz's language, 'the hoax of the twentieth century'. We now know a great deal about denialist writings, techniques and vehicles, and their effectiveness or lack thereof. Apart from tolerance of that especial brand of denialism, called 'comparative trivialisation', by Ernst Nolte (1985, 1988) and Andreas Hillgruber (1986) in Germany, there has been no denial by the German state, East, West or reunited. The *Schuldfrage* (guilt question) remains a central issue in daily German life, especially among the young. Perversely, perhaps, there has been a great deal of denial in the very democracies where freedom of speech is sacrosanct: France, the United States, Canada, Britain and Australia. Some of the reasons are becoming clear:

1. In the early postwar years, to facilitate the 'coming out' of Nazis and Nazis in hiding. Only the nullification of the Holocaust can make Naziness, and its derivatives, respectable or acceptable.

2. The re-legitimation of antisemitism as a political credo. This is only possible if antisemitism is sanitised of its ultimate practical 'model' – Auschwitz. Political and nationalistic antisemitism, and political parties devoted thereto, prevalent across Europe before World War II, are undergoing a resurgence in today's Europe.

3. To legitimise fascism as a worthy, organic political philosophy. This is only possible if you can divorce fascism from its associated death camp antisemitism. If the death camps didn't happen, then fascism and anti-

semitism can have nothing to be ashamed of and can, once again, be respectable.

4. To establish the illegitimacy of Israel if, indeed, Israel is the consequence and outcome of the Holocaust. This unfortunate and misleading Holocaust = Israel equation, strongly emphasised by former Prime Minister Menachem Begin, is still, regrettably, pervasive throughout Israel and the Diaspora. If, therefore, the Holocaust can be denied, then so, too, can any rationalisation for the foundation and continued existence of the Jewish state.

5. To establish the legitimacy of the Palestinian cause. By turning Palestinians into the victims, Jews are accused of behaving like the very Nazis whom the Jews falsely accuse of genocide.

6. To reconcile the Soviets' notion of the centrality of their own history of millions lost and their antagonism, especially after the 1967 war, to a Jewry, an Israel or a Zion that has, since 1945, had the pre-eminent claim of having lost six million of its people. To avoid that contradiction, Soviet academicians turned the Nazis into fascists and didn't mention the centrality, in the Nazi *Weltanschauung*, of antisemitism and the 'Final Solution'. In the end, for them, and for the ears of a world that may have been willing to listen, the only victims of fascism were communists. This phase – together with the Soviet system – has now passed, but it was, for decades, a state-sponsored enterprise in the major academies, more vigorous, more pernicious and much more effective, world-wide, than the 'free-enterprise' efforts of a handful of American denialists like Harry Elmer Barnes, Willis Carto and Arthur Butz.

7. To counteract fears of a breaking-up of social consensus in society, particularly when a society is in transition. To focus public attention on an alleged, ethnically identifiable fifth column of 'others' offers some grounds for a form of national unity.

8. To magnify, in some instances, a particular victim community's suffering without having to have it compared with, and found to be on a lesser scale than, the Holocaust. Deliberate flattening, or even minimising, of the Holocaust magnifies and equalises all atrocities. In a morbid sense, if everyone commits horrors, then not only is no person or group any more guilty than any other, but all humankind has suffered equally – and Jews, therefore, have no greater claim on humanity's conscience.

9. To express hatred of Jews.

10. To hurt, to shaft corpses with the added indignity of claiming that

there were no corpses, and to inflict on Jewish survivors the accusation, even the curse, that their nightmares are just that – very bad dreams. In the words of Vidal-Naquet: denialists 'are intent on striking a community in the thousand painful fibres that continue to link it to its own past' (Vidal-Naquet, 1992: xxiii–xxiv).

Certainly these denialists know what they're doing: they learn, refine, become more 'academic', more sophisticated, more credible as alternative explainers or revealers of 'truth', more subtle and less 'kooky' than they appeared immediately after the war. But while they remain professionally isolated within their communities, they are at the same time collectivised; that is, dispersed as they are geographically, they have turned themselves into a coterie, a cult, a collective who now meet publicly, or who are sometimes prevented from meeting publicly, as in Lebanon in 2001.[2] They are assembled in a fortress of their choosing, as purveyors of hate, as merchants of prejudice. While they may have a certain mass appeal, they are no longer viewed as discrete, independent scholars, worthy of attention or of a serious intellectual or academic hearing.

In 2000, and again in 2001, on appeal in senior British courts, the hubris of the new Crown Prince of ridicule, David Irving, 'the noted British historian, author of more than 20 books', ensured that a great many Humpty Dumptys fell off the wall (see Evans, 2002; Guttenplan, 2001). In July 2001, the three-judge Court of Appeal supported Justice Gray's initial ruling. They declared that Irving was 'one of the most dangerous spokespersons for Holocaust denial . . . No objective, fair-minded historian would have serious cause to doubt that there were gas chambers at Auschwitz and that they were operated on a substantial scale to kill hundreds of thousands of Jews.' In the libel case, Justice Gray concluded: 'Irving is anti-Semitic. His words are directed against Jews, either individually or collectively, in the sense that they are by turns hostile, critical, offensive and derisory' (Evans, 2002: 236).

In the end, for each work of Holocaust denial there are literally dozens of new works of careful, even ultra-careful, scholarship. It is the latter material that is used in public and private educational systems, both at the school and university levels.

Turkish denialism

Turkish denialism is always met with academic, journalistic, political and community counter-arguments, with barrages of facts, photos and testimonies to prove what the Turks so forcefully seek to disprove. The phenomenology of that denialism is never questioned: it is simply there. It has to be, and is, duly countered.

That masterly opponent of denialism, Pierre Vidal-Naquet, has written powerfully on the subject:

> the Turks ... do not stop there: they offer the very exemplar of a historiography of denial. Let us put ourselves in the position of Armenian minorities throughout the world. Imagine now Faurisson as a minister, Faurisson as a general, an ambassador, or an influential member of the United Nations; imagine Faurisson responding in the press each time it is a question of the Jews, in brief, a State-sponsored Faurisson combined with an international Faurisson, and along with it, Talaat–Himmler having his solemn mausoleum in the capital.
>
> Vidal-Naquet, 1992: 121

Richard Hovannisian's monograph on comparative denial is a profound analysis of these particular 'assassins of memory'. He succinctly analyses their methods and their objectives: 'to reshape history, to rehabilitate the perpetrators, to demonise the victims', 'justifying the present and shaping the future' (Hovannisian, 1997: 51). But we are still left with the question: why?

The pernicious, outrageous and continued nature of the Turkish denial industry saves it from being dismissed as comic hysteria. Here is a modern state, totally dedicated, at home and abroad, to extraordinary actions to have every hint or mention of an Armenian genocide removed, contradicted, explained, countered, justified, mitigated, rationalised, trivialised and relativised. The entire apparatus of the state is attuned to denial. It has created offices and officers abroad for the purpose. The actions are spectacular, often bizarre, and without any effort to distinguish between the serious and the silly: from pressures to dilute or even remove any mention of the genocide in the Armenian entry in the *Encyclopaedia Britannica*, to threats to sever diplomatic relations with France over the latter's recent parliamentary declaration that there was such a genocide, to replacing the Turkish Prime Minister's Renault car, to local Turks in Sydney seeking to have the ethnic-centred television station, SBS, recall and pulp its 25-year anniversary history for twice making passing reference to an event that 'never happened'.

I have been the recipient of the Turkish denialist endeavours. In 1987, I received an ambassadorial visit to try to stop me teaching my Politics of Genocide course, or at least the Armenian section thereof, and in September 1999, the Turkish Consul-General in Sydney sought to have our Macquarie University conference on 'Portraits of Christian Asia Minor' cancelled. When that failed, several conference delegates did everything possible to wreck the event.[3] World-wide, young, locally born Turks have been so influenced by the denial machine that they react with vehemence, aggression and disruption whenever and wherever the subject of what happened nearly ninety years ago is mentioned.

What motivates Turks around the globe? We don't know, and I don't believe anyone has published (at least, in English) the credible reasons for this deep-seated, obsessive and aggressive behaviour. I suggest the following:

1. A suppression of guilt and shame that a warrior nation, presenting itself as a 'beacon of democracy', slaughtered several ethnic civilian populations. Democracies don't commit genocide, *ergo*, Turkey couldn't and didn't commit genocide. The Turkish choice is to repress these emotions by aggressive denials rather than to purge them by any admissions.

2. A cultural and social ethos of honour, a compelling and compulsive need to remove any blots on the national escutcheon, a need to remove most or all of the epithets that have been used about Turkey over the last century – the 'Sick Man of Europe', the German ally, Muslim barbarians, the *genocidaires*, and so on.

3. A chronic and growing fear that any admissions will not be seen as symbolic but will result in massive financial reparations to Armenians, Assyrians and Pontian Greeks.

4. To conquer fears of fragmentation of social consensus in a society in transition, and Turkey is still in transition almost a century after its revolution in 1908.

5. An inner knowledge that the juggernaut of denial can't be stopped, even if they wanted it to stop. Starting in the immediate period after the Extraordinary Courts Martial in 1919, which established that many 'things'

happened, the denial industry has gained ever-increasing momentum, and is now quite beyond recall. To admit a seven-year period of genocide would be bad enough but to admit that the ensuing eighty-four years of denialism have been a cover-up would be even worse – because the state has invested its very soul in denial.

6. A 'logical' belief that genocide committed with impunity, the 1919 Extraordinary Courts Martial notwithstanding, is both warrant and licence to commit denial with impunity.

Turkish denialism will, therefore, become ever more vigorous and virulent in the next few decades. Turkey managed to subvert Shimon Peres, Israel's former foreign minister, into denying the enormity of the events. The *Turkish Daily News* reported Peres's one-day visit to Ankara on 10 April 2001 when he was reported to have said that 'Armenian allegations of genocide were meaningless'. Further: 'We reject attempts to create a similarity between the Holocaust and the Armenian allegations. Nothing similar to the Holocaust occurred. It is a tragedy what the Armenians went through but not a genocide.' In February 2002, Rivka Cohen, Israeli ambassador to Georgia and Armenia, declared that although what happened to the Armenians was a 'tragedy', it was unacceptable to draw a parallel with the Holocaust (*Australian Jewish News*, 8 March 2002). Not even Israel's geopolitical interests in a time of crisis can condone such public statements. Peres could, at worst, have said nothing. But if there is a defence of Peres, it may well lie in the fact that a handful of Holocaust historians, for example Steven Katz, Michael Marrus and Deborah Lipstadt, have given him *imprimatur* for such judgments.

Katz, in asserting the uniqueness of the Holocaust, appears to denigrate, and often diminishes, other genocides by defining their experience as (merely) 'tragedy' or 'calamity'. Marrus's important book, *The Holocaust in History* (1988), has fleeting references to the Romany people (Gypsies), and deals, in three pages, with the Armenian 'episode' as 'the horrors of the slaughter' but lacking 'the Promethean ambition that we have come to associate with the Holocaust'. Prometheus? The Holocaust was doubtless more Titanic than other genocides, but that doesn't mean the 'lesser' events were not genocide. Lipstadt's otherwise excellent *Denying the Holocaust* (1993) relegates the Armenian experience to a 'massacre', the result of a 'ruthless Turkish policy of expulsion and resettlement'. Her index item is 'Armenian massacres'.

Despite such seeming 'victories' for the Turkish denialists, the issue of a major genocide will be sustained as scholars pay more attention to those events. As Hovannisian rightly points out, 'concerned researchers and writers about both crimes are being drawn together by the threat posed' (Hovannisian, 1997: 53). A handful of Turkish scholars, particularly Taner Akcam and Halil Berktay, have now dared to enter the fray on behalf of reality rather than national honour. And a priest, Father Yusuf Akbalut, who insists that the 'alleged' events were real enough, was recently put on trial for 'inciting people to hatred and enmity by referring to religious, racial, sectarian and regional differences' (Diamadis, 2001: 19–21).

Australian denialism

The years 1992 to 2000 were crucial for admissions and apologies about the past. But amid these state and church apologies, the acknowledgements, the national and Senate inquiries, and despite the work of academics Raimond Gaita, Robert Manne and myself, a voluble denial industry was born.

An array of conservative critics refute both genocide and/or the gloom and mourning pervading Aboriginal colonial history. A few are reputable academics like political scientist Kenneth Minogue and anthropologists Ken Maddock and Ron Brunton. Senior politicians, like John Howard, John Herron, former federal cabinet minister Peter Howson, and former premiers Wayne Goss and Ray Groom have been joined by the former Governor-General, Bill Hayden. Fellow travellers include two former senior federal bureaucrats and an industrialist. There is a small journalistic group vehemently opposed to the *Bringing Them Home* material and, finally, a netherworld of radio talkback 'philosophers' incessant in their anti-Aboriginal chatter.

What many of these men have in common is that they do neither fieldwork nor homework. They are passionate in defence of national pride and achievement, indignant in denying any alleged 'racist, bigoted past'. Like so many genocide denialists, they assert but don't demonstrate, they disapprove but don't ever disprove; they assert that genocide never occurred here, or couldn't have occurred here, or could never occur here. More commonly, they nibble at the edges, sniping at weaker points, in the hope (or belief) that if they can demonstrate one error of fact or figure, the central and essential 'contention' of genocide will fall apart.

Goss, when Premier, insisted on the removal of such 'offending' words as 'invasion' and 'resistance' from Queensland school texts. Former Tasmanian Premier Ray Groom contended that there had been no killings in the island state, making him, in effect, Australia's foremost genocide denialist in the 1990s (*Australian*, 25 October 1994). Hugh Morgan, a mining executive, talks about crimes Australians 'did not commit, could not have committed or were not committed at all' (*Weekend Australian*, 3–4 April 1992).

From his assumption of office in 1996, the present Prime Minister began a systematic campaign against what historian Professor Geoffrey Blainey disparagingly calls the 'black armband' interpretation of Australian history (*The Bulletin*, 8 April 1997).This he defines as looking at the treatment of the Aborigines in a way which allows 'the minuses to virtually wipe out the pluses'. This swing, he says, 'has run wild', and even the High Court is 'that black armband tribunal'. Howard sympathises with those 'Australians who are insulted when they are told we have a racist, bigoted past' (*Sydney Morning Herald* editorial, 18 November 1996)

The 'Witnesses for the Defence', as journalist Padraic McGuinness styles himself and his colleagues, are remarkable for their anorexic arguments and, at times, quite uninformed and unintelligent explanations. In concert with a few academics, his small coterie contrives to claim – invariably in *Quadrant* magazine, which McGuinness edits – that the charge of genocide is either pedantry or mischief; that Australia didn't commit genocide by forced removal because, if we had, we would have prosecuted the crime (when committed by federal and state bureaucrats?); that many, or even most, removals were with parental consent; that only a 'small number' (12,500) were removed, citing an Australian Bureau of Statistics 1994 survey to support the mini-removal thesis; that removal was akin to sending white kids to boarding school; that many benefited from removal; that Aboriginal leaders were assimilationists; that since earlier anthropologists didn't find genocide, it couldn't have occurred; and, finally, that some, but an unspecified number, of those who assert genocide do so because they 'are of Jewish background and have an interest in the Holocaust'.

But why the denials? Robert Manne, who has devoted the past three years to a study of the stolen generations, has published a learned essay on denial (Manne 2001). A forensic counter to McGuinness's 'Defence' team, he does, as Lipstadt and others have done elsewhere, an impeccable dissection of their claims and assertions. In his final section, he asks 'why?'

Motives differ, he says: 'some of the anti-*Bringing Them Home* campaigners are now too old or proud to reflect on the cruelty of practices in which they were personally involved'. Others are 'former leftists who are so obsessed by the conduct of ideological combat against their former friends that they have come to believe that truth is simply the opposite of what they once believed'. 'Some are general purpose right-wingers who hunt in packs and can be relied upon to agree with whatever their political friends believe.'

Manne is less concerned with their motives than with what he calls the heart of the campaign, namely, 'the meaning of Aboriginal dispossession'. There is, he argues, 'a right-wing and populist resistance to discussions of historical injustice and the Aborigines'. Separation of mother and child 'deeply captured the national imagination': that '[stolen generations] story had the power to change for ever the way they saw their country's history' – hence the imperative to destroy that story. This is an astute observation. There is unlikely to be any other explanation of the virulence with which that 'story' has been savaged. However, this imperative doesn't explain their systematic attacks on the 'falsity' of the era of the physical killings.

We need to probe a little deeper than this. Are these people simply guilty officials, or just anti-Leftists, or indiscriminate pack-hunting Rightists? Are they not simply passionate defenders of national pride and achievement, *alla Turca*? Are they not just a collective St George slaying the author-dragons, black and white, who insist that we do, indeed, have a 'racist, bigoted past', because they know the truth – that we have no such past? Are they simply unable to accept that fellow Australians, albeit of earlier generations, committed such heinous offences or are they, more materialistically, concerned that an admission of the truth by today's Australians would open the floodgates of litigation and compensation?

There can be no doubt that reparation and restitution to Aborigines are anathema to the majority of Australians. Admitting a few 'past mistakes' is one thing, paying compensation for what was done is quite another. The Prime Minister and his servants have made this clear. In April 1996, Martin Bryant's shooting spree in Port Arthur, Tasmania, killed thirty-four people. Amid outcry, John Howard decided to spend $300 million on a nationwide gun buy-back scheme. Any similar or even much lower figure for Aboriginal reparation is considered outrageous. The enormous cost of the *Cubillo* and *Gunner* cases – two Northern Territory Aborigines who established their 'removal' but who lost their damages suit against the federal government – indicates that money is no object in winning a government cause. But it is not just the money or the quantum thereof that makes the denialists so mean-spirited: it has much more to do with their stereotyped and negative perceptions of the intended recipients of such money.

Motives also lie in an Australian insecurity about who and what we are, and where we are – a small number of predominantly white, Christian people surrounded by hundreds of millions of non-Christian Asians. The assimilationist tradition is powerful: we need to feel, and to be seen, as one, and, in such oneness, there isn't room for counter-cultures, let alone for divergent views of our history. We don't see ourselves as 'having a history' in any pejorative sense, only Gallipoli in a good sense. Aboriginal nationalism, with its insistence on an older civilisation and autonomy, and on an unequal present, is disturbing, even distressing, a threat to a nation worried about fracturing, about 'cracks appearing in the temple of homogeneity'. The nineteenth-century belief that Aborigines were dying out, or would die out, is an enduring one. Many would prefer that it endure for ever. We want noble origins, to feel that we are in a 'good' country, one dedicated to both the belief and the practice of egalitarianism, a nation born of, but distinct from, the class society which lingers on in Great Britain. A true-blue Australian deplores the notion of a privileged class. Raymond Evans and Bill Thorpe have successfully dissected Keith Windschuttle's 'massacre of history', his 'bowdlerised, mypoic version of Australia's past' (Windschuttle, 2000). They conclude that for Windschuttle and the other *Quadrant* 'Defence' team, the real history is 'intensely disconcerting', leading to a preference for 'an unsullied Union Jack proudly flying over the Australian continent' (Evans and Thorpe, 2001: 21–39).

The media flurry caused by Keith Windschuttle's *The Fabrication of Aboriginal History*, published in 2002, centred mainly on whether or not historians Henry Reynolds and Lyndall Ryan were correct about a handful of footnote references and attributions. There was also heat about Windschuttle's 'Tasmanian settler mentality', his lack of historical training, some possible 'neo-plagiarism', his alleged fudging and misrepresentation of the work of others, and the virtual self-publication of the work by a family business (*Australian*, 13 January 2003). Much space was devoted to the 'Black Debate' and to Windschuttle's threats to sue all who upset him.

What has been forgotten in this brouhaha is that genocide, whatever else it may be perceived as being, is a crime, not a debating point. It must be said that most of the disputants, including the journalists who have been gleefully reporting the 'stoush', don't come to this aspect of Australian history with a background in Holocaust and genocide studies, and so they argue, exclusively, about the extent of the numbers dead, in either the fields or the footnotes of Tasmania or Treblinka. In this 'debate', no mention is made of the legal definition which says that genocide is the attempt to destroy a specific group 'in whole or in part': the disputants always insist on 'the whole' or nothing. There is no mention of acts other than physical killing, or of attempts to commit the crime, conspiracies to do so, or complicity in the events. The opinions and beliefs of the commentators – whether Ron Brunton, Keith Windschuttle, Robert Manne, Henry Reynolds or Colin Tatz – don't matter. For some fifty years now, despite the elegant examination by genocide scholars of the admittedly flawed definition of this crime in international law, the crime remains as defined in 1948. The definition is now further cemented into the Statute of the International Criminal Court.

Australia's genocide isn't about this or that incorrect footnote or who said what, where and when. It is about who *did* what, where and when, and with what intent. Brunton (1998) insists that genocide demands malignancy. For once, I might agree with him. But our opinions are irrelevant. We did what we did, or so we like to believe, with 'good intentions'. That won't make genocide go away, and the law doesn't specify malignancy. Intent to destroy, not motive, is the key. Certainly Australians should engage with their history. But they should do it in an appropriate place: if not a criminal court, then in the next best venue, a civil court, under strict but somewhat more flexible forensic rules, *à la* the David Irving trial.

We want to feel good about ourselves, to know that being Australian is being a certain kind of decent people, even decent by way of being good colonists (or handlers of asylum-seekers). Historian Graeme Davison (2001) believes that Australians are forever playing to an imaginary grandstand, always looking upward and outward (never inward) for approval, always concerned about not failing: 'The habit of seeing ourselves through the eyes of the imaginary other is the most lasting mental relic of colonialism. Like children, colonial Australians were anxious to win the good opinion of their parents, so it was Mother England [and now, the United States] that young Australians first sought to impress.' The image of the 'nice guys', the informal, hospitable, laid-back guys was, he cites Mark Landler as saying, 'merely a camouflage for an Australian people more technically proficient, ambitious, aggressive – and yes, even more authoritarian and anxious – than we liked to admit, even to ourselves'. Although Davison and Landler made their comments in a context of sport and Australian identity, they are as pertinent here.[4] Any attack on what 'we' did in previous generations and centuries is an attack on what 'I' did, or didn't do: it is an assault on the collective narcissism and on the individual upholder of our clean, decent foundations. The very mention of an Australian genocide is, therefore, appalling and galling and must be put aside. The 'clean foundations' are the white, ethnic nation foundations. Australia, according to my colleague Winton Higgins, rests not on a civic nationalism – which insists on the inclusiveness of all and the dignity of citizenship as the measure of a nation's worth – but on an exclusive white, ethnic nationalism as the basis for belonging.

I have another suggestion: that denialism in Australia is also about the place of morality in Australian politics. It is either a promotion of an especial Anglo-nationalism, a particular Australian moral virtue, in which there is, by definition, no place for genocidal thoughts or actions, or it is an attempt to excise morality from political considerations, to create an amoral, economically centred body politic. I'm not quite sure which of these it is and it may well turn out to be both.

A curious national belief is that simply being Australian, whether by birth or naturalisation, is sufficient inoculation against deviation from moral and righteous behaviour. In January 2000, a reporter asked Senator Amanda Vanstone, (Liberal) Minister for Justice, whether Konrad Kalejs, formerly a member of the notorious *Arajskomando* killing unit in Latvia in the Holocaust years but later a naturalised Australian, would be welcome in Australia. The question was put as Kalejs, already deported from the United States and Canada, was about to leave London on the eve of British deportation proceedings. 'Would you expect a situation where any Australian citizen would not be welcome here?' replied the Senator. She is reported as saying that he was 'an innocent Australian until proven guilty' and that she would welcome him at the airport as she would any other Australian *(Daily Advertiser,* Wagga Wagga, 4 January 2000).

In the same year, at the height of Australian reaction to criticism by the United Nations and other international agencies – on apologies and reparations for stolen children, and on mandatory sentencing laws in

Western Australia and the Northern Territory – Foreign Minister Alexander Downer was indignant: 'We cannot', he declaimed to the ABC, 'breach human rights in this country – because we're Australians.' In July 2002, Australia refused to sign a protocol strengthening the international convention on torture. It was the only Western nation among the refusers, in company with China, Libya, Cuba, Sudan and Nigeria. Inspectors could not simply walk in and inspect our asylum-seeker detention centres, because as Australians we should not be suspected of doing 'those sorts of things.'

In April 2001, when *Obersturmführer* Karlos Aleksandrs (Karlis) Ozols, Latvian *compadre* of (the then late) Kalejs, died in Melbourne, the Australian Chess Federation posted a eulogistic 'Rest in Peace' on its website for this citizen, this former Australian chess champion, this 'witty and charming' alleged killer of at least 12,000 Jews in Latvia. His past was irrelevant; his *Australian* chess-playing was what mattered. Parliamentarians were aghast at being asked to ratify the Genocide Convention in 1949 – because 'the horrible crime of genocide is unthinkable in Australia . . . That we detest all forms of genocide . . . arises from the fact that we are a moral people.'[5]

Much of the denialism is, I believe, a propping up of this mythical national moral hygiene, of an idealised 'down under' way of life that is simply beyond comparison, or analogy, with the barbarisms of the Balkans or the murderous mindsets of the Nazis. As we see in daily sport *ad nauseam*, it is the Indian sub-continent, and other 'foreign elements' – like East Germans and the Chinese – who cheat, throw matches, accept bribes or take drugs. Australians don't, or can't, do these things because we're Australians. It has been suggested that, in order to 'clean up' Australia's history of race relations before the Sydney 2000 Olympic Games, the denialist journalists and former bureaucrats met in enclave and began publishing voluminously and simultaneously in *Quadrant* and the major newspapers in September 2000 (*Sydney Morning Herald*, 12 October 2000; *Australian*, 14 September 2000, *Sydney Morning Herald*, 14 September 2000). The timing was, otherwise, a curious coincidence.

Are they protecting the inherent 'moral gene' that runs through white (and naturalised) Australian veins? Or is it rather a case of their attempting to ridicule anything that acknowledges an underlying morality in politics, a moral nihilism which 'de-moralises' us all and leaves no room for issues of shame, guilt, atonement of any kind? In this way, for example, one doesn't have to think, or feel, about the refugees, the boat people and other 'illegals' imprisoned in camps in the deserts of South and Western Australia. (And if we do think about the desert incarceration of asylum-seekers, we don't see their location, or their conditions, as abnormal, let alone abhorrent. That is what you do, what we have always done with those other people, the Aboriginal peoples, in remote Australia.[6])

Impotence

The fall of Irving, the too-clever-by-half manipulator of fact and fiction, is a dismal signpost for Holocaust denialists. His demise – of reputation as historian, as 'expert' on the Holocaust and of financial security – won't stop their activities but it will nullify whatever gains they believe they were making. Their leader chose the most careful, precise, controlled and polite arena he could find to test his contentions – the most senior British civil court – and lost it all.

Perhaps most fateful for denialists is their linkage with the far Right. Irving is now indelibly connected with extreme right-wing individuals and organizations: *inter alia*, Ewald Althans, leader of the *Vertriebs bewege und Offentlichkeitsarbeit*, which had global links with neo-Nazis (until it closed in 1992); Thies Christophersen, a former SS guard at Auschwitz, a wanted man in Germany; Gunther Deckert, of the National Democratic Party, convicted for incitement to racial hatred and defamation of the memory of the dead; Robert Faurisson; Gerhard Frey, possibly the widest disseminator of denial propaganda in Germany; François Genoud, a Swiss banker and lawyer and an active Nazi since the 1930s; Wilhelm Staeglich, once stationed at Auschwitz, a man well ensconced in the portals of the Institute for Historical Review in the United States, whose manifesto includes the belief that 'The whole theory of the holocaust has been created by and promulgated by political Zionism for the attainment of political and economic ends, specifically the continued and perpetual support of the military aggression of Israel by the people of Germany and the US' (Stenekes, 2002).

Yet for all the company they keep, and for all their outpourings, these denialists assist rather than hinder genocide and Holocaust research. They have prompted a separate area of study – denialism – and have thereby exposed themselves, their methods, underpinnings, backgrounds and histories, and their connections to one another. They have, unwittingly, prompted studies by men and women of eminence – people like Professor Pierre Vidal-Naquet – who would otherwise not have written on genocide. He stepped outside his work as a classicist to give genocide scholarship a new and memorable phrase: 'the assassins of memory'.

Today, the Turks lose daily as country upon country, state upon state, and legislature upon legislature recognise the Armenian genocide. Despite their apparent 'gain' of the present Israeli government as an 'ally' in their obsessive denialism, my prediction is that two decades from now the tide will turn slowly but irrevocably against this Turkish industry. Awaiting 'the verdicts of history' – the catchphrase which the more modern Turkey insists upon – will result in more, not less, evidence of the attempted annihilation of the Armenians. The more they deny and decry, the more hitherto uninterested scholars become interested, and the more written by these scholars, the more Turkish scholars of a younger generation become curious.

Do denialists succeed? In Australia, denialists have brought immense pressure on Sir Ronald Wilson, chairman of the *Bringing Them Home* inquiry, attacking him, in ugly fashion, in every way possible. Their campaign no doubt led to his admission that it was a mistake to use the word genocide in his report, something he regretted: once you use that word, he said, 'you come up against the matter of intent' and he had erred in attributing such intent to Australian 'removalists' (*The Bulletin*, 12 June 2001: 26–30). With respect, the judge has confused intent with motive. (Motive is the personal or internal reason that guides one's actions, says Greenawalt (1999: 2275); intent is the basic volition required to perform a deliberate action or seek a specific result.) It matters not that Australian motives were 'good', 'pure' or 'Samaritan'; what matters is that the Genocide Convention deals with intent, not motivation, and child removers clearly intended that these children would cease to be Aboriginal. Sir Ronald was right to use the word in his report.

But for all this Lilliputian 'success', Australian denialists are clearly not of the equivalent stature, significance or intellect of the Noltes and Hillgrubers: they won't be writing the textbooks for our school and university curricula. They will hold their private and celebratory seminars, essentially to reinforce each other and their audience rather than to 're-educate' the public. They will produce *Quadrant* with an increase in *ad hominem* attacks, perhaps concentrating even more on those of 'Jewish background'. (If this is the case, I would prefer to be regarded as one of Jewish foreground, as it is that foreground of my existence which compels me morally to investigate all manners and matters of genocide.)

But whether they are senior political figures, once powerful bureaucrats, journalists or talk-back radio 'philosophers', they miss two essential by-products of their denialism: first, they keep issues alive that had begun to fade, or have or had the potential to fade, from public consciousness; and second, they provoke infinitely more interest among, and research by, those who have the real qualifications, skills and ethics to do such work. In a bizarre sense, denialists – who see themselves as prophylactics protecting our society from a moral re-appraisal of past behaviours – are fecund; they actually increase the fertility of research into those very behaviours. They can, however, take comfort in their one undisputed achievement – their ability to hurt the victim peoples.

Australian denialists won't make any serious or permanent inroads into what is now an almost universal recognition that this country has an unsavoury past. There is, today, a strongly conservative politics in Australia. Regrettably, under Prime Minister John Howard, conservatism has come to mean not preservation but the attempt to destroy, or the actual destruction of, institutions, as well as the rejection of all moves towards a recognition of present-day inequalities in matters of race, gender or sexual preference. Denialism appeals to John Howard, Phillip Ruddock (the Minister for Immigration) and John Herron, men who are uncomfortable with, and who accordingly disdain, the major social changes in values and attitudes of the past forty years. They are truly yesterday's men, unable to stop what is written, read, heard, seen, taught or preached by those who do, indeed, fashion the civic culture of our society.

MEMORY

The New York cataclysm of 11 September 2001 is burned into the psyche of Americans and, of course, many others. Americans (and the British, and Australians) will keep those images and memories alive, invoking 'the war on terror' for a long time to come – whether the enemy is real, merely hinted at, or imagined in order to preserve the image of an underhand, unexpected assault now graver than that of Pearl Harbor in December 1941, a cosmic American humiliation and unfathomable hurt at being so hated. The memory is important for many reasons, including personal grief, increased patriotic pride, the bravery of firemen, the history books, new alliances, foreign policy, increased military budgets, the 'war against terrorism' and Saddam Hussein. The event is re-played, in slower and slower motion, as if the better to freeze for ever those ghastly minutes. It will be a long time, indeed, before any commentators suggest that their country 'move on', that is, turn away from those events and what they represent.

In the same breath, Native Americans are urged to reconciliation, not only for past events but for those of recent and present-day memory. Contexts and circumstances, of course, differ widely; but it is worth reflecting on the interplay between history and memory; on just what levels of inhumanity people are asked to forgive, let alone forget; on the necessity of memory as a social cement that enables many victim groups to cohere; on how reparations may or may not 'assuage' memory; and on the way in which 'justice' is thwarted or defeated by politics or *realpolitiks*.

History and memory

A black American woman in Studs Terkel's book *Race* says: 'They never let you forget their history, but they want you to forget yours' (Terkel, 1993: 142). Memory is not simply a physiological or psychological phenomenon experienced by individuals. There is very much a common memory, with its own politics, especially on matters affecting a nation's geopolitical and national interests. Australians scrutinise, magnify, exhibit, venerate and strive to remember every square inch of Gallipoli, every wound, act of valour and every death in that 'birth of the nation'. Shrine-ology of many kinds is rampant and millions of medallions are struck, even for the non-heroic. When 103-year-old Alec Campbell, the last Anzac alive, died in May 2002, the entire nation was mired in a welter of nigh-hysterical memory about the nice sixteen-year-old who carried water at Gallipoli, who neither shot nor was shot at, and who was repatriated with enteric fever soon after landing. The Prime Minister even cut short a profitable gas-supply visit to China to attend this digger's state funeral. What leaders never do, as John Pilger has commented to me, 'is distinguish between the victimhood of the Anzacs and the vicious imperialism that sent them to their deaths'. On matters concerning Gallipoli, the striving is ever more towards 'moving back'. But on matters Aboriginal, the catchphrase is that the time has come 'to move on'. 'From what?' I ask.

There are two kinds of history: inside history and outside history. The first is personal and internal, with ingredients that are the essence of Aboriginality or Jewishness or Armenianness. This 'inside history' includes one's personal perception of the nature of, and one's attitudes towards, life and death, traditions, folkways, outlooks, idioms and, of course, memory. The outside history is usually the victor's record and the aggregate of past events, the narrative in time, the chronicle of what has befallen a people, with good and (mostly) bad faith, across the centuries. This outside history is often a chronology and collective memory of catastrophe.

History, even murderous history, can and does aid survival. 'Their doom is to be exterminated', wrote English novelist Anthony Trollope of the Aborigines in 1873; 'fragments of them only remain' (1966 [1873]: 134–42). The late Oodgeroo Noonuccal (Kath Walker) was acutely aware of how that kind of history becomes a force which binds people:

> Let no one say the past is dead
> The past is all about us and within.
>   in Gilbert, 1988: 99

'We cannot forget', say the Mothers of Plaza de Mayo in Argentina, the mothers of the *desaparecidos*: 'A people without memory has no future' (*Sydney Morning Herald*, 19 November 1984).

Outside history is not simply the chronicle of what white or perpetrator societies did to victim groups. It is also the history of turning them into an outside people, outside where everyone else lived and, importantly, outside the laws by which everyone else lived. Aborigines became not just different, or a people unlike us, but a people other than us. This geographic, religious and legal otherness, this quality of being 'other' than us and, therefore, other than human, was the first step along the road to the various forms of genocide.

Outside history, including the calamities, is a social cement that binds people, even faction-ridden and internecine people. It produces an element of cohesion, a sense of sharing and belonging. Ironically perhaps, genocidal efforts often reinforce the drive for survival and for the maintenance of value systems that had begun to weaken within the democracy of assimilation.

To ask victim peoples to surrender their internal historical memory is to misunderstand their psyches, souls and sociologies. The Romany peoples have a different cultural attitude from those of the Armenians and the Jews, who need to talk unceasingly about their catastrophes. The Romany see their destruction as a kind of shame, as something not to talk about, not to write about, not to lecture about. Yet the O Porrajmos – the 'Great Devouring', their name for their destruction – remains an indelible part of their inside and their outside contemporary history, their collective memory.

Choices about what is remembered and what is forgotten are both insidious and harmful. Paradoxes can come full circle, especially now that the heirs of the victims must forget while the heirs of the perpetrators seek rehabilitation:

> Since the collapse of communism, there has been a tendency in some of the former Soviet-bloc countries to glorify the memory of profascist groups and individuals who co-operated with the Nazis before and during World War II: streets and currency have been renamed in their honour; busts have been erected in their memory, and . . . periodicals glorify their patriotism.
>
> Gruber, 1995: 1

There can be no clearer example of this than the wholesale rehabilitation of Nazi war criminals in Lithuania in 1990–92. Self-confessed killers from Majdanek, and members of the notorious 12th Lithuanian Auxiliary Police Battalion, who killed approximately 47,000 Jews in Byelorussia and Lithuania, were given financial compensation for being convicted by Soviet courts (*Jerusalem Post*, 25 October 1995). Ukrainian collaborators with the Nazis are now resurrected as 'freedom fighters' and 'war heroes'. Ieng Sary – 'Brother Number Two' and Pol Pot's brother-in-law – was the killer at Tuol Sleng, 'Cambodia's Auschwitz'. In 1996, political deals allowed Sary and others to be readmitted to legitimacy and to the political fold (*Sydney Morning Herald*, 17 March 1997).

Much thought should be given to the nature and the speed with which outrage, revenge and retribution slide, or subside, into forgiveness, amnesty and, as we have seen above, into resurrection of the memory of the deed and the restitution of the reputation of the perpetrator.

Levels of inhumanity

All people rate their memories, that is, they remember and/or venerate big things and small things, major and minor events, in their lives and in their cultural histories. Some events are 'big' by any yardstick, others appear to be exaggerated beyond reason. But two issues infuriate, humiliate and fester within genocide victims: first, the failure by those who demand 'forgiveness' or 'closure' to see what is significant to the victims; second, the manner in which 'forgivers' insist on their own memories while relegating, even denigrating, both the victims' memories and their right to insist on their significance.

There is now a small but excellent literature on the interplay between memory and history (Darian-Smith and Hamilton, 1994: 9–32). We know that memory embellishes the past, often inflating and exaggerating it. The *Slachter's Nek* Rebellion in South Africa in 1815, which culminated in the grisly and botched British hanging of five Boer rebels, is momentous in Afrikaner eyes. The Great Trek from the Cape in 1834–36 is as sanctified in the Afrikaner psyche as is the Exodus in Jewish consciousness.

Comparing atrocities, engaging in what Michael Berenbaum (1990: 34) disparages as a 'calculus of calamity' between people's histories, and between their feelings about those histories, is fruitless. What is valuable is to attempt analysis, albeit with inexact and subjective tools, of what constitutes murder, mass murder, atrocity, crimes against humanity, war crimes and, at the top of the scale, genocide. Having done that, there is a crying need to examine the degrees or levels of genocide. Essential is a measure of the intensities of these events, an instrument, however crude, so that unlike events are not equated, and so that all inhumane behaviour is not conflated and then flattened to the point where all such crimes are equal. Robert Melson has pointed out the fallacies that confuse the issue of comparison (1996: 16). Uniqueness, he says, does not mean incomparability and comparability does not mean equivalence.

As discussed previously, the United Nations definition of genocide as an international crime is inadequate. It omits political groups, thus leaving Stalin's slaughter of between five and fifteen million *kulaks* (people who hired labour and who opposed collectivisation) and Indonesia's killing of between half a million and a million communists in the 1960s, beyond the compass of the offence. The UN definition, as we have seen, lists any one of five acts as constituting the crime of intending to destroy, in whole or in part, a national, ethnic, racial or religious group, as such. Grades or levels are not considered in the Convention. Yet, for me and, I dare say, for all of us, death is absolute: serious bodily or mental harm is something else; children forced into conversion may well become coerced Catholics or Muslims, but they live.

Is there not a difference in character between both the 1915–16 shooting of Armenian men and the forced death marches of women and children on the one hand, and, on the other, the forced transfer of Christian Armenian children to Turkish families? Is there not a qualitative difference between the slaughter – by club, poison and gun – of 10,000 Aborigines in Queensland between 1824 and 1908 and the assimilation of 'half-caste' Aboriginal children in the nineteenth and twentieth centuries? Is there not a difference in nature between Hitler's extermination of three million Polish Jews between 1939 and 1945 because he wanted every Jew dead and the mass murder in 1648–49 of 100,000 Polish Jews by General Bogdan Chmielnicki because he wanted to end Polish rule in the Ukraine and was prepared to use Cossack terrorism to kill Jews in the process? The genre of the crime is not contingent on arithmetic; it is intent which differentiates.

Britain's colonial attempt, under Lord Milner, to anglicise South African schools and to abolish the Afrikaans language at the beginning of the twentieth century is not a crime of the same genre as the killing of millions of Armenians, Jews or Russian land-owning peasants. I assert the need for precision in language and the necessary subdivisions of the crime, in terms of both its quality and its quantity. I cannot subscribe to Israel Charny's notion that 'if the deaths of 500,000 people occurred . . . because of a nuclear-plant accident that the government didn't plan, want or celebrate, it is still genocide, which to me means the murder of a mass of people, even though there was less intention than indifference, stupidity, and avarice at work in creating the evil' (Charny, 1994: 83). A leak occurred in an unpressurised nuclear reactor at a place called Chernobyl, Ukraine, in 1986: 250 died and thousands, perhaps tens of thousands, were irradiated. Poisonous methyl isocyanate escaped at the American Union Carbide factory at Bhopal, India, in 1984: 2,600 died there and some 300,000 suffered long-term ill health. Whatever we call these events, they weren't genocide, as intent was lacking.

It is important to identify aims, intent, method and outcomes so that we don't flatten the events in the manner of Dwight MacDonald and Ernest Nolte. In 1957, MacDonald, a liberal American analyst, wrote a book of essays called *The Responsibility of Peoples*. He managed to convey the message that Belgian bastardliness in the Congo and British bastardliness in bombing Dresden were, generically, on a similar plane or planet to German barbarism towards the Jews. Nolte, the contemporary German historian, equates what the Germans did at Auschwitz with what the Americans, or specifically Lieutenant Malcolm Calley, did at My Lai in Vietnam (1988). With such 'comparative trivialisation', we acquiesce in the demise of genocide and its meaning. If everything that results in the killing of more than a handful of people is genocide, then nothing is genocide. There is no need of the word, the idea, the crime or its analysis. It is essential to know what it is that we want to remember, or to forget or to forgive.

Officially recorded memory: war crimes trials

Every act of genocide in the twentieth century was met with fierce declarations that no stone would be left unturned in bringing the perpetrators to retributive justice. When, for example, the first news of the deportations and massacres of Armenians reached the West in May 1915, the Allied powers declared:

> In view of this new crime of Turkey against humanity and civilisation, the Allied Governments make known to the Sublime Porte that they will hold all members of the Turkish Government, as well as those officials who have participated in these massacres, personally responsible.
>
> Hovannisian, 1968: 147

'When the hour for legitimate reparations shall have struck', France declared she would not forget the 'terrible trials of the Armenians' (*Le Temps*, 7 November 1918). In September 1942, in the House of Commons, Winston Churchill expressed his horror at the deportations of the Jews from France: 'When the hour of liberation strikes Europe, as strike it will, it will also be the hour of retribution.'[7] These sentiments, in virtually identical terms, have come from Western governments ever since, except perhaps in the case of Rwanda.

It was the Turkish and German governments, rather than the Allied powers, which held war crimes trials after World War I. Therein, of course, lay their weakness. Vahakn Dadrian's analysis reveals the extent of the reluctance of domestic governments to prosecute their own for war crimes (Dadrian, 1989: 221–334; see also Yeghiayan, 1990). He also reveals how international political considerations quickly overtook the urge to punish and how ineffective a deterrent or preventive such trials can be when the accused fare so well.

Nevertheless, an Extraordinary Court Martial was instituted in Turkey in March 1919. It was meant to try 112 people, including the 'Big Seven', the leaders of the *Ittihad ve Terakki* Party, including Talat Pasha, Enver Pasha, Cemal Pasha, the medical killers Nazim and Sakir, members of two wartime cabinets, provincial governors and high-ranking military and political officers. The principal charges were 'massacres and unlawful, personal profiteering' therefrom. The trial was interrupted in May 1919 when the British insisted on removing sixty-four of the accused to Malta to await British justice. Very little happened to them. Of the forty-eight remaining, the 'execution of the crime of massacre' was proven against thirty-six; several were sentenced to death in absentia, others received fifteen years and a few were acquitted. Only three, all relatively minor officials, were executed. By January 1921, the courts martial had been abolished. Many of the accused escaped or were set free. It was left to Armenian 'avengers' to assassinate Talat, Sakir, Cemal and Enver. It is of interest that the self-confessed killer of Talat in Berlin, Soghomon Tehlirian, was acquitted by the German Criminal Court on the grounds of justifiable homicide for the atrocities committed by Talat.

What began as a strong cry for retribution ended in the weak whisper of amnesty, and a volume of denial thereafter. Nevertheless these courts martial were, in my view, as a Turkish newspaper editorial said in April 1919, 'the most important trial in the six-hundred year history of the Ottoman Empire'.

Was the (Holocaust) survivor right in lamenting 'And we shall be forgotten, drowned out by the voices of the poets, the jurists, the philosophers and the priests' (Borowski, 1976: 132)? Yes. And no. The *Takvimi Vekayi*, the official gazette of the Ottoman government, recorded the trials. And even if Ankara removed the gazette from circulation soon after its publication, the Armenian Patriarchate of Jerusalem has a copy which reminds us in perpetuity that the Turks themselves proved Turkish perpetration of the Armenian genocide.

Such has been the juggernaut of Turkish denial since then that the Permanent Peoples' Tribunal, founded by the Italian jurist Lelio Basso in 1976, was asked to sit in session in Paris in 1984 to determine whether Armenians were in fact victims of deportations and massacres in the Ottoman Empire, whether this constituted genocide, and if so, what were the consequences for the international community and the parties concerned (Permanent Peoples' Tribunal, 1985). The genocide by the Young Turks was confirmed and it was determined that present-day Turkey must 'assume responsibility without using the pretext of any discontinuity in the existence of the state to elude that responsibility'. Perhaps the most significant Tribunal conclusion was: 'This responsibility implies first and foremost the obligation to recognise officially the reality of this genocide and the consequent damages suffered by the Armenian people.' Here then, some sixty or more years after the events, was a re-trial, in effect a supplication to acknowledge, and to remember that something terrible had happened. It is also a struggle to reclaim the dignity of the victims (Adalian, 1991: 103).

The Leipzig trials of 1921–22 are not well enough known. The Allies had a choice: either occupy Germany, capture the men wanted for 'conventional war crimes' and try them, or allow the Germans to try their own. They allowed German jurisdiction. To placate Allied public opinion, the Germans prosecuted 901 cases of war crimes; 888 suspects were acquitted or summarily dismissed. Only twelve trials were held, half resulting in acquittals and half in ridiculously light sentences, 'dismal by any standard of retributive justice', as Dadrian observes. But they served a purpose. At the end of World War II, there could be no question of again permitting national jurisdiction. The way had been paved for the world's first international trial.

The Nuremberg Trials are well known. An international military tribunal, composed of two judges each from of the United Kingdom, the United States, France and Russia, tried twenty-two Nazi leaders for:

- crimes against peace, that is, waging war;
- crimes against humanity, that is, deportations and, in effect, genocide;
- war crimes, that is, violations of the laws of war; and
- conspiracy to commit these three kinds of criminal acts.

Twelve were sentenced to be hanged, three to life imprisonment, four were sentenced to fifteen to twenty years' imprisonment and three were acquitted. The importance of Nuremberg was that individuals as well as states were considered responsible and made punishable for crimes against international law. Much of the criticism of these trials has been that they were a veneer of legality to cover expressions of vengeance. But since when has controlled (rather than lynch-style) vengeance and retribution not been part of the criminal sanction system?

There were, in addition, trials of Germans in German courts for acts contravening German law. The majority of the judges were, or had been, Nazis: there were simply not enough 'clean' judges to try the cases. The general verdict is that too few were indicted, too many got light sentences and justice was not done. The Frankfurt Trial of the Auschwitz killers was perhaps the longest and most successful of the trials. Held between December 1963 and August 1965, only three of the twenty-one accused were acquitted, three were given 'life at hard labour' and most of the others received fairly severe sentences.

There is a tendency to disparage all efforts at judicial accountability for the World War II period. West Germany prosecuted over 106,000 cases between 1945 and 1995, with 6,198 receiving fifteen years or less, 166 sentenced to life and thirteen to death. True, some 98,000 cases were dismissed or resulted in acquittal due to cross-jurisdictional problems, defendants being unfit to stand trial, defendants dead by the time of the trial, defendants 'gone missing', and the absence of extradition treaties.[8] The East German courts did four times better, in terms of convictions; only 11 per cent of the 14,500 tried were acquitted, compared with 38 per cent of West German defendants.[9] Austria, the country with an inordinately high percentage of 'Final Solution' bureaucrats, began its trials before Nuremberg; 28,000 were brought to trial and some heavy sentences ensued, although most were pardoned or had their sentences reduced in the 1950s.[10] Importantly, all of these trials were based on the principle that crimes against humanity cannot be committed with impunity. They produced a judicial record, a tribute to history and a public awareness that something had happened. Historians now mine these resources, providing the evidence for such seminal works as Christopher Browning's *Ordinary Men* (1992) and Henry Friedlander's *The Origins of Nazi Genocide* (1995).

In 1993, the State of Bosnia-Herzegovina brought action against Yugoslavia (Serbia and Montenegro) before the International Court of Justice, charging:

> That Yugoslavia . . . must immediately cease and desist from all acts of genocide . . . including but not limited to murder; summary executions; torture; rape; mayhem; so-called 'ethnic cleansing'; the wanton devastation of villages, towns, districts and cities; the siege of villages . . . the starvation of the civilian population . . . the detention of civilians in concentration camps . . .[11]

The world's first international war crimes tribunal since Nuremberg, the Yugoslav War Crimes Tribunal, prosecuted its first case, in 1994, against a Bosnian Serb, Dusan Tadic, for serious offences too barbaric to describe (*Australian*, 9 November 1994). The Court, established by the UN Security Council, was funded to the extent of $15 million in 1994 and took a long eighteen months to constitute. By 2001, a number of prosecutions had succeeded, culminating in the arrest and indictment of Yugoslav President Slobodan Milosevic, and the sentencing of General Radislav Krstic to forty-six years in prison for the specific crime of genocide.

In 1996, the United States Holocaust Memorial Museum and the Library of Congress held a conference, 'Nuremberg and its Impact: 50 Years Later'. A key speaker was the brilliant and dynamic Benjamin Ferencz, the prosecutor in the *Einsatzgruppen* case. Bosnia, he said, represented two great disgraces: 'we let it happen' and while 60,000 NATO and 30,000 US troops were in the vicinity, 'they' – the perpetrators of genocide – 'walk the streets'. With some asperity, he says 'we are an uncivilised society': twenty million died in the first war in order to create the League of Nations; forty million died in the second one to create the UN Charter, and twenty million, at least, have died since then. In the end, we live amid a philosophy which says 'all of Bosnia is not worth one American soldier'. Auschwitz survivor and Nobel Laureate Elie Wiesel echoed these sentiments: 'It is [only] by condemning the executioners, by unmasking their dishonour, that we can bear witness for the victims' (*Time*, 7 August 1995).

Looking at the lack of progress fifty years on from Nuremberg, it is clear that war crimes tribunals are not the salvation of civilisation. Nor are they the vehicle for prosecuting the 'big fish', those who produce, inspire and implement the ideological imperative to annihilate. But, apart from their value in establishing a judicial record, they are humanity's appeal to law, and a major avenue to public awareness that something terrible indeed happened.

In November 1994, the UN created yet another international tribunal to try those responsible for genocide in Rwanda. Of interest is that Rwanda's opposition to the measure was based on the resolution's ruling out the possibility of a death penalty; the tribunal would, said Rwanda's UN ambassador, 'only appease the conscience of the international community rather than respond to the expectations of the Rwanda people' (*Australian*, 10 November 1994). One of the few pertinent questions about the world's attitude to these events was posed by British journalist Matthew Parris: 'Do Africans realise that the cruellest of the racisms they face lies not in the abuse they get from white trash, but in the tolerance [this racism] finds from the white elite?' (*The Times*, 11 April 1994). Since inception, at least 115,000 are awaiting trial, and by mid-2002, only eight had been convicted. The irony is that if these local trials go the full distance, they could result in the world's greatest instance of judicial killing.

Ethiopia has over a thousand men in the Addis Ababa jail awaiting trials for war crimes. Mahteme Solomon, the Minister of Justice, deemed trials essential to the post-genocide healing process: 'If we allow the perpetrators of the most horrendous deeds to go unpunished, we are simply inviting more terror' (*Australian*, 25 October 1994).

Since the 'success' of the Nuremberg process has been seen as scant, proponents of the 'truth' road to reconciliation in South Africa believed that that route would be more effective. In creating a Truth and Reconciliation Commission (TRC), the government wanted to establish 'as complete a picture as possible of the nature, causes and extent of gross violations of human rights' from 1 March 1960 to 1996. It gave amnesty to those confessing fully to crimes committed 'with a political objective', and talked of the need for reparations (estimated at R3 billion). Archbishop Desmond Tutu's TRC is a singularly Christian concept, one of sin, confession and absolution. He is committed to what he calls a new moral order, one in which truth prevails over lies, where it is 'not the Hitlers of the world who ultimately prevail, but its little people'. Why no spirit or system of retributive justice? Why allow the potentially disastrous practice of treating state crime as requiring no accountability and no responsibility? Why establish a political ethos which says, in effect, that state-organised criminality can be committed with impunity? Does it matter that one arch killer was Eugene de Kok – or is it more important to know that he (and so many others) worked for specific government agencies, entrusted with 'tasks'? There was no trial of the key issues: only voluntary confession that the killings and tortures were political, not criminal, that each confessor was acting on his own delusion that, for instance, some black children were terrorists, or would grow into terror- ists, usually of the communist variety. The state *qua* state is well and truly off the hook.

In December 1993, Australia disbanded the Special Investigations (or 'war crimes') Unit of the Attorney-General's Department. What began as a flurry of guilt for having so long denied that we ever allowed into the country so many Nazi officials, as part of our postwar immigration, ended in what many see as a whimper of three prosecuted cases, and a public hiss at the alleged costs – for nil returns.

More significant for my context than the outcome of the trials is the fact that we had trials at all. Within a week of my arrival in Australia in January 1961, I knew roughly how many Nazi war criminals were in Australia, several of them by name. So did the Jewish Council to Combat Fascism and Antisemitism. So did anyone who cared to know. (Someone needs to explain the silence between 1961 and April 1986, the month Mark Aarons, Pierre Vickery and John Loftus presented their research in a series, 'Nazis in Australia', broadcast in 'Background Briefing' on ABC radio.) But public policy differed markedly from that of the Jewish Council. Attorney-General Garfield Barwick refused a Russian request in 1961 for the extradition of Ervin Viks, chief of Security Police in the Tallin–Kharyus Prefecture, responsible for thousands of deaths. (In January 1962 he was tried in absentia by the Estonian Supreme Court and sentenced to death.) Barwick expressed his dilemma thus:

> On the one hand, there is the utter abhorrence felt by Australians for those offences against humanity to which we give the generic names of war crimes. On the other hand, there is the right of this nation, by receiving people into its country, to enable men to turn their backs on past bitternesses and to make a new life for themselves and for their families in a happier community . . . We think the time has come to close the chapter.
>
> Attorney-General's Department, 1993: 214–15

One can only wonder about Barwick's concerns for Viks's past bitternesses, the ones he should be free to turn his back on: was it that Jews existed, or that he had killed them, or that he hadn't killed enough of them?

The War Crimes Amendment Act 1988 must be remembered for the opposition it evoked from public figures (Bevan, 1994: 21–5). Senator John Panizza demanded to know why we were 'hauling these geriatrics before the court'. Senator John Stone contended that the legislation was (Prime Minister) Hawke wooing the Jewish vote. Senator David Brownhill said the Act had 'the potential to destroy the social fabric of Australian society'. The country, wrote the *Australian Financial Review*, 'was about to be torn apart'. A senior government adviser was upset that 'a nice 75-year-old German man who lived next door' turned into a 'dreaded Nazi'. Archbishop David Penman wanted to know if we were a nation of mercy and forgiveness or one of vengeance. Brigadier Alf Garland argued that you couldn't try 1940s' crimes with 1980s' morality. Judge Frank Moran predicted that the statute would become an ineradicable 'blot on Australia's criminal jurisprudence'. Justice Marcus Einfeld warned that justice would not flow from the bill.

Virtually the same sentiments were expressed in 1994 about the amendments to the Racial Hatred Bill, clauses seeking to criminalise hate propaganda and racial vilification. Ivan Polyukhovich's defence tried to invalidate the War Crimes Amendment Act on the grounds that it went beyond the external affairs power of the Commonwealth and that section 9 usurped the judicial powers of the Commonwealth, as provided in the Constitution.[12] By six votes to one, the Court ruled that the retrospective nature of the Act did not diminish the Commonwealth's power to deal with external and defence matters. But by four votes to three, it ruled, in effect, that the trial of World War II criminals did not usurp the judicial power of the Commonwealth.[13] Brennan J. said it would be wrong 'to select a specific group of persons *from a long time past* out of all those who have committed, or are suspected of having committed, war crimes in other armed conflicts' (my emphasis). Genocide, he argued, was not a crime until 1948, so the charge of that crime was not available at the time of the Jewish, Gypsy and other deaths. The Germany of 1941 to 1945, the killing Germany, was too far away, too remote from today's Australia. Toohey J. epitomised the moral issue: 'It would be to turn a blind eye to history to see no connection.' The survivors indeed came perilously close to being like Primo Levi's *sommersi*, drowned by the judicial voices. History, too, by one vote in seven, was nearly submerged (Jones, 1991).

Graham Blewitt's report on Australian war crimes trials provides a full background to reports of Nazis in Australia, to the work of Mark Aarons (2001), to the Menzies Review, to the major investigations, to the sources of the allegations, to details of trial issues abroad, to the details of the cases against Ivan Polyukhovich, Mikolay Berezovsky and Heinrich Wagner and to the issues still confronting Australia (Attorney-General's Department, 1993: 214–15).

What Blewitt doesn't mention, surprisingly, is the outstanding work of Sydney's Professor Richard Wright and his colleagues, undertaken to substantiate witnesses' claims. Here was the first forensic archaeology of modern genocide. In the absence of documentation about mass graves in parts of the Ukraine, here was skeletal and anatomical evidence beyond dispute. At the Serniki gravesite in the Ukraine, 553 bodies were examined; sixty-three belonged to females up to nine years of age; 410 had suffered bullet wounds to the head; the bullets were 9mm German ammunition, with cartridges stamped with years of manufacture, between 1939 and 1941. Hair subjected to carbon-dating showed death before the advent of hydrogen-bomb testing, therefore before the early 1950s. In short, there was irrefutable proof of mass murder of Jews, by Germans and their assistants, within specific time spans, impeccable corroborative evidence that one living witness did indeed see what he claimed to have seen (Bevan, 1994: 53–4, 84–5). (Some of these bullets are now displayed at the Sydney Jewish Museum.)

In spite of the weaknesses and so-called poor outcomes of past trials, for me the trials are much more than punitive prison sentences for men like Klaus Barbie. Irrespective of outcome, they posit a *prima facie* case that certain events were undertaken by specific individuals on behalf of specific nations. They establish who were victims and who were perpetrators. The Treblinka and Auschwitz trials in German courts[14] established that death for Jews and Gypsies was processed at places called Treblinka and Auschwitz, that these places and programmes were not and are not fabrications of Jewish hoaxers or fictions of Hollywood film-makers.

Trials produce contemporaneous documents, with an authenticity sometimes lacking in post-event materials. Trials produce eye-witnesses from among the victims, the perpetrators and 'third parties', that is, the 'associates' and bystanders. Those who, because of their 'sparse' outcome, oppose trials, misconceive the process: trials are not undertaken in the belief that every case will be won and that all those charged will be convicted. There is some deterrence in the mere fact of a trial, not simply in a conviction or heavy punishment. Trial is an articulation by the state that an evil of some kind is believed to have occurred. Trial is contention, debate, under strict rules of evidence, in a legal theatre. Trial is as much of a public declaration as we can get that there are moral and ethical values which society wishes, or needs, to sustain. Trial records – whether of Polyukhovich here or of Finta in Canada[15] – are, in my opinion, infinitely more powerful educative tools about contemporary social and political history than the passive voice and the indirect speech of history texts, or of books such as this one.

At the International Association of Genocide Scholars conference in Minneapolis in June 2001, Judge Gabrielle Kirk McDonald reflected on her role as president of the *ad hoc* Rwandan Tribunal. In her last adjudication, she said, she wrote a 350-page judgment – as the indelible record of what happened. That, she believes (as I do), will remain the best record of that history, an Everest that later denialists will have difficulty surmounting.

Given that organised forgetting and/or calculated denialism are rampant, such trials tell us what occurred, quite apart from the guilt or innocence of those nice old men living next door. Trial records last longer in archives than do superseded textbooks in libraries. Trials which produce the horrifically rich fruits of scientific archaeology will remain, if not in everyone's memory, then in the readily retrievable and displayable record of the past.

Dadrian speculates that the Young Turks were encouraged in their war against the Armenians precisely because there had been no trials or punishment following Sultan Hamid's massacres of Armenians between 1894 and 1897. He argues convincingly that genocidal behaviour without accountability led to an ethos of committing genocide with impunity.

The failures of the Turkish and Leipzig trials led the Allies to adopt very different procedures after World War II. Nuremberg was not only a military court of occupation but also an international court. However, Dadrian wonders 'whether Nuremberg might have been contemplated at all, let alone instituted, if only the Jews and to some extent the Gypsies [at that time two vulnerable minorities with no parent-state to press for punitive justice] had been the sole victims of the Nazis'. He reminds us of Oliver Wendell Holmes's dictum: there is no substitute for lived experience as an *animus* for law-making (Dadrian, 1997: 416). When our nation stands silent for two minutes, at 11 a.m. every 11 November, we experience just how much the lived experience of the past is the spur to something we so openly call Remembrance Day.

I join Dadrian in suggesting that genocide studies reveal an embodiment of the concept of 'worthy and unworthy victims'. In Europe, Jews and Gypsies were not worthy of serious rescue, or of serious bombing of the Auschwitz railway lines. (As to black Rwandans awaiting trial, one of my former students suggests that in relation to Africa there is an even more alarming Western concept emerging from the Rwandan events – 'unworthy perpetrators'.)

Wiedergutmachung *and reparations*

Is there any connection between memory and money, between victim insistence on the past and perpetrator insistence on the present and future, between their demands or cries for reparation and those on whom the demands are made? Yes, of course.

In Australia, the late Professor W.E.H. (Bill) Stanner asserted 'we can neither undo the past nor compensate for it: . . . the most we can do is give the living their due' (Harris, 1979: vii). The late Aboriginal poet, Kevin Gilbert, was tougher: 'Two hundred years after the original theft it is still possible for public opinion to make governments cease compounding the felony and to make restitution to the victims' (ibid.).

When I was young, I prized the German word *Wiedergutmachung*, 'making good again'. It sounded profound and exotic, more attractive than the dour word 'reparations'. With study, it became obvious what an appalling term it is. How, in God's name, does one make good again the Armenian *vilayets* of Erzurum, Bitlis, Trebizond, Sivas, Kharput, Cilicia and Anatolia? Or the communities of Vilna, Vienna, Shavli, Schitomir, Riga, Kovno, Nowogrodek, Belgrade, Warsaw, Lodz and Lublin, to name but a handful? Or the Romany of most of Europe? Or the great majority of black Australians? One needs the exquisitely painful poem of Don Pagis to tell us about making good again.

Draft of a Reparations Agreement

All right, gentlemen who cry blue murder as always,
nagging miracle-makers,
quiet!
Everything will be returned to its place,
paragraph after paragraph.
The scream back into the throat.
The gold teeth back to the gums.
The terror.
The smoke back to the tin chimney and further on and inside
back to the hollow of the bones,
and already you will be covered with skin and sinews and you will
    live,
look, you will have your lives back,
sit in the living room, read the evening paper.
Here you are. Nothing is too late.
As to the yellow star:
it will be torn from your chest
immediately
and will emigrate
to the sky.

Weissbort, 1993: 223

Stanner, Pagis and Elie Wiesel are 'emotionally correct' as there can be no amends to the maimed, the tortured and the slaughtered. Yet I am conscious of Gilbert's intellectual view; even when confronting Primo Levi's paths of ashes, I contrive to be, but don't always succeed in being, impressed by the genius of the late French writer Georges Perec, a Holocaust survivor: 'There is no epoch', he wrote, 'no condition, no crisis that the mind cannot grasp; there is no anarchy that cannot be ordered, no situation that cannot be mastered, no phenomenon that reason and language, feeling and rationality cannot conquer' (Bellos, 1993: 277). This echoes Dr Abraham Wajnryb, a man who had a defiant need to make sense of, and extract meaning from, the meaninglessness of the Holocaust (Hunter, 1997). I am swayed by the rationality, in 1919, of Australia's Prime Minister, Billy Hughes, who defined the issue before the Commission on (German) Reparation:

No wrong without remedy. Whatever the nature of the wrong – whether to life, limb, health, property, or any other right, the wrong-doer must, as far as he can, make reparation for the wrong. As it is between individuals, so it must be between states. That is the reign of law; that is the principle of justice.

Baruch, 1920: 289–315

I am persuaded by the pragmatic Scots who devised the notion of reparation as a civil law remedy, the payment of money for one who suffers injury or financial loss as a result of a legal wrong (Secretary of State for Scotland, 1977). I am convinced of some value in the remedy of restitution, by which a court orders a wrong-doer to restore moveable property, including money, to an aggrieved person. However, I do appreciate what victims mean by 'blood money'. In most instances, such money must be avoided.[16] But if you can't give back the ungivable, or restore the unrestorable, then we are left with only one thing – money. It was in 1625 that Grotius, a father of international law, said 'money is the common measure of all things'. To refuse the monetary compensation is to refuse the atonement. And that is what Hughes said we must never do: never let the wrong-doer escape his action, his confession, his guilt and his expiation.

The Allies duly sought reparations as a form of moral retribution, of atonement. The payments were as much moral–political as economic. The War Guilt Clause of the Versailles Treaty assigned responsibility for the war to Germany, a charge Germany acknowledged. There would be reparations to civilians for acts of cruelty, violence or maltreatment, including imprisonment, deportation and internment; for acts injurious to civilian health, to capacity to work, or to honour; for maltreatment of prisoners of war; for forced labour without pay; for damage to property by confiscation or destruction.

I don't have to traverse the Holocaust here. What is more important than any history I might recount are the documents consequent upon the Holocaust: the UN's 'Principles of International Law Recognised in the Charter and Judgment of the Nuremberg Tribunal', the UN Convention on Genocide, the German Federal Indemnification Law, and the Israeli–German restitution agreement. The first two of these are well rehearsed, but the last two are worth some elaboration.

The Indemnification Law begins by admitting that a wrong was committed upon people by reason of their race, faith or ideology. Claimants thus include those 'deliberately or frivolously killed or driven to death', or their successors; 'persecutees' who were subjected to treatment 'unworthy of a human being', who were deprived of liberty through 'preventive custody, penal imprisonment, detention in a concentration camp or forced to stay in a ghetto'. The very language shows how much graver the offences were the second time Germany was found guilty.

In September 1952, the German Federal Republic and Israel signed an agreement on reparation. Israel was to receive US$850 million in cash and goods over twelve years. A further DM450 million was to be paid to the Conference on Jewish Material Claims, which represented Diaspora Jewry, and to individuals who suffered under the Nazis, in the form of individual restitution. These payments were meant to end in 1964, but continued into the 1990s. As the new millennium began, major German industries began restitution payments for slave labourers, albeit fifty-eight or more years after the events.

What cannot be left unsaid here is that, in 1980, a West German official referred to the demands for reparation by Gypsies as both 'unreasonable' and 'slanderous'. Further, the Mayor of Darmstadt told the Council of Sinti and Romany (two of the tribes comprising the Gypsies) that their request to be included in remembrance ceremonies to mark the liberation of Bergen–Belsen 'insulted the honour' of the memory of the Holocaust (Young, 1997).[17]

The Armenian people have been denied any form of recompense since the Ataturk government began its step-by-step denialism in 1919.

The Aboriginal search for both acknowledgement and recompense has been long and painful (see, *inter alia*, Tatz, 1983: 291–306). Land rights, in all but Western Australia and Tasmania, have been achieved with varying degrees of reluctance on the part of, and legal challenge by, state and territory governments. Claims about possession and dispossession climaxed in the Mabo and Wik cases, the implications of which have yet to be fully worked out. There have been nearly two decades of rodomontade about a treaty, with continuing argument (Brennan, 1992). Elsewhere I have argued strongly that if we are serious about any kind of reparation, we need to avoid the oft-quoted Canadian model of a negotiated settlement (a continuation of the treaty-making process) as the *only* way to go forward (Tatz, 1983:

300–301).[18] It would help to look to the German models. Stanley Tipiloura, a former Aboriginal Australian Labor Party member of the Northern Territory Legislative Council, has argued: 'Compensation does not necessarily mean money. It means the creation of jobs, health services and so on' (Brennan, 1992: 54). This notion is shared by several Aboriginal leaders but, as I pointed out earlier, Aboriginal frustration at any real change in their conditions, at the continuing refusal of the federal government to establish a reparations tribunal (as recommended by a Senate committee), has led to a greater clamour for symbolic and substantial financial compensation.

John Howard, when Leader of the federal Liberal Opposition in 1989, declared, in the name of the just society, that there could be no special favours, no positive discriminations for any one group, especially not for Aborigines. He pledged repeal of the existing land rights legislation simply because no other group has such special benefits. In office, he didn't repeal these laws but he went a long way towards their diminution. More of this philosophy emerged from the Liberals and Nationals in the 1990s and early 2000s, essentially proclaiming that, as of today, all are equal and none should be advantaged over another.

Never mentioned by the conservative side of Australian politics are the original reasons for legislation which attempted to truly protect, advantage or compensate Aborigines and Islanders. Not mentioned is the fact that no other group has such a disadvantaged history. One could, with charity, dismiss much of the rhetoric as mere election 'Howard-speak'. But in one short sentence, Howard obliterated – as did Canadian Prime Minister Pierre Trudeau in the 1960s, before he changed his views in the 1970s – all indigenous personal, social, political, economic, cultural and legal history. The Howard–Trudeau 'just society' proposition clearly implies that, as of a certain date, all previous histories and legacies are expunged to make way for, at best, a clean slate, or, at worst, a post-reconciliation one.

There are two implications of this philosophy, each with devastating consequences. Aborigines, like new immigrants, have 'just arrived'; in order to share in the 'just' and 'equal' society they must compete on equal terms. All past violations are to be totally disregarded and therefore any form of atonement and compensation rejected. If the memories haunt, the remedy is simply to exorcise them. The unhappy historical periods are at a great distance, like a century ago. Meanwhile, as opposed to those of ill will but with long and resentful memories, the 'good' people preach reconciliation. They argue for a sharing of the future at the price of closing the chapters on the past. The victim must forgive the perpetrator, clearing the record and the perpetrator's conscience. 'Let's turn over a new leaf and begin again' is a commonplace in reconciliation rhetoric. Its proponents never acknowledge what the old leaf was or what it is that is to begin again. Nor do they ever spell out what it is that Aborigines should cease doing by way of injury to the mainstream. This must be the best imaginable bargain for the reconciliationists.

Where lies recompense for victims of genocide? There is the first-blush response of revenge and retribution, in the manner of Churchill. Then follows a military tribunal as at Nuremberg, soon overtaken by the newer considerations such as the Cold War and the *realpolitik* that it would be better to turn Nazi Werner von Braun and his ilk into American citizen-heroes. There is reparation for some Jews, but patently not for the dead and not for all those surviving. There is the Tribunal in Turkey of 1918–19, soon overtaken by fresh killings until 1922, since followed by the extra-ordinary denial machinery put in place by Turkey. There is denial, the refusal to concede a 'labour of mourning' through vigorous Turkish contention that there was and is nothing to mourn. Ultimately, in our context, there is refuge in the argument that we shouldn't judge yesterday by the standards of today – that, somehow, the passage of time, however short, exculpates and exonerates that which was manifestly evil even then.

THE POLITICS OF APOLOGY

Reconciliation in our time

'The past is a foreign country; they do things differently there' is how Leslie Hartley begins his novel *The Go-Between* (1953: 9). In similar vein, genocide is foreign to those of us who consider ourselves apart from 'them', the ones who did things differently, who perpetrated mass destruction of human life in some past time, in some other disconnected or unconnected place. This notion of foreignness reached its highest point when the world, including Australia, pointed, with undertones of racist simplicity, to the tribal nature of the Hutu–Tutsi conflict, something stemming from deepest and darkest Africa.

We live in times of sharp social, legal and economic divisions, here and abroad. We have started the new millennium with the belief (or the hope) that by the effluxion of time, experience and growth, it should be a much better one. We point to virulent nationalism and its legions of dead. We deplore the fact that bitter memories of recent past conflicts between clans, tribes, factions, ethnicities and nations led to catastrophes in Bosnia, Serbia, Somalia, Rwanda, Burundi, Sudan, the Middle East, Greece, Turkey, Spain, East Timor and Indonesia.

We deplore the recent violent politics of remembering so explicit in, for example, the Zulu Inkatha movement. We preach, instead, a politics of forgetting, of reconciliation and peace: Nelson Mandela and Desmond Tutu, the arch reconciliators of our time; Arafat, for a brief moment, then Barak and now even Sharon talking about 'the Middle East peace process'; Clinton and the North Koreans; Bush Jr and China; Jimmy Carter and Cuba; Gerry Adams, the IRA and British prime ministers; France still haunted by its collaborationist past; Chileans trying to put Pinochet behind them; (former) President Menem urging that no one look back to Argentinian military atrocities over a decade ago.[19]

The Vatican, as we have seen, has apologised for its responses during the Holocaust, East Germany said 'sorry' to the Jews minutes before reunification and Poland followed suit. 'One cannot dwell constantly on memories and resentments', pleaded François Mitterrand in 1994, while haunted by his labours for Vichy and his friendship with the infamous secretary-general of the Vichy Police, René Bousquet.[20] In Australia, the Aboriginal Reconciliation Council yielded little, after ten years, but a mantra for political party correctness.

Reconciliation appeals as a sane approach, ethical and moral, especially in colonial contexts like the United States and Australia. The word seems to resonate a merciful Christ rather than an unforgiving Jehovah. It offers hope, harmony and 'humane-ness'. It suggests an end to enmity and a settling of differences. And so a shibboleth is born, a catchphrase adopted by opinion-makers to discern those who, stubbornly and wrongly, resist the entwined and 'synonymous' notions of 'forgive and forget'. If the politics of remembering the feuds, the hatreds and the differences results in even more cataclysmic deaths, surely, they say, it must be replaced with an ideology of forgiving and forgetting.

There are costs in this new fashion, costs to the victims. It is they who must forgo the desire or need for retributive justice. It is they who must eschew notions of guilt and atonement and, all too often, any reparations, restitution or compensation for harms done to them. It is they who must agree to the diminution, or even abolition, of that shared historical memory that holds victim groups together. It is they who must concur in the substitution of their memory with our memory and their history with our history. It is they who must connive at ignoring the importance of accountability for the crimes against them, and agree to the blurring or obliteration of responsibility for who did what to whom. It is they who must cease being so hysterical about denialism, that major tributary of forgetting, which claims that there was nothing to remember in the first place.

Such are the unwelcome consequences of the philosophy of 'forgive and forget'. Such is the politics of conjoining two words with such different meanings, interpreted quite differently by the historians and the victims.

Saying sorry, Australian-style

Acknowledgement isn't necessarily apology, let alone remorse or restitution, but apology implies acknowlededgment. The Australian public has responded to the *Bringing Them Home* national inquiry in a quite unprecedented way: hundreds of thousands have signed 'sorry books', thousands stood in queues to listen to removed people telling their stories, many more thousands still plant small wooden hands, signifying their hands up to guilt or sorrow, on lawns and beaches across the country. The Australian Labor Party has pledged apology on its return to office. State governments, churches, mission societies, city and shire councils proclaim both sorrow and apology. Their sincerity is not the issue – it is their symbolism which matters. Minogue disparages this 'festival of National Sorry Day, with its apparatus of sorry books, tearfulness and a minute's silence'. Even if one concedes that this is 'trendy breast-beating', it is significant because so many Australians have actually done something by way of acknowledgement. And acknowledgement, however 'shallow' or 'chic', is one of the antidotes to denialism.

Acknowledgement is often an expression of regret, remorse, sorrow or a sense of shame, but not necessarily of personal guilt. Jeremy Weber suggests that while regret doesn't have to involve personal guilt, it does imply a deep sense of responsibility, 'the civic responsibility that comes from membership in a society that cares about its present moral character' (Weber, 1995: 10). Gaita (1998) says: 'We didn't know because we didn't care enough.' True, but with more knowledge of what indeed happened, now is a time for regret that we neither knew nor cared.

The outstanding and formidable exception to the flow and to this incipient social movement of regret is the present Coalition federal government. The then Deputy Prime Minister, Tim Fischer, didn't believe his generation 'should accept the guilt of the previous one' (*Sydney Morning Herald*, 14 January 1993). The Prime Minister offered a personal gesture but claims that to apologise formally is to open the way to huge claims of compensation. He also contends that he cannot apologise on behalf of Australia because the nation comprises many migrant groups who were or are innocent of any of these actions. Yet most ethnic groups have, on their own initiative, made official apology on behalf of their nation, Australia.

The Conservative government talks about these events as being removed from our time and values. Not discussed by anyone in this context is the reality that, in 1949, while Australia unambiguously ratified an international treaty which defined forcible removal of children as a crime in international law, it continued a vigorous practice of removal well beyond that date. Repeal of the 'removal' laws began only in 1964, and continued, one state at a time, until 1984. The last blatant removal of a child was in Perth in 1970, when the authorities defied a judge's order to restore a child to its natural parent. Others, not so blatant, went way beyond 1970. The 'assimilation factories' ceased only very recently: the St Francis Home and Colebrook in South Australia in 1957 and 1978 respectively, the Retta Dixon Home in Darwin in 1980, Sister Kate's Home in Perth in 1987, and lastly, Bomaderry in New South Wales in 1988.

How do we date 'yesteryear'? Many of the stolen are of the same age as the Prime Minister and his then Minister for Aboriginal Affairs, Senator Dr John Herron, and some are the ages of the Ministers' children. Barbara Cummings is alive and well, or as well as being raised in the Retta Dixon home has allowed her to be. Her *Take This Child* (1990) is the recognised history of removal, and recent removal at that, in the Northern Territory.

The problem of removal is not confined to past generations; it continues affecting many people who are alive today. Removal may affect future generations, especially if the ideas suggested by Western Australia's former Police Commissioner, Bob Falconer, ever come to fruition. Deploring what he called 'Fagin-like behaviour' – Aboriginal families sending children 'barely able to see over the counter' to rob fast-food outlets – he suggested that such children ('too young to be charged') be removed from their families and placed with suitable carers. (*Canberra Times*, 24 August 1998). His 'call' was backed by the then Premier, Richard Court. Falconer's suggestion was born out of realism, he claimed, not racism; further, 'this will not create another stolen generation.' He and his colleagues may well have a genuine concern for children likely to become 'hardened criminals by the time they are 14 or 15', but one has to ask whether such a suggestion could ever emanate from any police commissioner about white children. The mindset of Western Australians towards Aborigines has a long history. And it should be noted that throughout Australia, white children at risk are usually a welfare agency matter, whereas Aboriginal children are inevitably a police matter.

Since the early 1990s, an interesting development in the Western world has been the willingness of some governments to make sense of themselves as a people, to face their national history, to acknowledge it, to express regret, and to offer some form of reparation or restitution. Apart from those countries in Roy Brooks's book (1999), other countries have come to terms with their pasts. In New Zealand, the 1840 Treaty of Waitangi has been ruled a legally enforceable instrument, resulting in a special Waitangi Tribunal which listens to Maori claims and makes substantial compensations – such as the Ngai Tahu (South Island) settlement of 1997. The Crown has apologised for its failure 'to act towards Ngai Tahu reasonably and with the utmost good faith'; it has restored Maori authority over lakes, mountains and other properties; and provided, at least, $170 million in compensation (*The Press*, Christchurch, 24 September 1997).[21] South Africa has faced the horrific past, at least the past since 1960, through its Truth and Reconciliation Commission (TRC), and there is ongoing discussion about the size and nature of reparation. A possibly noble but very flawed exercise, the TRC at least exhibited the recent past and limited the outrageous lie that began in April 1994 – that only a handful of white South Africans were complicit and every other white citizen was either opposed to the system or was a closet freedom fighter. At least another twenty-seven nation states have justice and reconciliation mechanisms in operation.

In 1996, Canada's Royal Commission on Aboriginal Peoples concluded that 'there must be an acknowledgment that great wrongs have been done to Aboriginal people', the 506,000 First Nations and Inuit who now form 1.7 per cent of the population; that the premises of the philosophy 'all Canadians are equal are very wrong'; that the 'equality approach', which ignores inequalities, 'is the modern equivalent of the mindset that led to the *Indian Act*, the residential schools, the forced relocations, and the other nineteenth-century instruments of assimilation' (Minister of Supply and Services, 1996: 9). Ottawa has given some $350 million to community-based healing initiatives for victims of this schooling system. A further $30 million was made available for out-of-court settlements of individual cases. Above all, both Canada and the United States have accorded 'first nation' status to Indians, recognising them as people who had prior occupation, sovereignty and governance, and have engaged them in true conversation about renegotiating understandings, treaties and compacts. The creation of Canada's newest province, Nunavut, as home of the Inuit people, is the culmination of that fresh thinking.

We shrink and retreat from any and all such notions. For ten years we had an embattled official Aboriginal Reconciliation Council trying to work with a national government intent on deflecting, playing down or distorting the past, a government which was rigid in its adherence to a philosophy of 'One Australia' in which all are 'equal', irrespective of both historical and present-day inequalities. If the former colonial dominions were to be viewed as competing to address and redress the past as a way of confronting the present and handling the future, Australia would be running a clear last.

In the 'Four Corners' programme of the Australian Broadcasting Commission on the eve of the 1998 election, John Howard conceded that his greatest mistake in his first term of office was the tone of his speech, and his refusal at the National Reconciliation Conference in Melbourne in May 1997 to announce a formal Commonwealth apology for the removal of children.[22] 'Our history is not without blemish', he conceded, after two and a half years of asserting something very different.[23] Political analyst Gerard Henderson suggested that there are 'signs of a softer Howard' and the Prime Minister himself declared his 're-invention' for the new millennium (*Sydney Morning Herald*, 13 and 15 November 1998). The Prime Minister has, however, consistently refused to consider a treaty: that implies two nations, he argues, a notion he 'will never accept'. He contemplates a pact, 'a document which would attempt to, sort of, set some of these things out'. On the other hand, the Reverend Tim Costello has criticised Howard's desire for a written understanding from Aborigines that their 'first and foremost allegiance is to Australia and nothing else'. This, he says, sounds like *'Deutschland Uber Alles'* – 'it reveals a homogenising instinct' (*Sydney Morning Herald*, 7 November 1998).

Tim Costello's comment is a neat shorthand for what Higgins calls Australia's ethnic nationalism.[24] Australia, he contends, rests not on civic nationalism, which insists on the inclusiveness of all and the dignity of citizenship as the measure of a nation's worth, which Howard would claim, but on an exclusive white, ethnic nationalism which Howard himself represents, as the basis for belonging. Denialism, Higgins argues, is strongest in such societies, including Australia:

> Ethnic nationalism relies on unilinear, essentialist narratives that emphasise the ethnic group's unique destiny or chosenness, innocent victimhood, set of virtues and heroic deeds. The darker side of actual national pasts and presents contradicts this sort of narrative, and has to be suppressed.

It may be possible for a 'softer', re-invented Howard, or for his successor, to construct an observable strategy for 'reconciliation', one that enables better relations with Aboriginal leaders and communities. To this end, he made what at first (but only at first) looked like a significant Ministerial appointment. In 2001, Herron was effectively sacked as Minister for Aboriginal Affairs and the portfolio was given to Phillip Ruddock, Minister for Immigration, who would also be responsible for the separate portfolio of reconciliation.[25] Once upon a time, Ruddock had a sensitive and abiding interest in Aboriginal issues. No longer, it would seem. His appointment and the new strategy could not, and did not, work in the absence of a formal, national apology. An editorial view in the *Sydney Morning Herald* was that reconciliation implies a meeting of hearts and minds, 'not a patronising attempt to dictate the terms of a relationship', a relationship that must begin with apology (16 November 1998). Robert Manne described the Prime Minister's belief that he could deny the recent past, refuse to apologise and keep his reputation intact as being 'symptomatic of a kind of blindness which, in parts of Australia, has not yet been overcome' (*Sydney Morning Herald*, 19 November 1998).

With blindness, there is also deafness. The senior conservative leaders have no real conversation or dialogue with Aborigines and if there is 'consultation', any opposition to the ruling mindset is simply not heard. In 1998, Gaita's conference paper 'Responding to ancestors' made a pertinent reference to philosopher Martin Buber's *Ich und Du* (*I and Thou*).[26] Between humans, it is possible to enter a relationship, a true dialogue, with the fullness of one's being. Generally, Buber wrote, we enter relationships not with the fullness of our being but only with some fraction of it. The Aboriginal–non-Aboriginal relationship seems to me to be based on the minutest of fractions.

It seems unlikely that Prime Minister Howard can ever locate, within himself, a sense of real understanding and true appreciation of the recency and privity of so much Aboriginal mistreatment, let alone the legal connection between the sovereign Australia of yesterday and its successors in office today. Nor is he likely to 'find' a genuine respect or even liking for indigenous Australians, or come to see the truth of the venerable Aristotelian doctrine that treating unequals equally is as unfair as treating equals unequally.

Archie Cameron and Leslie Haylen were wrong fifty years ago. Australia's behaviour is now before the bar of public opinion, it is now on the international conference agenda, and now genocide in Australia is 'thinkable'. Minogue is quite wrong when he argues that Aborigines, or apologetic breast-beaters, or scholars like Professor Raimond Gaita have 'coined' the word genocide simply to escalate a national issue into an international one. The International Association of Genocide Scholars, meeting in Montreal in 1997, discussed the Australian case and passed strong resolutions addressed to the Prime Minister. The matter isn't, as the Prime Minister would have it, a relatively minor, purely domestic issue. It will continue to haunt him, and his place in Australian history.

In the *Kruger* case, Justice Mary Gaudron stated: 'If acts were committed with the intention of destroying the plaintiffs' racial group, they may be the subject of action for damages whether or not the Ordinance was valid.'[27] Indeed, a multitude of civil suits is under way.[28] In essence, these cases rest on several causes of action: wrongful imprisonment due to unlawful or *ultra vires* conduct, due to breach of duty of guardian, due to breach of statutory duty, due to breach of fiduciary duty, and due to breach of duty of care. The purpose of these cases won't be so much a matter of punitive damages as an acknowledgement that 'things' were done, that they were evil, worthy of an apology, even a token one, and a token of atonement (Schaefer, 1997: 22–4). Although two removed children, Gunner and Cubillo, lost their action in Darwin, the court found substantial evidence that many things had indeed 'happened', including sexual mistreatment in institutions. (The Christian Brothers, and several other church organisations, have now acknowledged the history of sexual abuse in their schools, have made reparation, albeit often as the price of silence, and expressed atonement.) The Commonwealth's defence in these cases will, however, continue to rest on the 'legitimacy' of the beliefs of the time, on the argument used in 1949 by federal Liberal MP Joe Gullett, about the German generals on trial, and how they 'carried out their duties as best they could', acting 'according to their lights' and 'in accordance with the ethics of their profession'.

Federal and state governments have steadfastly refused to entertain reparations or settlements. They insist that compensation will only be paid to those who can establish their claims in court, a costly exercise for all concerned, as the $11.5 million *Cubillo* and *Gunner* cases showed all too plainly. The $63 million finally allocated to Aborigines by the federal government is said to be not compensation, not restitution for what were, most dubiously, 'legitimate' beliefs at the time, but funding for counselling services, for efforts to reunite families and for the compilation of histories and genealogies of people affected by these practices.

EPILOGUE: TEACHING ABOUT GENOCIDE

Why reflect on genocide? Why spend so much time thinking, reading and teaching about this doom-laden side of the human condition? Why search for meaning in the 'unalloyed evil' – a term from my philosopher friend, the late Stanley Benn – that 'produced' some 174 million deaths in the twentieth century?[1]

Good enough questions, perhaps, as one laments the lack of punishment for those who committed the crimes, and the 'wilful impotence' of those who could do something but who do nothing, or very little, to prevent its constant recurrence.

Harold Lasswell (1958), the eminent American political scientist, once wrote that all of us should examine, at least once a year, who we are – in our houses, streets, suburbs, towns, states and nations. We ought to assess what values we hold, or can acquire, such as income, status, deference, physical safety, personality and skills, as in oratorical, technical, military, literary or sporting virtues. We would then be in a position to decide whether we wish to be contemplative or manipulative about who we are, what we have, or wish to achieve. He didn't use *manipulative* in a pejorative way: he simply meant that we should decide whether we are thinkers and accepters, or thinkers and doers. He made no judgment about which is the better approach, and nor do I.

By nature, I am a doer. But what can one do in this field? In 1981, Leo Kuper reflected that while 'the word is new, the concept is ancient'; and he had to, or we have to, try to break through both the condonation of, and indifference to, these cataclysmic events (1981: 9–11). It will be recalled that when Elie Wiesel was asked what anyone could do about the Holocaust, he replied that one must teach, and teach again. Teaching, of course, won't prevent genocide, but it will help lay bare that seemingly metahistorical phenomenon, which in the case of the Holocaust sometimes becomes an obscure, sacralised event. And so my contribution is to teach and to talk, perhaps even to preach.

What to teach?

Racism is a destructive, irrational behaviour rather than a mere mindset of prejudice. It is often translated into vicious practice and, often enough, into genocide. It has finally come to be seen for what it has long been, namely, the most important single cause of conflict in the modern era. Racism has displaced the confrontation between capitalism and communism, and the clash between conventional nationalisms. It may well culminate in the ultimate clash, 'the race war', as predicted by race scholars like Britain's Hugh Tinker (1979) and South Africa's Ronald Segal (1967).

The race problem is often diluted, masked or underrated by the social and socio-biological sciences. It isn't a subset of class or caste, or of 'social problems' or 'deviance' in sociology and anthropology courses. Moreover, antisemitism, in many ways the most radical form of racism, is frequently ignored altogether by social scientists. This primary case of racism is relegated to an intellectual ghetto – to a separate literature, a separate shelf in the library and a separate place in the curriculum, if it appears at all. Racism is thereby short-changed and miscast in most curricula; antisemitism, where it is acknowledged, is sidelined. Genocide, often a racial terminus, is hardly taught at all, and is still seen as the somewhat aberrant hobby-horse of several dozen enthusiasts around the world. Only twenty-two years ago Leo Kuper was battling for genocide to be recognised as a legitimate area of study at the University of California in Los Angeles.

I have taught many courses on racism and its manifestations. For years I examined the similarities and differences between the 'racisms' of South Africa, Australia, Canada, the United States, New Zealand, Israel and Britain. These are the societies I know best and where I have undertaken fieldwork. Inevitably, the focus has had to be on minorities of colour, on the policies and practices relating to them and on finding ways by which discrimination might be ended. Within this framework, there is a limited scope for the consideration of antisemitism. Not because there hasn't been any in the societies with which I have dealt. Among many others, such factors as eugenics, the use, abuse and politics of IQ testing, and immigration restrictions alone would provide ample material for an exploration of Wistrich's (1992) 'longest hatred'.

Inevitably, in students' minds, antisemitism loses out to the plight of the underprivileged: Jews in these particular contexts are always seen as privileged. It is the underprivileged who struggle for human rights, for freedom, citizenship and land rights; it is they who have to find, or 'we' who sometimes try to help them find, ways of attaining civil rights, slum clearance, equal opportunities, affirmative action mechanisms and anti-discrimination legislation.

Obviously, all of this is valid, and vital. But what is lacking, by the nature of the material, is a sense of distinction in the levels and degrees of racism. Disfranchisement, alcohol prohibition, the pass laws and the evils of migratory labour in South Africa; the imposition or destruction of tribalism; the Jim Crow laws and their application in the United States; the forcible removal of Aboriginal children; the experiences of 'coloured minorities' in Britain or Israel; and the gross inequalities in access to sport are seen and taught as being on a single plane of inequality. There is little appreciation that, at bottom, these issues are inevitably existential issues of *being, half-being,* or *simply not being.* Rather, we study *having* and *not having.* Rights are 'things' the oppressed seek, something you get or are denied, like packaged goods. This is the kernel of my being as a teacher and student: to illuminate that, at best, several victim groups had a life imposed on them that was second rate; but that at worst, other groups – Jews, Armenians, Aborigines – were denied life itself.

In the search for the right *to be* rather than *to have,* I turned to genocide studies. While the study of genocide must seek out its levels or degrees, at least there is no displacement of antisemitism; and such study is a vehicle, perhaps the best one, for showing the relativities of what befalls those who are perceived as different, castigated as different, treated as different and eliminated as anomalous human forms.

The teaching agenda

We – my colleagues from the Australian Institute for Holocaust and Genocide Studies and I – teach university, secondary school and adult education courses. What we do helps reflect genocide. We provide a mirror which gives an image of what happens when mass death and/or destruction of a people is intended. We try to make these events not merely apparent but plain. In another sense, we reflect on genocide by way of 'remembering with thoughtful consideration', a nice phrase from Noah Webster's dictionary.

The Judeocide presents us with the totality of, and the ultimate in, the human experience: from the unalloyed evil of Heydrich to the humanistic, even optimistic, hope inspired by some 19,141 (or more) righteous gentiles. In a grandiose way, wrote the eminent historian J.L. Talmon (1980: 30), the Holocaust confronts us with two diametrically opposed world views: between morality and paganism, between the sanctity of life and the cult of warfare, between equality of all and the supremacy of the select few, between justice and the discharge of uninhibited impulses.

Such universal issues demand serious attention in all educational and professional programmes. Matters of this magnitude cannot be squeezed into, at best, ten chronological lessons, from Haman to Hadrian to Hitler, in a separate school package called Jewish Studies. Nor can justice be done in university courses of one semester duration, usually of, at best, forty hours of face-to-face teaching. Further, if Holocaust education is to have both meaning and lasting impact, perhaps even just a fleeting impact, it should be incorporated into mainstream disciplinary teaching and not segregated into 'area' studies, 'special studies', 'Jewish Studies', 'special pleading studies'. Even then, the Holocaust, and genocide generally, is not the sole preserve of history, or sociology, psychology, politics or literature, but a proper subject for discussion in each of these disciplines.

First of all, we delve deeply into the two major genocides of the twentieth century, the attempted annihilation of the Armenians and the Jews. Only when we have explored those events as a template do we begin to assess whether other cases are, indeed, genocide or attempted genocide rather than mass murder, massacre, atrocity, war crimes or crimes against humanity.

Holocaust centres have little regard for definitions. For those who establish them, the very word *Holocaust* is enough. Most Holocaust scholars have concentrated on the interpretation of the event rather than on its definition. I accept this, but I am critical of the many centres and museums which forget, or even deny, that the Holocaust belongs in the category of genocide, even if it is writ large. Genocide scholars engage in a legal-social scientific discourse about the use and meaning of the term. Students address definitional questions in undergraduate assignments and in postgraduate theses.[2] We 'play' with the problem, looking for the core of the crime, trying to find a universally acceptable definition, one limited to the intended destruction of defined groups, and rectifying the acknowledged deficiencies of the extant definition in the UN Convention. We are less concerned with definition as with what Henry Huttenbach calls 'a common guiding schemata', an anatomy, of genocide (2002: 167). Our approach remains essentially historical and we avoid what some Holocaust scholars disparage as sociological 'model-building'.

In the end, we remain stuck with the Convention's definition: because it patently has the force of international law and is now further enshrined in the schedule of the International Criminal Court; because we emphasise responsibility, accountability and even punishment for the crime; and because we value trials as educative and as productive of evidence that events happened. (Denialism, I believe, is best dealt with forensically. Professor Richard Evans's 28-hour stint in the witness box in David Irving's High Court libel suit produced by far the most effective exposé and record of the plaintiff's motives and machinations than any other medium to date.)

A key to unravelling the legal perspective of genocide is to analyse the intentions behind, and the ideological bases of, such group-specific killings and destructions across the spectrum of antiquity, the Middle Ages and the modern era. We distinguish those elements that are so often inextricable – motive and intent. Our reflection, and conclusion, is that intent is the best and only way to proceed. I argue that the *genocidaire*'s intent to destroy can even be arrived at via a moral alibi of acting in 'good faith' and 'in the best interests' of the victims or of the nation as a whole.

Genocide is, of course, contextual. To this end, we reflect an essentially politico-historical framework, emphasising the relationship between racism and genocide and between modernity and genocide. In short, we examine the socio-political conditions under which such mass killings and attempted destructions can and do occur. This means evaluating the prerequisites for the perpetration of the crime. Those established by Yehuda Bauer and Richard Dekmejian appear to be Euro-centred, based on their respective studies of the Jewish and Armenian genocides. Dekmejian (1980) says that the distinctive features of genocide include organisational specificity; planning, programming and timing; bureaucratic efficiency and comprehensiveness; technological capability; and the ideological imperative. Bauer, in more or less the same idiom, suggests that there must be an ancient hatred, a brutal dictatorship, a war setting, a compliant bureaucracy, and the use of technology.[3] They are not alone in suggesting that almost all genocides occur in a war setting and are usually perpetrated by totalitarian or authoritarian regimes. The question is whether these templates fit all African, Asian and South American cases, let alone the Australian one. The answer is probably 'no'. There is also value in studies of societies that appear to be genocidal but on reflection are not, as I contend in my chapter above on South Africa.

The uniqueness of the Holocaust is a constant theme. With students, we examine Bauer's insistence on two key aspects of the Holocaust: the planned total annihilation of the Jews, and the quasi-religious, apocalyptic ideology that motivated the massive murder machine. His *Rethinking the Holocaust* (2002) adds newer questions and his recent preference for the term *unprecedented* rather than *unique* opens up a whole new area for discussion in view of the several Holocaust precedents to be found in the Armenian case.

We are emphatic about locating legal and moral responsibility for genocidal policy and practice. However, I insist that students always seek the microscopic black pinhead of malignancy that caused the whole cancerous condition. 'Must we always do so?' students ask. My answer is 'yes', but not all of my teaching colleagues agree with this personal, and perhaps idiosyncratic, emphasis, explained in chapter 1. (In recent years, German professors have addressed the question; for example, Jorg Wollenberg (1996) at the University of Bremen has subtitled his book 'No One Participated, No One Knew'.) One way of framing this difficult issue is to have students look at a passage from Abby Mann's television play, which Stanley Kramer adapted for his 1961 film *Judgment at Nuremberg*. The theme is the last of the Nuremberg trials, that of the Nazi judges.

'The trouble with you, Colonel', said Ives heatedly, 'is that you'd like to indict the whole country. That might be emotionally satisfying for you, but

it's not exactly practical. And hardly fair'. Colonel Lawson looked at Ives
. . . then spoke quietly: 'Hare, hunter, field. Let's be fair. Then, still smiling,
he said, 'The hare was shot by the hunter in the field. It's really quite
simple.' . . . Then he bent over [American Judge] Haywood and spoke
quietly, sardonically. 'There are no Nazis in Germany. Didn't you know
that, Judge? The Eskimos invaded Germany and took over. That's how all
those terrible things happened. It wasn't the fault of the Germans. It was
the fault of those damn Eskimos.'

Who, indeed, was responsible? Only those who, in legal terms, contravened
Geneva Conventions, or committed 'war crimes', or 'crimes against
humanity'? Can a line be drawn between being a 'companion' to such
actions and being an 'accomplice', a 'participant'?

In the matter of bystander behaviour and rescue attempts, a case can be
made for the study of 'worthy and unworthy victims' and, in one or two
instances, 'unworthy' perpetrators. Worthy victims – or rather, the people
who are deemed worthy of assistance in a particular phase of the politics of
those nations capable of helping – are fairly rare, but we do have the
inspiring story of the rescue of 7,000 Jews by the Danes, some noble Italian
behaviour during World War II, and the more recent cases of 'humanitarian intervention', as in Somalia in 1994–95, or military action, as in Bosnia
between 1992 and 1993, or prevention, as in the case of the no-fly zone in
Iraq in 1993 to protect Kurds.

In an earlier era, few nations made any serious efforts to assist Armenians
or Jews. Discussing the bystanders during World War II, Saul Friedländer
said that they may have been motivated by self-interest, or by pseudo-
ideological choices, or by traditional antisemitism. But whatever the reason,
the result – except perhaps in the 19,141 instances of 'righteous gentile'
behaviour (recorded as at January 2002)[4] – was always a choice 'in which
the Jew was less than whatever other consideration he was weighed against'.
On the 'righteous', students always wonder why there were so few. Yet
historian Christopher Browning once remarked to one of my student
groups that he was puzzled as to why there were so many. And he is not a
cynical man.

Most students are attracted to the 'bystander' phenomenon, to the
indifference that allows genocides to occur. In the case of the Jews, Bauer
calls it 'hostile indifference'. We now know more about the rescue of some

Armenians, and this evidence now enables comparisons between the few attempts at Jewish and Armenian rescue and between 'righteous gentile' and 'righteous Muslim' behaviour.

We examine the 'historical revisionism' that seeks to hide or deny genocide, particularly in the case of Turkish behaviour towards Armenians, Pontian Greeks and Assyrians. The Australian denial industry – rather than the neglect of history, in which Australians have excelled – is fairly recent and struggles to obtain both a coherent voice and an eager or influential audience. Refreshingly, many Australians have recently shown a new willingness to buy the notion that there is an ugly history out there.

Despite their omission from the UN Convention definition, but certainly within Webster's definitional compass, we pay attention to the genocidal fates that sometimes befall political groups. Perhaps our weakest endeavour lies in the field of possible safeguards against potential genocides and repetitions of genocide. Political prediction is often a matter of collecting a great many factors and variables, processing them and presenting models for communities at high, medium and low risk of genocide. American scholars Barbara Harff and Ted Gurr do this kind of work very well indeed (Gurr and Harff, 1995).

Robert Jay Lifton's (1986) presentation of the Nazis' 'biomedical vision' of the Holocaust, and of the 'biocracy' that gave effect to it, interests students. Vahakn Dadrian (1989) has presented evidence of a similar Turkish vision, one in which the 'microbes' within the Turkish body politic required removal. Students evaluate Daniel Goldhagen's (1996) critique of this biomedical model: he argues that few genocides have conformed to it.

The 'intentionalist' *versus* 'functionalist' view of the Holocaust, as discussed in chapter 2, is always popular with students, partly because they have to assess my intrusion of an 'inevitabilist' approach, one which asserts that genocidal engines almost always have to be in place before they can be put into operation, and need only a radical leader or government to switch them on.

We give students an angry passage from Cynthia Ozick's article in *The New Yorker* (6 October 1997) and ask what lessons can be learned from the Anne Frank 'industry'. Specifically, why are there such frantic efforts to falsify a perfectly clear exposition of her vision of darkness? The passage reads:

The story of Anne Frank in the fifty years since 'The Diary of a Young Girl' was first published has been bowdlerized, distorted, transmuted, traduced, reduced; it has been infantilized, Americanized, homogenized, sentimentalized; falsified, kitschified, and, in fact, blatantly and arrogantly denied. Among the falsifiers have been dramatists and directors, translators and litigators, Anne Frank's own father, and even – or especially – the public, both readers and theatregoers, all over the world. A deeply truth-telling work has been turned into an instrument of partial truth, surrogate truth, or anti-truth. The pure has been made impure – sometimes in the name of the reverse. Almost every hand that has approached the diary with the well-meaning intention of publicizing it has contributed to the subversion of history.

We see our undergraduate students, most of whom are experienced and who are in their final year of study, as equal partners in the enterprise of trying to answer some of these questions arising from the two major case studies. One can hardly do fieldwork in this domain, and so analyses and evaluations must come from documents, testimonies, news reports, scholarly works and trial transcripts, sources as available to intelligent students as to their teachers. Most of our questions have no immediate answers. One can't find the 'right' answers in any one or two texts, or on the internet. They have to do what Yehuda Bauer urges all students to do, namely, learn to tell the story, then analyse it and evaluate it. His other urging, our urging, is the better sense of sociological inquiry, the why as well as the what. Over the years, students have produced profound responses in their essays, especially on the topics discussed below. Several have been published in our journals and books, especially those on Rwanda and East Timor. Some students have gone on to doctoral programmes based directly on their undergraduate interests.

Following the major assignment on the Jewish and Armenian cases, we ask students to tackle one of thirty-four seemingly similar or divergent events. They may elect to study other victims of the Nazi regime: for example, the treatment of Gypsies (the Roma or Romany people), Jehovah's Witnesses or Russian prisoners of war. In these contexts, it is possible for students to appraise the validity of Daniel Goldhagen's thesis that it was only German antisemitism that was 'exterminatory'.

In genocide studies, there is a noticeable avoidance of the fates of those colonised in Africa, Asia and South America. Much of the smallish literature on 'colonial ethnocide' is often unhelpful: either the case is relegated to the too-hard basket and left for (unspecified) others to consider; or it is described simply as a matter of 'progress' extinguishing a culture; or explained away as a contest for land and what the land held, a struggle in which the (inferior) local inhabitants were, and are, always destined to succumb to (civilised) progress, whether it be mining, agriculture, re- or de-afforestation. Colonial oppression is most often seen merely as loss of ethnicity, language or material culture, a lesser phenomenon, inevitable, well-intended, as in the 'white man's burden', deplorable, regrettable, but somehow not heinous. We need to remember that Aboriginal Australians were deemed expendable not just because they were considered 'vermin', or because they sometimes speared cattle or settlers, but because they failed the Lockean test of being a people capable of a polity and a civility, to wit, they couldn't or wouldn't exploit the land they held, at least not in the European sense.

Students choose from a variety of Asian case studies: mass killings of communists in Indonesia 1965–66, or the killings in Cambodia (Kampuchea) in 1976–81; the treatment of the Baha'i in Iran, or what it was that characterised the creation of Bangladesh, involving three million dead, in 1971. They may look at what is called 'the rape of Nanking' or undertake the difficult task of determining what has happened to Tibetan people under Chinese rule.

From Africa, they may investigate genocide in Rwanda and Burundi (the 1972 and the 1994 events); the treatment of Jehovah's Witnesses in Central Africa; what followed the secession of Biafra from Nigeria; or assess the trial of dictator Macias Nguema, overthrown in 1979 by his nephew, to see if what happened in Equatorial Guinea (formerly a Spanish colony) was genocide. The fate of the black Jews of Ethiopia is certainly worth examination and students may care to take on board Frantz Fanon's verdict, written in 1959, about 'the genocide that is rife in Algeria' (in Kuper, 1981: 60). The treatment of the Herero peoples of what was South-West Africa (now Namibia) by the German colonisers cries out for serious study.

There is no shortage of South and Central American case studies. In particular, we suggest students approach the fate of the Aché Indians in Paraguay or that of the Indians in Brazil.

Europe has enough cases: to assess what the Ukrainian General Bogdan Chmielnicki was trying to achieve against Polish rule when his pogroms killed 100,000 Jews and destroyed 300 communities in 1648–49; to determine whether the man-made famine in Soviet Ukraine and the fates of the 'wreckers' and 'the enemies of the Soviet Union' during Stalin's purges, or the Russian treatment of Chechens, Ingush and Crimean Tatars in the 1940s, constitute the crime of genocide. Students can elect to analyse 'ethnic cleansing' in what was Yugoslavia or the contention that organised rape has been an instrument of genocide in Bosnia.

As to the Middle and Near East, there is the question of the treatment of Kurds since 1980 and, of course, the fate of the Pontian Greeks in Smyrna in 1923. The Palestinian issue is not on the agenda, and even Muslim or anti-Israel students have, by this point in their course, learned enough about genocide to refrain from asking why it isn't. (There may soon be a case for examining whether some Palestinian organisations have not only the dismantling of the Israeli state as their objective, but also the 'removal' of all Jews from that domain. Israeli actions may become near-genocidal. Deplorable attacks on Palestinians are a matter of record, but – and in spite of some anguished cries by Israelis who deplore their govern-ment's stances and actions – this is a course on genocide, not one on the history of violence and counter-violence, terror and anti-terror.) Closer to home, students can elect to study the case of East Timor, or the treatment of either mainland Australian or Tasmanian Aborigines.

Antiquity and the Middle Ages pose a problem of choices and sources. We offer the case study of the annihilation of the people of Melos in 416 BCE, or the Roman destruction of Carthage, or the mass murders of witches in Europe in the Middle Ages. (Several of our doctoral students have come to genocide studies via ancient history.)

Some cases may not be genocide, and remain in the 'to-be-decided' basket: the Irish potato famines in the 1840s, and the atomic bombing of Hiroshima and Nagasaki in 1945. Several eras and regimes have yet to be put on our students' agenda: what Ghengis Khan did to the Tanguts in China in the years 1226 to 1233; what the generals have done to the Karen and other tribes of Burma since 1962; what happened to ten million Chinese under Chiang Kai-shek's rule between 1928 and 1949, before Mao took control of the mainland and what Mao did thereafter. There is hardly a shortage of genocide material for study.

'Mission' accomplished?

Students are attracted to the subject of genocide. Perhaps the exhilaration lies in having to use every ounce of one's intellectual and emotional resources to tackle the topic, and being able to unravel that which at first seems so incomprehensible, so inexplicable. Some good phrasing has come from my colleague, Winton Higgins. When I asked him for his 'take' on what it is that we do, he replied:

> In the social sciences we get a sanitised version of how our (western) societies work. We thus build up a particularly anodyne self-image of ourselves as westerners, as heirs of the Enlightenment – humane, rational and reasonable. Genocides are atrocities that 'others' commit, so revealing their backwardness and Otherness (that is, the antithesis of what 'we' are like). The study of genocide exposes the Enlightenment-based self-image as dangerous complacency. This is so especially when we look at colonial genocides (what 'we' got up to not so long ago and, in some cases like Australia, the morally repugnant foundations of our nationhood), and at the Holocaust (what some of 'us' did within the lifetimes of many of us).
>
> Thus, delving into genocide helps our students and ourselves to come of age and confront the real dangers and as-yet-unaccounted-for collective responsibilities that we badly need to be aware of. Among other things, we learn to recognise that what might at first blush seem like minor insensitivities and grotesqueries in public life actually belong to a pattern that can extend to devastating crimes. [Australian Immigration Minister Phillip] Ruddock's vilification of refugees, and his incapacity to relate to their suffering before they came here and in his own Wackenhut[5] camps, are both cases in point. The one behaviour belongs in a continuum with Goebbels, the other in a continuum with Eichmann and the banality of evil.
>
> Our satisfaction, then, is a bit like the canary's in the mine. We indicate the danger when it is in its infancy. More broadly, we are producing students (and so citizens) who are socially aware in a morally informed way – ones whose consciences haven't been lulled by social sciences elaborately built up around a denial of genocide. We teach, above all, those most central of all modern western values (à la Charles Taylor): justice, the dignity of the individual human life, and sensitivity to the suffering of others. We run the ultimate finishing school in civics.

I deplore the whole 'mission statement' circus that universities so eagerly embrace – as a way of 'corporatising' themselves and their 'product' which makes cheap and shallow virtue out of pretty-sounding 'objectives' and jargon-riddled 'outcomes' and 'throughputs'. But, as a mission statement, Higgins's response is just fine – that is what we do rather than what we preach or prattle.

The student responses are not dissimilar. This is one student's neat encapsulation:

This course opens students' intellects, sometimes through shocking revelations, to the real world they are responsible for. It insists on examining historical antecedents to see how history, geography, politics, biology, medicine, engineering, architecture and philosophy contribute to deadly outcomes. The spiral contains irrefutable documentation about dates, deeds and doers, and the legal transcripts at the end of a genocide that tie up that trio. At the conclusion of the course, students are able to differentiate degrees of atrocity, to read early-warning signs, to judge, and thereby to take responsibility for the world they inhabit. Their future contributions – as advisers, teachers, researchers, parents or neighbours – should help diminish the deadly impulses in certain peoples. It proved the dictum: 'You can't stop what you don't understand'.

Final thoughts

Like Alexander Baron, thoughts about genocide assail me daily. I read about it, think about it, teach about, and in the end, develop a macabre sense of humour in order to stay wedded to it. Even the students learn to smile – not broadly, but wryly – as we try to make sense of the seemingly insensible.

Perverse, perhaps, but genocide is inspiring enough to make me want to examine it, explore it, deconstruct it, explain it, lay it out for the world to see, and perhaps to learn from it. Exhilaration and pain come from discovery of fact, fiction, motive, intent. Acute discomfort – as in self-doubt and doubt about humankind – arises when seeking to understand how genocides come to be humanly possible. Explanations of how genocide is technically, economically, politically and militarily possible are an easier task.

Earlier, I explained why I am not interested in what is called 'psycho-politics', especially of the 'what-made-Hitler-tick' variety. More importantly, I am forever trying to find what Saul Friedländer called the 'transmission belts' that drove the Nazis (and other perpetrators). Was it 'their insane impulses' or the 'pathology of their exterminatory drive'? Obedience? Fear? Was it what Christopher Browning believes drove the 'ordinary men' of Police Reserve Battalion 101 from Hamburg – the non-soldiers, the non-Nazis, the non-real police for that matter – to become the most proficient killing unit in the Lublin district of Poland, namely, conformity? Or is it what Ze'ev Mankowitz[6] speculates: the invention of a new political religion in which normal values are reversed, where the injunction is to hate rather than love, to make war rather than peace, to produce death rather than preserve life; one in which God is displaced by (Nordic) Man, one who is just as capable as the Deity of producing death at whim as life at whim, and in whose new universe the *manufacture of death* rather than the death of particular peoples becomes the real end purpose?

No one has yet solved the riddle of 'the soul of the suicide'. Nor is anyone likely to. I don't regret the energy recently spent in three years of trying to find the heart of that particular darkness, namely, why so many Aboriginal and Maori youth prefer death to life (Tatz, 2001a). Some of what I have written in that context has been of some value, a practical challenge for an understanding and for some alleviation, but never for prevention. Discovering or, rather, uncovering the *genocidaire* is a challenge. I don't regret the energy spent there either, and some of what I have written over the years has led to a realm of understanding among many students and members of the public. But I doubt if any of that energy and activity have led to any alleviation, let alone prevention – even of child removal in Australia, in this 'lucky country'. Sandwiched between these two -*cides*, my interest lies in writing about sport because it has some important qualities: it is transitory, transient, illusory, frothy, futile most of the time, fun sometimes, and it doesn't usually end in cemeteries. But even the sports material, at least in the Australian Aboriginal case, reflects genocidal phases, images, horrors and outcomes.

NOTES

Prologue

1. I have opted for denialism and denialist rather than the conventional denial and denier for this genre of genocide negation or disavowal.

I Breaking the Membrane: Journey Towards Genocide

1. *From the City, From the Plough*; *There's No Home*; and *The Human Kind*.
2. In his website, this Baron describes himself as 'an independent researcher . . . exposing Zionist and other mendacity and disinformation', including 'a book-length exposé of Zionist agent and sexual deviant David Irving'.
3. *Churban/Hurban*, or *Shoah*, the Hebrew words for the destruction of European Jewry. Today, the term *Churban* is used mainly by Orthodox Jews in Israel.
4. In the nineteenth century, people of 'European–Hottentot' mix were known as Bastards, then as Griquas, with an offshoot people called Bergenaars. Many were of mixed union with Khoikoi people. In the twentieth century they were recognised as a distinct people and categorised as 'Cape Coloureds'.
5. 'Blood libel' covers the continuing saga, from antiquity to the present, in which Jews have been falsely accused of committing murder, or ritual murder, mutilation murder or crucifixion murder of Christians, in order to consume the flesh or obtain the blood of their victims. The belief was

that these 'offences' were for 'medicinal' purposes or to obtain blood for making *matzot*, the unleavened bread used at Passover and Easter time.

6. Donald Watt, an Australian soldier in World War II, has published his memoir, *Stoker: the Story of an Australian Soldier Who Survived Auschwitz-Birkenau*. He claimed, *inter alia*, that he was a stoker of furnaces. Acclaimed by many, the book is nevertheless an 'appropriation', perhaps a misappropriation, albeit a well-intentioned one. Darren O'Brien has demonstrated that he simply could not have been where he was, doing what he claimed to be doing.

2   Approaches to Genocide

1. Remarkably, Marion Harland (1897: 415) referred to 'this gigantic holocaust with all its attendant horrors of flame, rapine and violation' in the case of the Armenian massacres under Sultan Hamid II in the 1890s; and J. Castell Hopkins wrote about 'the full glare of the national holocaust upon the altar of Mahometan cruelty' (1896: 313).

2. Objections to his Jewish origins were met by Göring declaring: 'I determine who is a Jew.' At Nuremberg, he was a witness against Göring. Milch was sentenced to life imprisonment, reduced by pardon. Released in 1954, he became a consultant to industry.

3. There are 613 commandments (*mitzvot*) as to moral and religious being, conduct that regulates relationships to God and to fellow human beings.

4. See Bibliography for Berkovits, Fackenheim, Jakobovits, Katz, Peli, Rubenstein, Soloveitchik.

5. This much maligned man was assassinated in Israel following a libel trial involving these negotiations. Bauer says he and his group may well have rescued 200,000 Budapest Jews and saved a further 10,000 who were deported to the area around Vienna instead of to Auschwitz (Bauer 2002: 239).

3   Germany: The Genocidal Engine

1. Most of the material in this chronology derives from lectures by David Bankier at Yad Vashem. Most of the documentary sources used are in Arad *et al.* (1981: 102–14).

2. Goebbels needed a trigger for this pogrom. Conveniently, seventeen-year-old Polish-born Herschel Grynzspan had entered the German embassy in Paris on 7 November and shot Ernst vom Rath in what was most likely a lovers' quarrel. The diplomat died two days later.

3. There are many sources on the German churches and antisemitism. I have made use of the entries in Zentner and Bedürftig (1997).

4   Australia: Defining and Interpreting Genocide

1. See also Huttenbach's editorial 'Towards a conceptual definition of geno-cide' (2002: 167–75) and the reviews of Charney's two-volume reference book by Richard Goldstone and by Henry Theriault in the *Journal of Genocide Research* (4)2, June 2002, at 261–5 and 266–70 respectively.

2. The 'Ten-Point Plan' was the Conservative government's response to the High Court Wik case which found that Aboriginal land rights could co-exist with those of the pastoralists. The Howard legislation wound back these Aboriginal rights, particularly the right to negotiate about future development on traditonal lands.

3. *Nulyarimma and Others v Phillip R Thomson* was initially an application for a writ of *mandamus*, ACT Supreme Court, 1998, before Justice Ken Crispin. The Registrar of the Magistrates' Court refused to issue the initial summons as he believed it did not disclose any offence known to Australian Capital Territory law as genocide. Hence the writ against the Registrar to compel him to issue summons against the named persons. Three judges (Wilcox, Whitlam and Merkel JJ.) held that the stated facts did not fall within the genocidal framework and definition in the Convention.

4. The best single source of information on Aboriginal society is the two-volume *Encyclopaedia of Aboriginal Australia*, edited by David Horton (1994).

5. For a full account of the views of Peter Connolly QC, S.E.K. Hulme QC and Sir Walter Campbell, former Supreme Court judge and Governor of Queensland, see Association of Mining and Exploration Companies (1993: 23–61).

6. The German bacteriologist Robert Koch postulated his germ theory in 1882.

7. First formed in Victoria in 1837, in New South Wales in 1848, in South

Australia in 1852, in Queensland in 1859 and the Northern Territory in
1884, these white-officered black troops were infamous for their butchery.
The trial of the notorious commander William Willshire, tried and
acquitted of murder, caused the disbanding of these 'legions'. See Kimber
(1997).

8. For a rigorous documentation of all legislation affecting Aborigines, see
   John McCorquodale, *Aborigines and the Law: a Digest* (1987). The full list
   of protection legislation is too long to present here. The key statutes are:
   NSW – Aborigines Protection Act 1909; Victoria – Aborigines Protection
   Act 1869, Aborigines Protection Act 1886; Queensland – Aboriginals
   Protection and Restriction of the Sale of Opium Act 1897, Aboriginals
   Preservation and Protection Act 1939; Tasmania – Cape Barren Island
   Reserve Act 1912; Western Australia – An act to prevent the enticing
   away the Girls of the Aboriginal Race from School or from any Service
   in which they are employed 1844, Aborigines Protection Act 1886,
   Aborigines Act 1905; South Australia – Aborigines Act 1911, Northern
   Territory Aboriginals Act 1910 [South Australia administered the Territory
   at that time]; Northern Territory [administered by the federal government]
   – Aboriginals Ordinance 1911.

9. The Canadian sociologist Erving Goffman (1968) coined these terms for
   North American mental institutions. He called them 'places of residence
   and work where a large number of like-situated individuals cut off from
   the wider society for an appreciable period of time, together lead an
   enclosed, formally administered round of life'. Prisons, he wrote, serve as
   a clear example, providing we 'appreciate that what is prison-like about
   prisons is found in institutions whose members have broken no laws'.

10. The *Bringing Them Home* document attributes this quotation to one of
    Gale's staff, James Isdell, a travelling Protector.

11. Granuloma is not a disease but an aggregation of cells usually associated
    with chronic inflammation. Certain infections, such as tuberculosis, bru-
    cellosis, leprosy and syphilis give rise to infective granulomas in many
    different organs of the body. Granuloma *inguinale* is a sexually trans-
    mitted disease, while granuloma *annulare* is a harmless skin disease. The
    Citizenship Act didn't specify and didn't differentiate. Yaws (or fram-
    boesia), found throughout tropical and sub-tropical zones, is caused by a
    spirochaete very similar to that which causes syphilis. But yaws, while
    infectious, is *not a sexually transmitted disease*, knowledge available at that
    time.

12. Henry Reynolds has written elegantly – in *The Whispering in Our Hearts* (1998) – about the people who couldn't satisfy their consciences, who worried about the Aboriginal–white relationship, who said so publicly and who attempted some kind of action to try to change the way things were.

13. *Kruger, Bray v Commonwealth*, 1997, 146 Australia Law Reports 126 or 1997, 71 ALJR 991.

14. Cited as 'Anonymous: Commonwealth Government', October 1996.

15. The endocrinologist I consult tells me that this disease was undoubtedly present earlier on, but that diagnostic tools were primitive, or were not used in Aboriginal communities, until as recently as the early 1980s.

16. In the *Encyclopaedia*, cited above, the appendix material includes statistical evidence of most of these social indicators. The 1996 census, for example, shows an unemployment rate of 22.7 per cent as opposed to the national 8.1 per cent; a weekly income of $502 per week (for an average household of 3.7 people) as opposed to $736 for households of 2.7 people, and an adult take-home pay packet 25 per cent lower than non-Aborigines.

17. The current crises in Aboriginal life are examined in my article on Aboriginal violence (1990: 245–60); in my (1995) book, especially chapter 13; my (1994b) chapter in Baxi and Mendelsohn, 159–77; the article in *The Sydney Institute Quarterly* (1998: 3–11); and in my book on Aboriginal suicide (2001a).

5   South Africa: Genocide or Not?

1. Most of the material in this chapter is drawn from my *Shadow and Substance in South Africa* (Tatz, 1962) and subsequent articles.

2. The material in this paragraph is drawn from Davenport (1997: 191).

6   Reflecting on Genocide: Denialism, Memory and the Politics of Apology

1. I avoid the word revisionism. It is an essential part of French history, going back to the Alfred Dreyfus case, and was once used positively: the *revisionnistes* were those who pressed for a judicial inquiry or reopening of that infamous case. It has subsequently come to be used, as a nice euphemism, by those who deny the Holocaust.

2. In March 2001, fourteen Arab intellectuals denounced the projected denialist conference scheduled to be held in Lebanon. The influential London Arab newspaper, *Al-Hayat*, editorialised that such conferences 'disgraced Lebanon' (*Ha'aretz*, English edition, 20 March 2001). However, in June 2001, such a conference was held in Jordan.

3. Dr Salahi Sonyel of London presented a denialist paper entitled 'Christian Minorities and the Destruction of the Ottoman Empire, with particular reference to the 20th Century'. His supporters, including diplomatic staff, were ill-behaved.

4. Davison, 'The imaginary grandstand: international sport and the recognition of Australian identity', Australian Society for Sports History conference, Adelaide, 10 July 2001.

5. Leslie Haylen, *Hansard*, House of Representatives, vol. 203, 30 June 1949, 1871.

6. The majority of government-run settlements and church-established missions of the nineteenth and twentieth centuries were established on the basis of their isolation, in places described as 'splendidly secluded', rather than in the natural habitats of the native people. See chapter 4 (and deMayo 1990).

7. Winston Churchill, *Hansard* (Parliamentary Debates, House of Commons), 8 September 1942.

8. Dr Helge Grabitz, Senior State Attorney, District Court of Hamburg, at 'Nuremberg and its Impact: 50 Years Later', Library of Congress and US Holocaust Memorial Museum Conference, Washington DC, 13 November 1996.

9. Professor C. Frederik Rüter, Deputy Judge, Amsterdam Criminal Court, at 'Nuremberg and its Impact' Conference.

10. Dr Winfried Garscha, research officer, *Dokumentationsarchiv des österreichischen Widerstandes*, Vienna, at 'Nuremberg and its Impact' Conference.

11. International Court of Justice, 8 April 1993, General List no. 91.

12. *Polyukhovich v The Commonwealth* (1991) CLR 501.

13. Six of the seven judges voted on this question. Brennan J., who had voiced the sole dissenting opinion on the 'external powers' question, didn't judge the 'usurpation' issue. As he had already expressed his opposition to the Act, I have counted his 'absence' as placing him with the two dissenting judges, thus a four to three majority in favour.

14. These were two Treblinka trials in Dusseldorf, one in 1964–65, of ten SS men, including Kurt Franz, and the second in 1970, when Franz Stangl

was on trial. There were three Auschwitz trials in Frankfurt between 1963 and 1966.

15. By a three to two majority, the Ontario Court of Appeal dismissed the Crown's appeal against the acquittal of Imre Finta, a camp guard at Szeged in Hungary, on charges of crimes against 8,617 Jewish prisoners. The case raised a veritable mountain of constitutional and criminal law, and of evidentiary and moral issues. See *Dominion Law Reports* 92 DLR (4th) Part 1, 3 September 1992, 1–160.

16. For a hypothetical instance, if the I.G. Farben company were to offer Macquarie University millions of dollars to create a Centre for the Propagation of Jewish Life and Culture. (Since this essay was first published, Macquarie accepted a $2 million gift from the self-confessed 'world's richest fascist', Ryoichi Sasakawa, jailed for three years by the US army of occupation after World War II because of his alleged war crimes. The *Sydney Morning Herald* (14 December 1994) joined my protest at the University's controversial step in the absence of a full campus debate.)

17. See also Young's thesis (1994), and his chapter in Tatz (1997a).

18. It is of interest that, at the very end of 1994, the New Zealand government offered to settle all Maori land compensation claims for NZ$1 billion (A$830 million) over ten years. As could be expected, this 'settlement envelope' offended both conservative whites, who claim that Maori have already had too much, and Maori leaders, who were insulted by what one commentator called a 'late twentieth century axe-and-blanket deal'.

19. Of significance (and considerable courage) was the November 1994 decision by Judge Oscar Garzon Funes in the Buenos Aires district court to award US$3 million to Daniel Tarnopolsky, whose mother, father, sister, brother and sister-in-law disappeared on 15 July 1976: $1 million was to come from the State and $1 million each from the two former military chiefs of staff, Emilio Massera and Armando Lambruschini, whose connection with the murders had been established in earlier trials. See *New York Times*, 12 December 1994.

20. Tony Judt, 'Vichy's Ghost Returns', *Weekend Australian*, 5–6 November 1994.

21. Two years earlier the Tainui Federation of Tribes of the North Island won compensation of $170 million and restoration of 15,400 hectares.

22. 'Four Corners', screened 28 September and Channel 9 *Sunday*, with Laurie Oakes, 27 September; see also the editorial, *Sydney Morning Herald*, 30 September 1998.

23. Televised speech, 27 September 1998.
24. Higgins, paper entitled 'Could It Happen Again? The Holocaust and the National Question', Academy of Social Sciences Workshop, 'The Genocide Effect', St Paul's College, University of Sydney, 4–5 July 2001.
25. See 'The Reconciliation Issue', special edition of the *Melbourne Journal of Politics*, vol. 25, 1998, comprising eleven essays on the concept. I share the view of some critics who see 'reconciliation' as an impossible achievement where there is such wealth and power disparity between the parties. Further, the reconciliation efforts to date have not addressed a single one of the myriad social, economic, health and legal problems besetting Aboriginal communities, as described in the section 'Near-extermination' in chapter 4 above.
26. Paper given at the 'Aborigines, the Arts and Reconciliation' conference at the Victorian College of the Arts, 23–24 October 1998.
27. *Kruger and Bray*, 1997, 71, ALJR 991, 1037.
28. In early 1999, the cases of *Peter Gunner v Commonwealth* and *Lorna Cubillo v Commonwealth* began in Darwin, subsequently lost by the plaintiffs in 2001. These were the lead cases handled by the Melbourne firm of Holding Redlich. At least 550 claims for common law damages have been filed in the Darwin Registry of the High Court.

Epilogue: Teaching about Genocide

1. R.J. Rummel's draft article for the *Enciclopedia Italiana*.
2. For example, Jennifer Balint's Honours thesis (1991), listed in the Bibliography.
3. Lectures at Yad Vashem.
4. Yad Vashem insists that this is only a representative, not a true, figure.
5. Named after the American entrepreneur who developed a system of privatised incarceration centres, the Australian subsidiary of which is Australian Correctional Management.
6. Lectures at Yad Vashem.

BIBLIOGRAPHY

Aarons, Mark (2001), *War Criminals Welcome: Australia, a Sanctuary for Fugitive War Criminals since 1945*, Melbourne: Black Inc.

Adalian, Rouben (1991), 'The Armenian Genocide: context and legacy', *Social Education*, 55(2).

Allen, William Sheridan (1984 revised edn), *The Nazi Seizure of Power: the Experience of a Single German Town, 1942–1945*, New York: Franklin Watts.

Aly, Götz, Peter Chroust and Christian Pross (1994), *Cleansing the Fatherland: Nazi Medicine and Racial Hygiene*, Baltimore, MD: The Johns Hopkins University Press.

Arad, Yitzhak, Yisrael Gutman and Abraham Margaliot (1981), *Documents on the Holocaust*, Jerusalem: Yad Vashem.

Ascherson, Neal (1987), 'The Death Doctors', *The New York Review of Books*, May 28.

Association of Mining and Exploration Companies (1993), essays by Peter Connolly QC, S.E.K. Hulme QC and Sir Walter Campbell, in *The High Court of Australia in Mabo*, Melbourne.

ATSIC (1993), *International Year of the World's Indigenous People: Speeches [by Paul Keating, Lois O'Donoghue and Sol Bellear] to mark the national and international launch*, Canberra.

Attorney-General's Department (1993), *Report of the Investigations of War Criminals in Australia*, Canberra: AGPS [The Blewitt Report].

Balint, Jennifer (1991), 'That odious scourge, Genocide: towards a definition', BA Honours thesis, Politics Department, Macquarie University.

Bankier, David (1996), *The Germans and the Final Solution: Public Opinion under Nazism*, Oxford: Blackwell Publishers.

Barkan, Elazar (2000), *The Guilt of Nations: Restitution and Negotiating Historical Injustices*, New York: W.W. Norton and Co.

Baron, Alexander (1980), 'Jewish preoccupations', in Jacob Sonntag, ed., *Jewish Perspectives: 25 Years of Jewish Writing*, Jewish Quarterly Omnibus, London: Secker and Warburg.

Barta, Tony (1985), 'After the Holocaust: consciousness of genocide in Australia', *Australian Journal of Politics and History*, 31(1) (special issue edited by Konrad Kwiet and John A. Moses: *On Being a German-Jewish Refugee in Australia*).

Baruch, Bernard (1920), *The Making of the Reparation and Economic Sections of the Treaty*, New York and London: Harper and Bros.

Bauer, Yehuda (1994), *Jews for Sale?: Nazi–Jewish Negotiations, 1933–1945*, New Haven, CT: Yale University Press.

Bauer, Yehuda (1994b), 'In search of a definition of antisemitism', in Michael Brown, ed., *Approaches to Antisemitism: Context and Curriculum*, New York: American Jewish Committee.

Bauer, Yehuda (2002), *Rethinking the Holocaust*, New Haven, CT: Yale University Press (Nota Bene paperback edition).

Bellos, David (1993), *Georges Perec: a Life in Words*, London: Harvill.

Bemporad, Jack (1968), 'The concept of man after Auschwitz', in Albert H. Friedlander, ed. (1968).

Berenbaum, Michael, ed. (1990), *A Mosaic of Victims: Non-Jews Persecuted and Murdered by the Nazis*, New York: New York University Press.

Beresford, Quentin and Paul Omaji (1998), *Our State of Mind: Racial Planning and the Stolen Generations*, Fremantle: Fremantle Arts Centre Press.

Berkovits, Eliezer (1976), 'The hiding God of history', in Yisrael Gutman and Livia Rotkirchen, eds, *The Catastrophe of European Jewry*, Jerusalem: Yad Vashem.

Bevan, David (1994), *A Case to Answer: the Story of Australia's First European War Crimes Prosecution*, Kent Town, SA: Wakefield Press.

Bleakley, J.W. (1929), *The Aboriginals and Half-Castes of Central and North Australia*, Canberra: Commonwealth Parliamentary Papers, II(74).

Borowski, Tadeus (1976), *This Way for the Gas Chambers, Ladies and Gentlemen*, New York: Penguin.

Bozovic, Miran, ed. (1995) *Jeremy Bentham: the Panopticon Writings*, London: Verso.

Brennan, Frank (1992), *Sharing the Country: the Case for an Agreement between Black and White Australians*, Ringwood, Vic: Penguin.

Brookes, Edgar H. (1927), *The History of Native Policy in South Africa from 1830 to the Present Day*, Pretoria: J.L. van Schaik Ltd, reprinted as (1974), *White Rule in South Africa 1830–1910*, Pietermaritzburg: University of Natal Press.

Brooks, Roy, ed. (1999), *When Sorry Isn't Enough: the Controversy over Apologies and Reparations for Human Injustice*, New York: New York University Press.

Browning, Christopher (1992), *Ordinary Men: Reserve Police Battalion 101 and the Final Solution in Poland*, New York: HarperCollins.

Brunton, Ronald (1998), 'Genocide, the "stolen generations", and the "unconceived generations"', *Quadrant*, May.

Buber, Martin (1984 edn), *I and Thou*, Edinburgh: T. & T. Clark Ltd.

Buffum, Consul David H. (21 November 1938), doc. L202, in *Nazi Conspiracy and Aggression* (8 vols), Office of United States Chief of Counsel for Prosecution of Axis Criminality, Washington DC: US Government Printing Office, vol. VII.

Butlin, Noel (1983), *Our Original Aggression: Aboriginal Populations of Southeastern Australia 1788–1850*, Sydney: Allen and Unwin.

Cannon, Michael (1990), *Who Killed the Koories?*, Melbourne: William Heinemann.

Chalk, Frank and Kurt Jonassohn (1990), *The History and Sociology of Genocide: Analyses and Case Studies*, New Haven, CT: Yale University Press.

Charny, Israel, ed. (1984), *Toward the Understanding and Prevention of Genocide*, Proceedings of the International Conference on the Holocaust and Genocide, Boulder, CO: Westview Press.

Charny, Israel (1992), 'A contribution to the psychology of denial of genocide: denial as a celebration of destructiveness, an attempt to dominate the minds of men, and a killing of history', *Journal of Armenian Studies*, 16(1 and 2), 289–329.

Charny, Israel (1994), 'Toward a generic definition of genocide', in George Andreopoulos, ed., *Genocide: Conceptual and Historical Dimensions*, Philadelphia: University of Pennsylvania Press.

Charny, Israel *et alii*, eds (1999), *Encyclopedia of Genocide*, Santa Barbara, CA: ABC CLIO Press, two vols.

Charny, Israel (2001), 'The psychological satisfaction of denials of the Holocaust or other genocides by non-extremists or bigots, and even by known scholars', *IDEA – a Journal of Social Issues*, 6(1).

Chater, Melville (1925), 'History's greatest trek', *National Geographic*, XLVIII(5), 533–83.

Chisholm, Richard (1985), *Black Children: White Welfare? Aboriginal Child Welfare Law and Policy in New South Wales*, SWRC Reports and Proceedings, 52, Social Welfare Research Centre, Kensington: University of New South Wales.

Churchill, Ward (1998), *A Little Matter of Genocide: Holocaust and Denial in the Americas, 1492 to the Present*, San Francisco, CA: City Lights Books.

Churchill, Winston (1933–34), *The Great War*, vol. 3, London: G. Newness.

Churchill, Winston (1952), *The Second World War*, V, *Closing the Ring*, London: The Reprint Society.

Cohen, Stanley (2001), *States of Denial: Knowing About Atrocities and Suffering*, Cambridge (UK): Polity.

Cole, Tim (1999), *Selling the Holocaust: from Auschwitz to Schindler, How History is Bought, Packaged, and Sold*, New York: Routledge.

Commonwealth of Australia (1913), *Preliminary Report on the Aboriginals of the Northern Territory*, Parliamentary Papers, III – as part of the Report of the Administrator for the year 1912.

Commonwealth Parliament (1997), 'In the National Interest – Australia's Foreign and Trade Policy', *White Paper*, August.

Cummings, Barbara (1990), *Take This Child*, Canberra: Aboriginal Studies Press.

Dadrian, Vahakn (1989), 'Genocide as a problem of national and international law: the World War I Armenian case and its contemporary legal ramifications', *The Yale Journal of International Law*, 14(2), Summer, 221–334.

Dadrian, Vahakn (1997), *The History of the Armenian Genocide: Ethnic Conflict from the Balkans to Anatolia to the Caucasus*, Providence: Berghahn Books.

Darian-Smith, Kate and Paula Hamilton (1994), *Memory and History in Twentieth-Century Australia*, Melbourne: Oxford University Press.

Davenport, T.R.H. (1977), *South Africa, a Modern History*, Toronto: Toronto University Press.

Davis, Mike (2001), *Late Victorian Holocausts: El Niño Famines and the Making of the Third World*, London: Verso.

Dawidowicz, Lucy (1975), *The War Against the Jews*, New York: Holt, Rinehart and Winston.

de Jong, Louis (1990), *The Netherlands and Nazi Germany*, Cambridge, MA: Harvard University Press.

Dekmejian, R. Hrair (1980), 'Determinants of genocide: Armenians and Jews as case studies', in Richard Hovannisian, ed., *The Armenian Genocide in Perspective*, New Brunswick, NJ: Transaction Books.

deMayo, Catherine (1990) 'Splendidly secluded: the location of Aboriginal mission sites in Australia', Master of Arts thesis, Politics Department, Macquarie University.

des Pres, Terrence (1976), *The Survivor: an Anatomy of Life in the Death Camps*, New York: Oxford University Press.

Deutscher, Isaac (1968), *The Non-Jewish Jew*, London: Oxford University Press.

Diamadis, Panayiotis (2001), 'Trials of denial', *International Network on Holocaust and Genocide*, 15(1), 19–24.

Drost, Pieter (1959), *Genocide* (Volume I) and *The Crime of State* (Volume II), Leyden: A.W. Sythoff.

Evans, Raymond, Kay Saunders and Kathryn Cronin (1975), *Exclusion, Exploitation and Extermination: Race Relations in Colonial Queensland*, Sydney: Australia and New Zealand Book Company.

Evans, Raymond and Bill Thorpe (2001), 'Indigenocide and the massacre of Aboriginal history', *Overland*, 163, Winter, 21–39.

Evans, Richard (2002), *Telling Lies About Hitler: the Holocaust, History and the David Irving Trial*, London: Verso; also published as (2001) *Lying About Hitler*, New York: Basic Books.

Fackenheim, Emil (1970), *God's Presence in History: Jewish Affirmations and Philosophical Reflections*, New York: New York University Press.

Fackenheim, Emil (1985), 'The Jewish Return into History: Reflections in the Age of Auschwitz and a New Jerusalem', in *Contemporary Jewish Theology – a Reader*, ed. Elliott N. Dorff, New York: Oxford University Press.

Fein, Helen (1979), *Accounting for Genocide*, New York: Free Press.

Fein, Helen (1993), *Genocide – A Sociological Perspective*, London: Sage Publications.

Fenner, Frank *et al.* (1988), *Smallpox and its Eradication*, Geneva: World Health Organization.

Finkelstein, Norman (2000), *The Holocaust Industry*, London: Verso.

Fletcher, C. (1984), 'European–Aboriginal relations in Western Australian history', *Studies in WA History*, 8, 1–16.

Friedlander, Albert H., ed. (1968), *Out of the Whirlwind: a Reader of Holocaust Literature*, New York: Doubleday and Co.

Friedlander, Henry (1995), *The Origins of Nazi Genocide: from Euthanasia to the Final Solution*, Chapel Hill: University of North Carolina Press.

Friedländer, Saul (1977), 'Some aspects of the historical significance of the Holocaust', *Jerusalem Quarterly* reprint, Middle East Institute.

Friedländer, Saul (1997), *Nazi Germany and the Jews*, vol. 1, *The Years of Persecution, 1933–1939*, New York: HarperPerennial.

Furlong, Patrick J. (1991), *Between Crown and Swastika: the Impact of the Radical Right on the Afrikaner Nationalist Movement in the Fascist Era*, Hanover, NH: Wesleyan University Press.

Gaita, Raimond (1997), 'Genocide and pedantry', in *Quadrant*, July–August, 41–5; 'Genocide: the Holocaust and the Aborigines', November, 17–22.

Gaita, Raymond (1998), 'Reply to Kenneth Minogue', *Quadrant*, November, 39–43.

Gale, C.F. (1909), 'Report of the Chief Protector', WA Parliament, *Votes and Proceedings*, vol. 2.

Gilbert, Kevin, ed. (1988), *Inside Black Australia, an Anthology of Aboriginal Poetry*, Ringwood: Penguin.

Ginsberg, Morris (1965), *On Justice in Society*, London: Penguin.

Glassman, Bernard (1973), *Anti-Semitic Stereotypes without Jews: Images of the Jews in England 1290–1700*, Detroit: Wayne State University Press.

Goffman, Erving, (1968), *Asylums*, London: Penguin.

Goldhagen, Daniel (1996), *Hitler's Willing Executioners: Ordinary Germans and the Holocaust*, London: Little, Brown and Company.

Goldsmid, John (1988), *The Deadly Legacy*, Sydney: University of NSW Press.

Goldstone, Richard (2002), review of *Encyclopedia of Genocide* in *Journal of Genocide Research*, 4(2), June, 261–5.

Gollancz, Victor [probable author] (1936), *The Yellow Spot: the Outlawing of Half a Million Human Beings . . .*, London: Victor Gollancz.

Green, Neville (1984), *Broken Spears: Aborigines and Europeans in the Southwest of Australia*, Perth: Focus Education Services.

Greenawalt, A.K.A. (1999), 'Rethinking genocidal intent: the case for a knowledge-based interpretation', *Colombia Law Review*, 99.

Grose, J. (1927), *WA Historical Society: Journal and Proceedings 1927*, 1(91), 30–35.

Gruber, Ruth Ellen (1995), *The Struggle of Memory: the Rehabilitation and Reevaluation of Fascist Heroes in Europe*, New York: The American Jewish Committee.

Gurr, Ted Robert (1993), *Minorities at Risk: a Global View of Ethnopolitical Conflict*, Washington DC: US Institute of Peace Press.

Gurr, Ted Robert and Barbara Harff (1995), *Early Warning of Communal*

Conflicts and Humanitarian Crises, New York: United Nations University Press.

Guttenplan, D.D. (2001), *The Holocaust on Trial*, New York: W.W. Norton and Co.

Haebich, Anna (1988), *For Their Own Good: Aborigines and Government in the Southwest of Western Australia, 1900–1940*, Perth: University of Western Australia Press.

Hancock, W. Keith (1961), *Australia*, Brisbane: Jacaranda Press.

Hansard, House of Representatives (1949), vol. 203, 30 June, 1871.

Harff, Barbara (1984), in *Genocide and Human Rights: International Legal and Political Issues*, vol. 20, book 3, Monograph Series in World Affairs, Denver: Graduate School of International Studies.

Harland, Marion (1897), *Under the Flag of the Orient: The Thrilling Story of Armenia*, Philadelphia: Historical Publishing Company.

Harris, Stewart (1979), *'It's Coming Yet . . .': an Aboriginal Treaty within Australia between Australians*, Canberra: Aboriginal Treaty Committee.

Hartley, L.P. (1953), *The Go-Between*, London: Hamish Hamilton.

Hillgruber, Andreas (1986), *Zweierlei Untergang: Die Zerschlagung des deutschen Reiches und das Ende des europäischen Judentums*, Berlin: Siedler.

Hopkins, J. Castell (1896), *The Sword of Islam or Suffering Armenia*, Brantford: The Bradley-Garretson Co. Ltd.

Horowitz, Irving Louis (1976), *Taking Lives: Genocide and State Power*, New Brunswick: Transaction Books.

Horton, David, gen. ed. (1994), *The Encyclopaedia of Aboriginal Australia*, Canberra: Aboriginal Studies Press.

Hovannisian, Richard (1968), 'The Allies and Armenia, 1915–18', *Journal of Contemporary History*, III(1).

Hovanissian, Richard (1992), *The Armenian Genocide: History, Politics, Ethics*, New York: St Martin's Press.

Hovannisian, Richard (1997), 'Denial of the Armenian Genocide with Some Comparisons to Holocaust Denial', inaugural Armenian Genocide commemorative lecture, Macquarie University, Centre for Comparative Genocide Studies.

Human Rights and Equal Opportunity Commission (1997), *Bringing Them Home: Report of the National Inquiry into the Separation of Aboriginal and Torres Strait Islander Children from their Families*, Sydney.

Hunter, Ernest (1997) 'At the healer's limits: three medical survivors of Auschwitz', in Tatz (1997a), 231–62.

Huttenbach, Henry (1988), 'Locating the Holocaust on the genocide spectrum – towards a methodology of definition and categorisation', *Holocaust and Genocide Studies*, 3(3), 289–303.

Huttenbach, Henry (2002), 'From the Editor: towards a conceptual definition of genocide', *Journal of Genocide Research*, 4(2), June, 167–75.

Isaac, Jules (1964), *The Teaching of Contempt: Christian Roots of Anti-Semitism*, New York: Holt, Rinehart and Winston.

Jäckel, Eberhard, (1969), *Hitlers Weltanschauung: Entwet einer Herrschaft*, Tübingen; also *Hitler's World View: a Blueprint for Power*, Cambridge, MA: Harvard University Press.

Jäckel, Eberhard (1988), 'The miserable practice of the insinuators: the uniqueness of the Nationalist-Socialist crime cannot be denied', in Aharon Weiss, ed. (1988).

Jakobovits, Immanuel (1987), 'Religious responses to the Holocaust', *Jewish Tribune*, London, 10 December.

Johnston, Elliott, QC (1991), *Royal Commission into Aboriginal Deaths in Custody, National Report*, vol. 2, chapter 10, 'The Legacy of History'.

Jonas, Hans (1968), 'The concept of God after Auschwitz', in Albert H. Friedlander, ed. (1968).

Jones, Angela (1991), 'More than a memory: Australia's war crimes trials', BA Honours thesis, Macquarie University.

Kaplan, Mordecai (1934), *Judaism as a Civilization*, New York: Thomas Yoseloff.

Katz, Steven T. (1976), 'Jewish faith after the Holocaust: four approaches', *Encyclopaedia Judaica Yearbook*, 1975–76.

Katz, Steven T. (1989), 'Essay: Quantity and interpretation – issues in the comparative historical analysis of the Holocaust', *Holocaust and Genocide Studies*, 4(2), 127–48.

Katz, Steven T. (1994), *The Holocaust in Historical Context*, vol. 1: *The Holocaust and Mass Death before the Modern Age*, New York: Oxford University Press.

Keppel-Jones, Arthur (1950 edn), *When Smuts Goes: a History of South Africa from 1952–2010, First Published in 2015*, Pietermaritzburg: Shuter and Shooter.

Kimber, Richard (1997), 'Genocide or not? The situation in Central Australia, 1860–1895', in Tatz, ed. (1997a), 33–65.

Kirst, Hans Helmut (1968), *The Fox of Maulen*, London: Collins.

Kociumbas, Jan (2001), 'Smallpox and genocide', Academy of Social Sciences

Workshop, 'The Genocide Effect: New Perspectives on Modern Cultures of Killing', St Paul's College, University of Sydney, 4–5 July.

Kundera, Milan (1985), *The Unbearable Lightness of Being*, London: Faber & Faber.

Kunitz, Stephen (1994), *Disease and Social Diversity: the European Impact on the Health of Non-Europeans*, New York: Oxford University Press.

Kuper, Leo (1981), *Genocide: Its Political Use in the Twentieth Century*, London: Penguin.

Kwiet, Konrad (1984), 'The ultimate refuge: suicide in the Jewish community under the Nazis', *Year Book XXIX*, New York: Leo Baeck Institute, 137–67.

Kwiet, Konrad, ed. (1986), *From the Emancipation to the Holocaust*, Kensington: Kensington Studies in Humanities and Social Sciences, University of New South Wales.

Lasswell, Harold D. (1958), *Politics: Who Gets What, When, How*, New York: Meridian Books.

Lemkin, Raphael (1944), *Axis Rule in Occupied Europe*, Washington DC: Carnegie Endowment for International Peace.

Levi, Primo (1988), *The Drowned and the Saved*, New York: Summit Books.

Lewis, Bernard (1986), *Semites and Antisemites*, New York: Norton.

Lewy, Guenter (1964), 'Pius XII, the Jews, and the Catholic Church', *Commentary*, 37(2), 23–35.

Lifton, Robert Jay (1986), *The Nazi Doctors: Medical Killing and the Psychology of Genocide*, London: Macmillan.

Lippman, Matthew (2002), 'A road map to the 1948 Convention on the Prevention and Punishment of the Crime Genocide', *Journal of Genocide Research*, 4(2), June, 177–95.

Lipstadt, Deborah (1993), *Denying the Holocaust: the Growing Assault on Truth and Memory*, New York: Free Press.

Loos, Noel (1982), *Invasion and Resistance: Aboriginal–European Relations in the North Queensland Frontier, 1861–1897*, Canberra: ANU Press.

MacDonald, Dwight (1957), *The Responsibility of Peoples and Other Essays in Political Criticism*, London: Victor Gollancz.

MacDonald, Rowena (1995), *Between Two Worlds: the Commonwealth Government and the Removal of Aboriginal Children of Part Descent in the Northern Territory*, Australian Archives, Alice Springs: IAD Press.

Macleod, Colin (1997), *Patrol in the Dreamtime*, Sydney: Random House.

Maddock, Kenneth (1998), 'The "stolen generations": a report from experience', *Agenda*, 5(3), 347–53.

Maddock, Kenneth (2000), 'Genocide: the silence of the anthropologists', *Quadrant*, November, 11–16.

Mandela, Nelson (1995), *Long Walk to Freedom*, London: Abacus.

Manne, Robert (1999), 'The stolen generations' in his *The Way We Live Now: the Controversies of the Nineties*, Melbourne: Text Publishing.

Manne, Robert (2001), *Quarterly Essay: In Denial – the Stolen Generations and the Right*, Melbourne: Morry Schwartz, Black Inc.

Markus, Andrew (1990), *Governing Savages*, Sydney: Allen and Unwin.

Marrus, Michael (1988), *The Holocaust in History*, London: Weidenfeld and Nicolson.

Mason, Tim (1981), 'Intention and explanation: a current controversy about the interpretation of National Socialism', in Gerhard Hirschfeld and Luther Kettenacker, eds, *The Fuhrer State – Myth and Reality*, Stuttgart, 23–40.

Mayer, Arno (1990), *Why Did the Heavens Not Darken?: The 'Final Solution' in History*, New York: Pantheon Books.

McCorquodale, John (1987), *Aborigines and the Law: a Digest*, Canberra: Aboriginal Studies Press.

McGrath, Ann, ed. (1995), *Contested Ground: Australian Aborigines under the British Crown*, Sydney: Allen and Unwin.

McGuinness, P.P. (2001), 'The erosion of the "stolen generations" slogan', *Quadrant*, April.

Medawar, Jean and David Pyke (2000), *Hitler's Gift: Scientists who Fled Nazi Germany*, London: Richard Cohen Books.

Melson, Robert (1992), *Revolution and Genocide: on the Origins of the Armenian Genocide and the Holocaust*, Chicago: University of Chicago Press.

Melson, Robert (1996), 'On the Uniqueness and Comparability of the Holocaust: a Comparison to the Armenian Genocide', the second Abraham Wajnryb Memorial Lecture, Centre for Comparative Genocide Studies, Macquarie University.

Miller, Alice (1991), *Breaking Down the Wall of Silence, To Join the Waiting Child*, London: Virago Press.

Minister of Supply and Services, Canada (1996), *Royal Commission on Aboriginal Peoples, People to People, Nation to Nation, Highlights from the Report of the Royal Commission on Aboriginal Peoples*.

Minogue, Kenneth (1998), 'Aborigines and Australian apologetics', *Quadrant*, September, 11–20.

Moody, Roger, ed. (1988), *The Indigenous Voice, Visions and Realities*, vol. 1, London: Zed Books.

Müller-Hill, Benno (1988), *Murderous Science: Elimination by Scientific Selection of Jews, Gypsies, and Others, Germany 1933–1945*, London: Oxford University Press.

Nettheim, Garth (1973), *Outlawed: Queensland's Aborigines and Islanders and the Rule of Law*, Sydney: Australia and New Zealand Book Company.

Nettheim, Garth (1981), *Victims of the Law: Black Queenslanders Today*, Sydney: Allen and Unwin.

Nolte, Ernst (1985), 'Between myth and revisionism: the Third Reich in the perspective of the 1980s', in H.W. Kock, ed., *Aspects of the Third Reich*, New York: St Martin's Press.

Nolte, Ernst (1986), 'Vergangenheit, die nicht vergehen will' [A past that will not pass away], *Frankfurter Allgemeine Zeitung*, 6 June.

Nolte, Ernst (1988), 'A past that will not pass away', in *Yad Vashem Studies XIX*, Jerusalem: Yad Vashem.

Novick, Peter (2000), *The Holocaust in American Life*, New York: Houghton Mifflin.

O'Brien, Darren (1997), 'Donald Watt's "Stoker": the perils of testimony', *Newsletter*, 3(3), Centre for Comparative Genocide Studies, Macquarie University.

Parsons, William and Margot Strom (1994), *Facing History and Ourselves*, Brookline: Facing History and Ourselves National Foundation.

Peli, Pinchas (1983), 'Where was God during the Holocaust?', *Jerusalem Post International Edition*, 17 and 24 April.

Perez, Eugene (1979), *North of the 26th*, Perth: Artlook Books [ed. Helen Weller].

Permanent Peoples' Tribunal (1985), *A Crime of Silence: the Armenian Genocide*, London: Zed Books.

Poliakov, Leon (1972–76), *A History of Antisemitism*, 4 vols, New York: Vanguard Press.

Power, Samantha (2002), *A Problem from Hell: America and the Age of Genocide*, New York: Basic Books.

Queensland Parliament (1896), *Report on the Aborigines of North Queensland*, Votes and Proceedings, 4(85).

Read, Peter (1983), *The Stolen Generations: the Removal of Aboriginal Children in New South Wales 1883 to 1969*, occasional paper number 1, Sydney: NSW Ministry of Aboriginal Affairs.

Reynolds, Henry (1981), *The Other Side of the Frontier: Aboriginal Resistance to the European Invasion of Australia*, Ringwood, Vic: Penguin Books.

Reynolds, Henry (1998), *The Whispering in Our Hearts*, Sydney: Allen and Unwin.

Reynolds, Henry (2001a), *An Indelible Stain? The Question of Genocide in Australia's History*, Ringwood, Vic: Penguin.

Reynolds, Henry (2001b), 'The Question of Genocide in Van Dieman's Land', Academy of Social Sciences Workshop, 'The Genocide Effect: New Perspectives on Modern Cultures of Killing', St Paul's College, University of Sydney, 4–5 July.

Rinderle, Walter and Bernard Norling (1993), *The Nazi Impact on a German Village*, Lexington: University of Kentucky Press.

Rose, Peter (1968), *The Subject is Race: Traditional Ideologies and the Teaching of Race Relations*, New York: Oxford University Press.

Roth, John K. and Elisabeth Maxwell-Meynard (2000), *Remembering for the Future: the Holocaust in an Age of Genocide*, London: Palgrave, 3 vols.

Roth, W.E. (1905), *Annual Report for the Chief Protector of Aboriginals for 1905*, Queensland.

Rowley, Charles (1970), *The Destruction of Aboriginal Society; Aboriginal Policy and Practice*, vol. 1, Canberra: ANU Press.

Rubenstein, Richard (1966), *After Auschwitz: Radical Theology and Contemporary Judaism*, Indianapolis: Bobbs-Merrill.

Ryan, Lyndall (1981), *The Aboriginal Tasmanians*, Brisbane: Queensland University Press.

Sartre, Jean-Paul (1995 edn), *Anti-Semite and Jew*, New York: Schocken Books.

Schaefer, Michael (1997), 'The stolen generations: in the aftermath of Kruger, Bray v the Commonwealth', University of New South Wales *Law Journal Forum*, 22–4.

Schindler, Pesach (1984), 'Rabbi Issachar Teichtal on *Hurban* and redemption', Rabbinical Council of America: *Tradition*, 21(3).

Schindler, Pesach (1990), *Hasidic Responses to the Holocaust in the Light of Hasidic Thought*, New Jersey: Ktav Publishing.

Schleunes, Karl (1970), *The Twisted Road to Auschwitz*, Chicago: University of Illinois Press.

Scholem, Gershom (1966), 'Jews and Germans', *Commentary*, 42(5), November.

Secretary of State for Scotland (1977), *Reparation by the Offender to the Victim in Scotland*, Report by the committee appointed by the Secretary and the Lord Advocate, HMSO, July.

Segal, Ronald (1967), *The Race War: the World-wide Conflict of Races*, Harmondsworth: Penguin.

Seidel, Gill (1986), *The Holocaust Denial: Antisemitism, Racism and the New Right*, Leeds: Beyond the Pale Collective.

Shain, Milton (1994), *The Roots of Antisemitism in South Africa*, Johannesburg: University of Witwatersrand Press.

Shermer, Michael, Alex Grobman and Arthur Hertzberg (2000), *Denying History: Who Says the Holocaust Never Happened and Why Do They Say It*, Berkeley: University of California Press.

Soloveitchik, Joseph B. (1999), 'A halakhic approach to suffering', *Torah U-Madda Journal*, vol. 8.

St Thomas More Society and the New South Wales Society of Jewish Jurists and Lawyers (1999), *A Remembrance and Reflection on the Holocaust (The Shoah)*, Sydney.

Stannard, David (1992), *American Holocaust: Columbus and the Conquest of the New World*, New York: Oxford University Press.

Starkman, P. (1984), 'Genocide and international law: is there a cause of action?', Association of Students' International Law Society *International Law Journal*, 8(1).

Stenekes, Willem (2002), 'History denied: a study of David Irving and Holocaust denial', MA Honours thesis, University of Western Sydney.

Storey, Matthew (1997), 'Kruger v the Commonwealth: does genocide require malice?', University of New South Wales *Law Journal Forum*, 'Stolen children: from removal to reconciliation', December, 11–14.

Strauss, Herbert A. (1980), 'Jewish Emigration from Germany: Nazi Policies and Jewish Responses' (I) in *Leo Baeck Institute Yearbook*, XXV, 313–61.

Talmon, J.L. (1980), 'European history as the seedbed of the Holocaust', in Jacob Sonntag, ed., *Jewish Perspectives*, London: Secker and Warburg.

Tatz, Colin (1962), *Shadow and Substance in South Africa: a Study in Land and Franchise Policies Affecting Africans, 1910–1960*, Pietermaritzburg: Natal University Press.

Tatz, Colin (1963), 'Queensland's Aborigines: natural justice and the rule of law', *Australian Quarterly*, XXXV (3), September.

Tatz, Colin (1964) 'Aboriginal administration in the Northern Territory of Australia', doctoral thesis, Australian National University, Canberra.

Tatz, Colin (1972), *Four Kinds of Dominion: Comparative Race Politics in Australia, Canada, New Zealand and South Africa*, Armidale: University of

New England, reprinted in *Journal for Contemporary History*, 2, Bloemfontein: the Institute for Contemporary History.

Tatz, Colin (1982), *Aborigines and Uranium and Other Essays*, Melbourne: Heinemann Educational.

Tatz, Colin (1983), 'Aborigines and the age of atonement', *Australian Quarterly*, 55(3), Spring, 291–306.

Tatz, Colin (1985), 'Racism, responsibility and reparation: South Africa, Germany, and Australia', *Australian Journal of Politics and History*, 31(1), 162–72.

Tatz, Colin (1989), 'Racism: the role and responsibility of intellectuals', in *The Gift of Life*, Sydney: Australian Association of Jewish Holocaust Survivors.

Tatz, Colin (1990), 'Aboriginal violence: a return to pessimism', *Australian Journal of Social Issues*, 25(4), November, 245–60.

Tatz, Colin (1994), 'Aboriginal rights and wrongs', in Upendra Baxi and Oliver Mendelsohn, eds, *The Rights of Subordinated Peoples*, Oxford: Oxford University Press.

Tatz, Colin (1995), *Obstacle Race: Aborigines in Sport*, Sydney: University of NSW Press.

Tatz, Colin, ed.-in-chief (1997a), *Genocide Perspectives I: Essays in Comparative Genocide*, Sydney: Centre for Comparative Genocide Studies, Macquarie University.

Tatz, Colin (1999), *Genocide in Australia*, research discussion paper no. 8, Australian Institute of Aboriginal and Torres Strait Islander Studies, Canberra; reprinted under the same title in *Journal of Genocide Research*, 1999, 1 (3), 315–52.

Tatz, Colin (2001a), *Aboriginal Suicide is Different: a Portrait of Life and Self-Destruction*, Canberra: Aboriginal Studies Press.

Tatz, Colin (2001b), 'Confronting Aboriginal genocide', *Aboriginal History* (2001), 16–36.

Terkel, Studs (1993), *Race: How Blacks and Whites Think and Feel about the American Obsession*, New York: The New Press.

Tinker, Hugh (1979), *Race, Conflict, and the International Order: from Empire to United Nations*, London: Macmillan.

Totten, Samuel and Steven Jacobs, eds (2002), *Pioneers of Genocide Studies*, New Brunswick: Transaction Publishers.

Totten, Samuel, William Parsons and Israel Charny, eds (1997), *Century of*

Genocide: Eyewitness Accounts and Critical Views, New York: Garland Publishing.

Trollope, Anthony (1966), *Trollope's Australia, a Selection from the Australian Passages in Australia and New Zealand by Anthony Trollope*, ed. Hume Dow, London: Nelson.

Vansittart, Lord (1943), *Lessons of My Life*, New York: Alfred A. Knopf.

Vidal-Naquet, Pierre (1992), *Assassins of Memory*, New York: Columbia University Press.

Watt, Donald (1996), *Stoker: the Story of an Australian Soldier Who Survived Auschwitz-Birkenau*, Sydney: Simon and Schuster.

Weber, Jeremy (1995), 'The jurisprudence of regret: the search for standards of justice in Mabo', *Sydney Law Review*, 17.

Weiss, Aharon, ed. (1988) *Yad Vashem Studies XIX*, Jerusalem: Yad Vashem.

Weissbort, Daniel, ed. (1993), *The Poetry of Survival, Post-War Poets of Central and Eastern Europe*, London: Penguin.

Wiesel, Elie (1965), 'A plea for the dead', in Nathan Glatzer, ed., *The Dynamics of Emancipation*, Boston: Beacon Press.

Wiesel, Elie (1985), *Against Silence: the Voice and Vision of Elie Wiesel*, ed. Irving Abrahamson, New York: Holocaust Library, 3 vols.

Windschuttle, Keith (2000), 'The myths of frontier massacres', *Quadrant*, October, 8–21; 'The fabrication of the Aboriginal death toll', *Quadrant*, November, 17–24; 'The enemies of assimilation', *Quadrant*, December, 6–20.

Windschuttle, Keith (2002), *The Fabrication of Aboriginal History*, Sydney: Macleay Press.

Wistrich, Robert (1992), *Antisemitism: the Longest Hatred*, London: Thames Mandarin.

Wollenberg, Jörg, ed. (1996), *The German Public and the Persecution of the Jews, 1933–1945: 'No One Participated, No One Knew'*, New Jersey: Humanities Press.

Yeghiayan, V. (1990), *The Armenian Genocide and the Trial of the Young Turks*, La Verne, CA: American International College Press.

Young, David (1994), 'A *Mulano* place: paradox and ambivalence in the Romani holocaust', BA Honours thesis, Politics Department, Macquarie University.

Young, David (1997), 'The trial of remembrance: monuments and memories of the *Porrajmos*', in Tatz (1997a), 109–37.

Zentner, Christian and Friedemann Bedürftig (1997), *The Encyclopedia of the Third Reich*, New York: Da Capo Press.

Zuccotti, Susan (2000), *Under His Very Windows: the Vatican and the Holocaust in Italy*, New Haven, CT: Yale University Press.

ACKNOWLEDGEMENTS

My warm and profound thanks to Sandra Tatz, who believes in and supports what I do; to my children – Paul, Karen and Simon – who are kind in that they accept that my time is so often devoted to things other than the family; to Dr Peter Arnold, editor and friend, for his care, insights and fat blue pencil; to John Pilger, for encouraging this book and introducing me to Jane Hindle at Verso; to Michael Harrington for his index; to Maggy Hendry for her copy editing; and to my students and fellow teachers in a variety of Holocaust and genocide courses over the years.

The book is an amalgam and rearrangement of some published and some new material. Chapter 1 is an amended, and shortened, version of an essay of that title which was published in Samuel Totten and Steven Leonard Jacobs's edited *Pioneers of Genocide Studies* (2002). Chapter 2, 'Approaching the Judeocide', is an expansion of an essay which appeared in the *Australian Journal of Jewish Studies*, V(2), in 1991. Chapter 3 is based on a short article that appeared in the *Australian Jewish News* in the late 1990s; on my oration given to the community at the Great Synagogue, Sydney, on 9 November 1999, the sixtieth anniversary of the '*Kristallnacht*' pogrom; and on my response, in July 1999, to the presentation by Sydney-born Edward Idris, Cardinal Cassidy, of the Vatican's *We Remember: a Reflection on the Shoah*. Some ten years in the making, this eleven-page Vatican 'more-than-an-apology' document needed a response – given by Rabbi Raymond Apple and by me.

Chapter 4 is a revision and elision of two essays on genocide in Australia. The first was published under that title as a research discussion paper (number 8) by the Australian Institute for Aboriginal and Torres Strait Islander Studies in 1999, and reproduced in Henry Huttenbach's *Journal of Genocide Research*, 1(3) of 1999. A second article, 'Confronting Australian Genocide' was published in the journal *Aboriginal History*, volume 25, in 2001. Chapter 5 is essentially the lecture I give to students as the case study of what appears to be genocide but is not. Chapter 6 comprises a major revision of a public lecture – the first Abraham Wajnryb Memorial Lecture – given at Macquarie University in December 1994. It was published as a monograph of the Centre for Comparative Genocide Studies in that year. It is combined with a revised conference paper on denial, first published in *Genocide Perspectives II* in 2003. The Prologue and Epilogue were written for this work.

INDEX